The Language of Business Meetings

THE CAMBRIDGE APPLIED LINGUISTICS SERIES

Series editors
2007–present: Carol A. Chapelle and Susan Hunston
1988–2007: Michael H. Long and Jack C. Richards

The Language of Business Meetings

Michael Handford
University of Tokyo

CAMBRIDGE UNIVERSITY PRESS
Cambridge, New York, Melbourne, Madrid, Cape Town, Singapore,
São Paulo, Delhi, Dubai, Tokyo

Cambridge University Press
The Edinburgh Building, Cambridge CB2 8RU, UK

www.cambridge.org
Information on this title: www.cambridge.org/9780521133432

First published 2010

Printed in the United Kingdom at the University Press, Cambridge

A catalogue record for this publication is available from the British Library

Library of Congress Cataloguing in Publication data
Handford, Michael, 1969-
    The language of business meetings / Michael Handford.
        p. cm. – (Cambridge applied linguistics)
Includes bibliographical references and index.
ISBN 978-0-521-11666-4 (hardback) – ISBN 978-0-521-13343-2 (pbk.)
1. Business meetings. 2. English language—Business English. 3. Business
communication. I. Title. II. Series.

    HF5734.5.H36 2010
    658.4'56–dc22   2010014049

ISBN 978-0-521-13343-2 Paperback
ISBN 978-0-521-11666-4 Hardback

For Mayu

Contents

Series editors' preface

This book makes a substantial contribution to the growing body of research on business communication. It uses a unique spoken corpus, the Cambridge and Nottingham Business English Corpus (CANBEC), to study the language of business meetings.

Business meetings are an important part of ordinary working life for many people, and these meetings take place, increasingly frequently, in English. They are not the easiest of situations to study. Meetings are often confidential, may include a large number of people, and frequently involve discussion of people, events and values that are referred to in inexplicit terms. They also vary considerably depending on factors such as the size of the company, the purpose of the meeting and the relationships of the people involved. Obtaining recordings of meetings, then, necessitates a personal relationship with the organization concerned, both to establish trust and to gain an understanding of the issues and relationships that are important in each meeting event. It is difficult to satisfy these requirements and still collect the large quantity of varied data that a detailed study of business meetings needs.

As principal researcher on the CANBEC project, Dr Michael Handford succeeded in collecting one million words from a variety of business contexts. This is a corpus large enough to make authoritative statements about language frequency, but small enough for the author to have familiarity with each of the texts in it and the relationship with the producers of the texts, as mentioned above. This dual perspective is a key feature of this book. Dr Handford is able to investigate the corpus as a large collection of pieces of language, treating them as independent of their original contexts. Looking at the corpus in this way, he obtains frequency lists of words and clusters, and by comparing CANBEC with a more general corpus of spoken English (The Cambridge and Nottingham Corpus of Discourse English, or CANCODE) also identifies the items that are the relatively most frequent in the business meetings. Each identified word and cluster then forms the basis for further study, with its role in achieving particular discursive strategies identified from its use in multiple contexts. The focus on what is typical allows also the identification of the unusual. Creative language use, which is a theme in current approaches to spoken discourse, forms the basis for one chapter (Chapter 7).

Dr Handford also treats the corpus as a group of individual discourse events, each situated in a social context, and undertakes a qualitative interpretation of a large number of individual episodes. He notes that, in such meetings, goals and relationships are not static categories but are constantly shifting. An approach that is attuned to subtle changes in footing is a necessary corollary to the quantitative work. The two perspectives intersect under the themes of interpersonal and relational meanings and the indexing of discursive strategies.

The book ends with a chapter on teaching, and here also Dr Handford takes a refreshingly personal stand. Rather than holding up native speaker interaction as the model for all non-native speakers, he deconstructs the notions of 'expert' and 'novice' speaker, noting that expertise in business or technical matters may intersect with degrees of language proficiency in the language in interesting and often unexpected ways.

The Language of Business Meetings will be of interest to researchers, teachers and materials writers concerned with the language of business and language in the workplace, as well as those concerned with researching the interface between corpus and discourse studies. Offering a rich and detailed study of an important area of Applied Linguistics, Dr Handford's book is a valuable addition to the *Cambridge Applied Linguistics* series.

Carol A. Chapelle and Susan Hunston

Acknowledgements

In writing this book, I have come to profoundly appreciate the following cliché: 'I am responsible for all its faults, but whatever value the work has is thanks to the help, education and encouragement of others'. While I was highly fortunate to be asked to develop the CANBEC corpus, the corpus itself is very much the brainchild of Ronald Carter and Michael McCarthy. I thank them for allowing me to be part of their work, and continue to learn from their rigour, stamina and enthusiastic openness of mind towards spoken discourse. I also benefited greatly from having Mike as my primary PhD supervisor, with the PhD research providing many of the findings discussed in this book. These findings were carefully commented on by my examiners, Angela Chambers and Ronald Carter. And thank you to Mike and Jeanne McCarten for their warm hospitality, music and fresh produce in Toft.

Several other staff and students of the School of English Studies at Nottingham also helped me understand the ideas and methods applied here. These include John McRae, Zoltán Dörnyei, Svenja Adolphs (who was also my secondary PhD supervisor and first tutor in the ways of corpus linguistics) Peter Stockwell, Louise Mullany and Norbert Schmitt. Fellow PhD students, with whom there was never enough time to talk, include Jane Evison, Sarah Grandage, Kevin Harvey, Alex Gilmore, Gila Schauer, Sarah Atkins, Dawn Knight and Steve Kirk. And the same goes with friends from IVACs, such as Anne O'Keeffe, Brian Clancy, Elaine Vaughan, James Binchy, Aisling O'Boyle, Bróna Murphy, Fiona Farr and Steve Walsh. Also, thanks to Rosanne Richardson and Rebecca Peck.

To my friend and fellow researcher Almut Koester I owe a huge debt of gratitude. Her PhD and research initially showed me how corpus business data can be exploited, and I continue to learn a great deal from our collaborations. I must also sincerely thank both Chris Candlin for disabusing me of my mistaken view of what discourse analysis involves, and for introducing me to social practices, and James Paul Gee for his kindness, insights and ethical example. Hiro Tanaka has shown me many new ideas and ways of researching, teaching and training, and is a constant source of support and sanity in Japan. Also, Francesca Bargiela-Chiappini has helped my understanding of what business discourse is, and why it is worthy of study, and Lynne Flowerdew has greatly encouraged my work on practices and corpora.

Both my PhD and this book would have been completed much later were it not for the flexible understanding I have enjoyed at the University of Tokyo over the past five years. In particular, I would like to express my appreciation to Sato-sensei, Fujino-sensei, Ozawa-sensei, Horita-sensei, Yamazaki-sensei, Paul Rossiter-sensei, Sudo-san, the FSO and Osada-san, and to Petr Matous-sensei for enlightening and motivating conversations and collaborations. Furthermore, the domestic and overseas students I have worked with at Tokyo and Nottingham, as well as the trainees at several companies, have helped me to uncover what is useful in a corpus, and more importantly to continue to appreciate the value of talking to each other. Also in Japan, a special thank you to David Peace for his interest in my work and companionship over the past few years.

While maintaining the anonymity of the 261 people who comprise the corpus is essential, several people were extremely helpful in terms of providing contacts and obtaining recordings, firstly Russ and Jane Evison, as well as Simon Gibbs, Justin Wateridge, Maria Handford, Tony Watson, Kiyoko Naish, Paul Marshall, Reno Mueller, Graham Webb, Raza Rizvi and Richard Stringer. Without the aid of these and many others, the corpus would never have been created.

I owe an immeasurable debt of gratitude to the editorial staff at Cambridge University Press. Firstly Jane Walsh, Commissioning Editor, who decided the initial proposal from a green researcher was worth pursuing. Once accepted, Anna Linthe's meticulous and incisive comments and suggestions, along with those of Geraldine Mark, have improved the book far more than I could have expected. Also, several suggestions and insights by the series editor Susan Hunston meant that the chapters are more coherent, more accessible and far less flawed than they were originally.

Several people kindly commented on early chapters, firstly Almut Koester, who read and helped improve a number of chapters, and also James Paul Gee, Ronald Carter, Francesca Bargiela-Chiappini, Hiro Tanaka, Douglas Forrester, and my co-authors and editors on the other side of the office at Cambridge University Press, Martin Lisboa, Angela Pitt, Neil Holloway and Chris Capper. Martin Lisboa in particular has helped me develop a stronger business-studies element.

The biggest thank you goes to my wife, Mayu, who was actively involved at all stages of the corpus development. Your loving belief and encouragement over these years have made this book possible, and it is therefore dedicated to you. And a little mention for the joy, humour and contested patience of my daughters, Julia and Maya. Finally, I should thank John Worrall at LSE and my parents Mike Handford and Kathleen Smith for getting me over those big first hurdles.

Transcription conventions

Dialogue

…	noticeable pause or break of less than one second within a turn
=	sound abruptly cut off, e.g. false start
+	speaker's turn breaks and continues
[ ]	words in these brackets indicate transcriber's comments
( )	pauses of one second or longer (the number of seconds is indicated)

Speakers

S1	speaker
S1?	transcriber's best guess at speaker
SM	unidentified male speaker
SF	unidentified female speaker

Features of speech

gotta	got to
gonna	going to
wanna	want to
d'ya	do you
wouldn'ta	wouldn't have
dunno	don't know
cos	because
aggro	aggravation
yep	yes
t'	the
'em	them
'specially	especially

1 CANBEC: *Corpus and context*

The term 'business meetings' can provoke many reactions, some of them not very positive. This seems especially true for those who spend a considerable amount of their working lives talking, listening and not listening in meetings; and yet Boden's (1994: 8) assertion that talk, and especially talk in meetings, is 'the lifeblood of organizations' still seems valid, despite recent advances in electronic communication. Managers regularly have meetings with subordinates to review, check, delegate and plan tasks and duties. Colleagues regularly meet to solve or defer problems, and sometimes to create them. Representatives from different companies meet at all stages of the inter-organizational relationship, and face-to-face introductions and discussions are still widely seen as a requisite step in developing such a relationship. This book is an exploration of the language people use in business meetings, and how this language may relate to and constitute the immediate and wider contexts[1] in which the meeting unfolds. In other words, it examines how people in commercial organizations communicate 'in order to get their work done', that is, 'business discourse as social action in business contexts' (Bargiela-Chiappini et al., 2007: 3).

As Bargiela-Chiappini et al.'s (ibid.) comprehensive survey of the field of business discourse shows, this is a growing, important and exciting area of interdisciplinary analysis. The contribution this book hopes to make is to show how a fully transcribed, ethnographically informed corpus of real business meetings can be described and interpreted using insights and methods from discourse analysis, not least in the inferential extraction of recurrent meeting practices and their realization through language. Other disciplines used in the interpretation of the data include applied linguistics, corpus linguistics, genre analysis, conversation analysis, pragmatics, linguistic anthropology, and various aspects of the umbrella term 'business studies', including management studies and organization studies. The findings presented in this book show some of the constraining and enabling language and conventions that are repeated across different business meetings by different speakers in different businesses. CANBEC, the Cambridge and Nottingham Business English Corpus, is the corpus that will be examined in detail over the forthcoming chapters.

CANBEC comprises various genres of business discourse, but this study will analyse the 912,734 fully transcribed words of authentic internal and external meeting data, taken from 64 meetings recorded in 26 companies in the UK, continental Europe and Japan, including several multinationals as well as many smaller enterprises. Data were provided by the manufacturing industry (for example, makers of pharmaceuticals, vehicles, industrial equipment and foam), the service industry (including hotel and pub chains), the IT industry and the financial industry. Meeting topics include sales, marketing, technical issues, procedure, logistics and strategy. The majority of speakers are from the UK (226); there are 35 speakers from other countries, and approximately 10 per cent of the speakers in CANBEC use English as an L2. Most of the recordees are male (79 per cent), and a majority are either upper or middle managers. A more detailed description of the corpus is given in the following sections.

Throughout this study, the meeting portion of CANBEC will be analysed in an attempt to answer the following questions:

- How can meetings be classified as a genre, and what are the characteristics of this genre?
- What are the statistically significant words and multiword clusters in meetings? .
- What role does such language play in the construction of meetings?
- What practices does this language seem to invoke?
- What are the important interpersonal language features in meetings?
- What language is used in problem-solving, hypothesizing and evaluating?
- What turn-taking practices seem prevalent in meetings?
- How can these findings inform teaching and the design of teaching materials?

In addition to these questions which are dealt with in succeeding chapters, several themes run through the book. These include issues of power, obligation, face and speaker goals. Another theme concerns how business-meeting discourse compares to other registers, particularly everyday English. How language relates to the communities of practice in which it is used and signals membership is also a recurring theme. For example, in extract 1.1 between the sales director (S2) and a trainee sales manager (S1), the director is discussing the difference between inexperienced and experienced sales staff. In order to contextualize extracts, relevant background information on the meeting in question and on the participants is provided for all meeting extracts (see section 1.3 of this chapter).

(1.1)

> *Internal meeting*
> Relationship of speakers: manager–subordinate
> Purpose: giving and receiving information/advice
> Topic: sales

S2: +because (2 seconds) I suppose with more junior sales people they're afraid you know they think "Oh I've gotta give discount you know because otherwise I won't get the deal".
S1: Hmm.
S2: And= but I think if you hold your own (1 second) as a quality supplier+
S1: Hmm.
(1 second)
S2: +erm ... people have respect for it.

The extract is interesting from a language perspective, because it shows S2 fulfilling his role as a manager through the expository evaluation of the difference between staff members within the company's community of sales staff in terms of how they communicate with clients.

The remainder of this chapter will discuss the collection of the data, the constituency of the corpus, the transcription and anonymization processes, and the issue of size and generalizability.

1.1 Data collection

CANBEC, like CANCODE (the Cambridge and Nottingham Corpus of Discourse English[2]), was conceived, proposed and is jointly directed by Professors Ronald Carter and Michael McCarthy at the University of Nottingham. Both corpora form part of CIC (the Cambridge International Corpus), which at the time of writing totals more than a billion words. CANCODE was a unique corpus at the time of its creation, because it was to contain only spoken data from a range of mostly informal contexts, and the intention with CANBEC was to develop a smaller corpus of purely spoken business discourse. Whereas CANCODE totals five million words, the target number of words for CANBEC was set at one million. Both projects were funded and supported by Cambridge University Press, with whom copyright for the data resides.

In 2001, I was employed as the sole corpus compiler, and was responsible for arranging and collecting the appropriate amount and type of data, organizing and carrying out transcription and anonymization of the data and developing a categorized database.

The most challenging part of the CANBEC enterprise was persuading companies to allow recording, with roughly 95 per cent of companies who were approached refusing permission. Companies were especially concerned about confidentiality. Despite written assurances and agreements guaranteeing thorough, systematic anonymization, most companies refused to allow microphones in their buildings. In other cases, feedback and a training session on effective communication were offered in exchange for permission to record, but this was also often rejected. Occasionally, after recordings had been made, the company asked to have the tapes back, because it was felt the conversations were too sensitive, or involved potentially illegal advice or decisions. Despite these issues, mainly through personal contacts, or contacts of contacts, the corpus was successfully compiled.

Cambridge University Press and Michael McCarthy, Ronald Carter and Svenja Adolphs at the University of Nottingham gave the following guidelines for what would be an appropriate sampling strategy:

- Recordings should be from a range of different private and publicly owned companies (for example, multinational corporations) in terms of size and type of business, including the manufacturing, service and financial sectors.
- There should be no recordings from NPOs or NGOs, public or government-funded institutions, such as universities or hospitals, nor should there be communication between professionals and laypeople, as between a lawyer and client. This was partly because such recordings already form part of CANCODE, and partly because these organizations are generally not profit-oriented to the same degree as 'traditional' businesses.
- Recordings should involve a range of speakers in terms of position, job, age and background.
- The majority of speakers should be British L1-English speakers, but up to 20 per cent could be 'non-native' English-speaking employees of companies to allow for comparisons.
- Recordings should mainly be from the UK, given that CANBEC is complementary to CANCODE. A further reason concerned the costs of travelling overseas to record data.
- Up to 20 per cent of the data could be from academic business contexts, such as business lectures in a university business department[3].
- Relevant background information about the speakers and their companies should be collected.

- The audio recordings must be carefully transcribed according to Cambridge University Press transcription codes, and fully anonymized so as to protect the speaker and the institution's identity.
- The use of video recordings was rejected because of the potential intrusiveness in meetings, and the probability that companies and participants would be unwilling to be recorded. There are also obvious anonymization and confidentiality issues with video data.

Another thorny issue concerning the actual recording procedure was whether the person making the recording should be present at the recording, or whether the equipment should be handed over to the participants who would then switch the machine on and return the tapes to the researcher. The latter approach was the one adopted by the team for the *Language in the Workplace* corpus project (LWP) in New Zealand, which provided the data for Holmes and Stubbe's (2003) book *Power and Politeness in the Workplace*. The approach chosen for CANBEC was to have the researcher present in the room, looking after the equipment and taking notes on the proceedings, while trying to be as anonymous as possible.

Discussing the Observer's Paradox, Labov (1972) reasons that the presence of a researcher constrains the production of language being researched, yet it is necessary for the researcher to systematically observe the unfolding discourse in order to fully understand it. However, unlike Labov's research, during CANBEC recordings the researcher was not actively involved in the discourse, and the presence of a microphone on the table during a meeting 'is not likely to cause much consternation' (Farr, 2005: 134) in our technological world. Furthermore, it was reasoned that having the researcher present would secure data which was more complete. In the absence of the researcher, the participants might not turn the equipment on until a meeting had formally started, thereby missing any crucial pre-meeting discourse (Mirivel and Tracy, 2005), or they might forget to turn the tape over, or they might turn it off if some delicate topic were to be discussed, and then forget to turn it on again. These problems did actually arise on the few occasions when the researcher was not present and responsibility for the recording was handed over to the employees of the company, and have been reported as systematic issues of the approach taken during the LWP research project (Stubbe, 2001). As has been reported by Duranti (1997), on asking participants about the effect of having an observer present, all responded that they forgot after a few minutes that he or she was present. It may be the case that this is a feature of observing goal-driven institutional discourse, in that the participants focus on achieving their goals, and therefore the presence of the researcher becomes irrelevant to their task in hand.

Probably the greatest advantage of having a silent witness present at the CANBEC recordings was that any points of interest or possible confusion for the analyst which arose in the course of the real-time dialogue could be addressed in a subsequent follow-up session with an available and suitable participant. While it was also possible to contact participants via email after listening to the recordings or reading their transcripts, the danger here was that there was sometimes a considerable time lag. Therefore, the point in question may have been forgotten by the participants. Such points included non-linguistic issues, but more usually specialized terms, most often nouns that were industry- or company-specific, and also what seemed to be deliberately non-specific, highly deictic uses of language, for example the turn by the chair in extract 1.2.

(1.2)

Internal meeting
Relationship of speakers: peer
Purpose: task-/problem-oriented; planning
Topic: technical; procedure

> S1: We just find it very hard to you know agree that that's possible with the people in this room so why don't have a chat afterwards with with you know who and er we'll sort that out.

By asking follow-up questions it was possible to clarify such details, but confidentiality, a respect for the individual's and the company's privacy, and the possibility of being seen to be prying also had to be borne in mind.

A related issue concerned obtaining more general background information. Some companies were happy to provide information on the company and the speech activity itself – for example, agendas, relevant emails, company management structures, organizational charts and strategic company goals – whereas others were not. While such documents usually cannot be reproduced in this study because of confidentiality issues, they have provided ethnographic information which allows for a thicker description of the data. Obtaining speaker information in terms of age, position, seniority in the company, first language and so on was not difficult, and generally the participants filled the information sheets out themselves or jointly with the researcher. Participants were also encouraged to contribute to decisions about meeting topic, purpose and speaker position in the company, thereby ensuring a level of emic input in the categorization process. This provided an insider's view of what was happening, which would not have occurred had the researcher been solely responsible for choosing the categories.

Such contextual information allows for a level of interpretation that a purely quantitative approach would not allow; in the field of business communication, solely quantitative approaches have been seen as inadequate in accounting for what is going on (Murphy, 1998). Indeed, to the uninformed outside observer, business discourse can range from seeming indeterminate to outright unintelligible. The issue of context will be further discussed in Chapter 2.

1.2 Corpus constituency

This section describes the companies, meetings, speakers and number of words that make up the CANBEC corpus. Figure 1.1 shows that a wide variety of company sizes was involved in the project, ranging from multinationals with over 50,000 employees to small businesses with a few employees. In terms of the types of business the companies were involved in, the following industries are most represented: manufacturing, pharmaceutical, IT, leisure, finance and consultancy. The total number of 26 companies who participated were located mostly

Figure 1.1 Company size

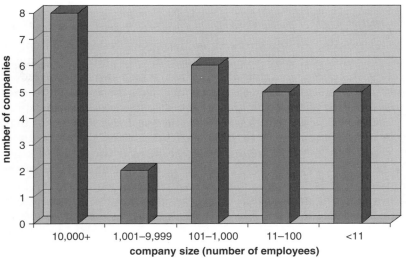

within the UK, although data were also collected in Japan, Ireland and continental Europe.

For all meetings, in addition to company size, type and location, information was collected on the departments where the recordings were made, the date of the recording, and whether the meeting was spontaneous or scheduled, face-to-face or otherwise. The number of speakers present and their individual profiles (for instance, their age, first language, level in the company, title and department) were consistently noted. As stated above, the majority of speakers in the corpus are British (226 out of a total of 261), although the non-British speakers are from 16 other countries, representing each continent of the globe.

One of the distinguishing features of CANBEC is the amount of external (inter-organizational) data, as the lack of such data in other comparable corpora attests. This totals just under 250,000 words, while the internal (intra-organizational) data comes to just over 670,000 words. Although parity between the two data types would have been ideal, the presence of both – even in unequal quantities – allows for interesting comparisons and discussions. Section 1.3 outlines the three contextual aspects that are arguably the most useful and relevant in understanding meetings, and are therefore provided for each corpus extract in the book: the relationship of the speakers, the purpose of the meeting and the topic of the meeting.

1.3 Contextual information

Relationship of the speakers

The relationship of the speakers in business meetings is often the most relevant contextual factor in understanding unfolding business-meeting discourse. In internal meetings, which are categorized as either manager–subordinate or peer meetings, the relationship was decided by considering the goal of the meeting and the institutionally sanctioned power relation between the speakers. This means that, while meetings tended to be categorized according to the status of the speakers, the social action being performed was also relevant. For example, in extract 1.3, a managing director and owner of the company (S3) is having a meeting with a technical manager (S2). Without looking at the data, we may assume that this is a manager–subordinate relationship. However, the managing director is asking advice from the technical expert about costing services, and therefore their official positions within the company are not as relevant as might be initially expected. This meeting was therefore categorized as a peer meeting. Peer meetings would also usually involve colleagues of the same or similar management status.

(1.3)

Internal meeting
Relationship of speakers: peer
Purpose: giving and receiving information/advice
Topic: technical

S3: But if that's daily then you need to do+
S2: [clears throat]
S3: +per per twenty four hour period.
(3 seconds)
S2: Yeah.
S3: Isn't it.
S2: Okay.
S3: Is that right? Am I getting my maths right?
S2: Yeah.
S3: Because I don't wanna screw up on this one.
S2: You'd have to look at the graph at exactly the right time.

For relationships in external meetings,[4] the contractual status of the two companies was interpreted as the key distinguishing factor. This distinction divides the data into either contractually bound or non-contractually bound relationships. Contractually bound relationships involve two organizations which have a formal, legally binding agreement concerning the nature of their business. In non-contractually bound meetings there is no legally binding contract. Instead, their business may be on a one-off or ad hoc basis, or the meeting may be exploratory, with one or both businesses looking to check the viability of starting a formal, contractually bound relationship. Both relationships may take the form of a partnership or alliance, in which the individual parties are joint principals in the business, or it may be a client–vendor (or subcontractor) type of relationship, in which the client will tend to direct or make requests to the vendor. A related distinction is that of Charles' (1996) analysis of sales negotiations, between established-relationship negotiations and new-relationship negotiations. The relationship between participants in this latter type closely resembles that of certain non-contractually bound meetings in terms of being new or ad hoc, although Charles' distinction refers solely to sales negotiations, whereas CANBEC involves other meeting purposes and topics as well (for example, 'planning' or 'reviewing').

While categorization of the relationship of speakers is extremely useful, it is essentially a heuristic device that imposes a structure on a dynamic, changing reality. This reality may change in the course of a speaker turn, and also over the long term. Gee et al. (1996: 68) argue that the ideology behind modern western corporations 'blatantly blurs traditional identities e.g. between "workers" and "managers"'. In inter-organizational discourse, the identities of brands, companies, manufacturers, subcontractors, distributors and clients have similarly become blurred over time (Klein, 1999). Nevertheless, differences are apparent in the actions business people are sanctioned to perform, and the language employed to perform them, which can be interpreted from a relationship perspective.

Meeting purpose

It is possible to categorize meetings in terms of purpose, goal or function in several ways (Holmes and Stubbe, 2003: 63), as was indeed the case with the participants' feedback on the meetings. It should be noted, however, that this was the most problematic of the various categorizations to apply to the data, and a high degree of fuzziness seems inevitable. The classification developed by Holmes and Stubbe (ibid.) outlines three main meeting types:

- planning, or prospective, meetings (forward-oriented)
- reporting, or retrospective, meetings (backward-oriented)
- task-oriented, or problem-solving, meetings (present-oriented)

While most meetings in CANBEC would fit easily within this categorization, certain external meetings in particular would not. For instance, buying, selling and promoting a product, and exploratory meetings, which often involve giving and receiving information and/or advice, are arguably supposition-oriented, in that they are largely concerned with hypothetical situations and possible outcomes (such as the potential development of a relationship between the companies). Therefore, they can resemble an early or pre-stage of negotiations, a form of communication usually associated with inter-organizational discourse. Interestingly though, participants themselves never used the word 'negotiation' to categorize any recorded encounter in CANBEC. To further complicate matters, many internal meetings, particularly between managers (or peers – see below), exhibit characteristics akin to negotiations, in that they involve the resolution, or negotiation, of conflicting interests, at least for part of the meeting. This is also compatible with Charles and Charles' (1999: 80) definition of a negotiation as 'a situation where the power relationship is symmetrical in that both negotiators have every right to control the situation and influence the other party'. Boden (1995) also argues that negotiating takes place in everyday business encounters, and not just staged, formal negotiations. We can therefore say that negotiating can take two forms: it can be a staged, usually inter-organizational meeting or series of meetings termed 'negotiations' (see Chapter 3 for discussion of negotiation stages), and the action of negotiating, which is synonymous with the resolution of conflicting goals; and it can arise in many internal peer meetings.

In addition, although the participants never labelled the purpose of any meeting as 'negotiating', various forms of the lemma do appear within meetings, most frequently in internal manager–subordinate meetings, and usually as a collocate of *they* or *them*, with the manager giving advice or information to the subordinate. In extract 1.4, for example, the sales manager (S2) is explaining about negotiating with potential clients.

(1.4)

> *Internal meeting*
> Relationship of speakers: manager–subordinate
> Purpose: giving and receiving information/advice
> Topic: sales

S2: "Expensive in comparison to what?" (1 second) you know. But erm … the other thing I I th= I mean I love it when it gets to negotiation stage cos you know they wanna buy.
S1: Well=
S2: If they start to negotiate with you … they want you.
S1: Absolutely.

In contrast, when the forms of *negotiate* are used in external meetings, they often signal a conflictual situation. For example, in extract 1.5, the buyer (S5) is refusing to agree to the new rates proposed by the seller (S3), and the refusal is followed by an extremely long silence of seven seconds.

(1.5)

> *External meeting*
> Relationship of speakers: contractually bound
> Purpose: negotiating; buying/selling/promoting a product
> Topic: production

S3: Is there any room for negotiation in this?
(2 seconds)
S5: Mick. There's already negotiation. We're just not buying.
(7 seconds)

Similarly, in a highly conflictual external meeting (see Handford and Koester, 2010) which will be discussed further in Chapters 7 and 8, we see the visiting representative (S2) in extract 1.6 baldly clarifying the non-negotiable status of the outlined contractual obligations.

(1.6)

> *External meeting*
> Relationship of speakers: contractually bound
> Purpose: task-/problem-oriented; buying/selling/promoting a product
> Topic: procedure; logistics

S2: So it seems (1 second) and (5 seconds) er= (1.5 seconds) it seems as if I'm here not to offer you any erm any negotiation way out of this at all.
S1: Yeah. [laughs]
S2: And that would be= that would be correct er we're not really looking to= (1 second) well (1 second) we aren't going to vary the (1 second) proposal that we've given to you.

To follow a purely emic categorization of meeting purposes or goals, whereby the meeting is categorized exactly in accordance with the participants' post-meeting description, would thus entail rejecting the term 'negotiating'. Therefore, the advice of Swales (1990: 39–40) was followed, who argues the analyst should 'develop sets of *a posteriori* categories, ones based on empirical investigation and observation, within which eliciting the community's category-labels plays a central role'. Through a consideration of the emic categories, the relevant literature and my own observations, the following six categories were selected to describe meeting purpose: 'reviewing', 'planning', 'negotiating', 'task-/problem-oriented', 'buying/selling/promoting a product', and 'giving and receiving information/advice'. There is obvious potential for overlap here (for instance, buying a product or giving and receiving information/advice can both occur during negotiations, as in Graham, 1983), which was often the actual case in meetings, and many meetings had more than one purpose. In addition, the categories are all applicable to both internal and external meetings – for instance, internal meetings could also be concerned with giving or receiving professional advice, as in extract 1.4.

Figure 1.2   Meeting purpose (all meetings in CANBEC)

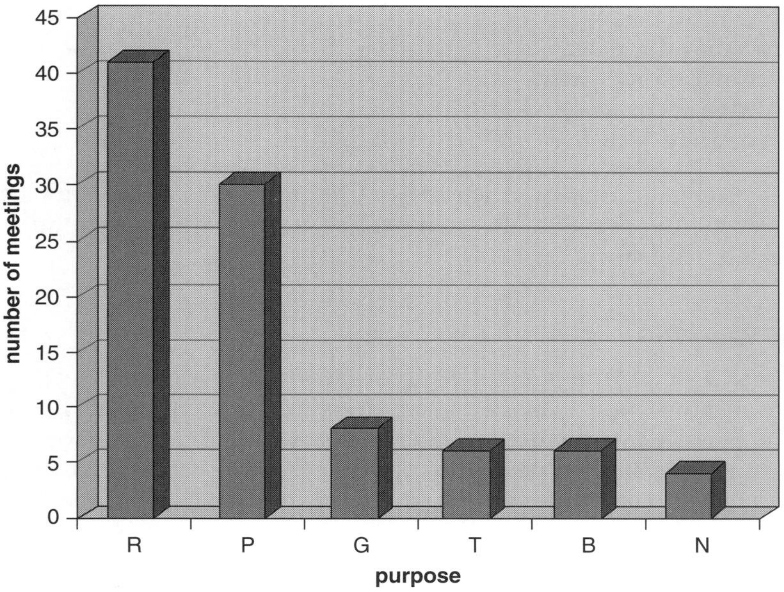

R: reviewing   P: planning   G: giving and receiving information/advice
T: task-/problem-oriented   B: buying/selling/promoting a product   N: negotiating

Figure 1.2 gives a breakdown of the main meeting purposes across meetings. In some cases, meetings were attributed two purposes. As this figure shows, the majority of meetings in the corpus involve reviewing and planning. A closer examination of the data reveals that most reviewing and planning meetings are internal, and that the majority of reviewing meetings in particular are between managers and subordinates. Planning meetings tend to occur in meetings between managers of equivalent status (peers). This makes sense intuitively, because we would expect planning to be more frequent among upper management and less common in manager–subordinate communication, given that planning will often involve deciding on procedural and strategic future directions of the company or department in question. Managers often review what subordinates have done as part of their job description, hence the higher frequency of reviewing in the manager–subordinate meetings. Equivalent empirical findings have also been reported by Holmes and Stubbe (2003: 68–70), which suggests that the results may be generalizable. The categories are spread more evenly across external meetings than internal meetings.

A more etic categorization of the data is also possible, as in the following example:

- procedure-focusing
- information-focusing
- decision-focusing
- negotiating-focusing

For teaching purposes, discussed in Chapter 9, this option may be more attractive, as the smaller number of categories may appear more distinct to the learner.

Meeting topic

Figure 1.3 shows the number of recordings that were made according to meeting topic. The categories in figure 1.3 were those chosen by the participants themselves. The reason why the total number of recordings as stated on the graph is greater than the actual number of recordings is that many meetings involved more than one topic (for example, 'sales' and 'technical').

Figure 1.3   Meeting topic

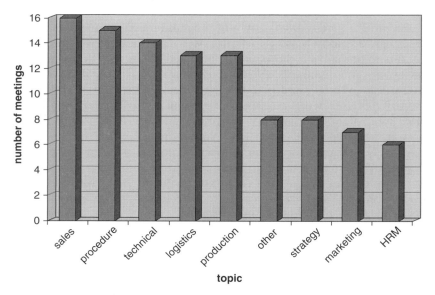

The following is a list of brief definitions of the topic categories.

Sales   Sales meetings in CANBEC are either external, with the companies discussing the buying and selling of products (usually in the form of one company trying to sell something to another company), or internal, with staff discussing some aspect of sales (for example, a new salesperson being given an introductory talk about clients' needs).

Procedure   Put most simply, these meetings focus on the way things are done. In contrast to strategy meetings, procedural meetings usually involve short-term goals.

Technical   These meetings involve communication about some technical aspect of the business (for example, the IT systems).

Logistics   Talk in these meetings is concerned with management of the physical-distribution side of the business, which controls the goods flow.

Production   Focus on this topic involves some discussion of the production process by the company. Production could also involve a service as well as a manufactured object.

Other   This category includes several topics, such as AGMs (annual general meetings), expenditure, accounts and discussing clients.

Strategy   These meetings are concerned with the long-term goals or objectives of the company. They are usually internal, and may involve the chief executive officer or managing director and an executive team.

Marketing   Marketing meetings involve some aspect of product or service promotion, placement or pricing.

HRM   The abbreviation stands for 'Human Resource Management', sometimes known as 'Personnel'. These meetings discuss the effective management of human resources.

1.4 Transcription and anonymization

According to Cook (1990:1), the problem of capturing relevant contextual information in transcription is twofold, in that 'it is infinitely delicate and infinitely expandable'. For example, the extent to which we interpret and acknowledge prosodic changes in our recording of the data relates to the delicacy of the transcription. In terms of expandability, the participants' relative position in a company might be as relevant to their use of language as what they had for breakfast. However, as Maxwell (1992) states, it is not possible to include everything which might be relevant, and, furthermore, an interpretation based on discourse analysis is in reality a reinterpretation (Jaworski and Coupland, 1999).

Despite these problems, 'spoken language is tied to its context for meaning and authenticity' (Farr, 2005: 135) and as such it was necessary to decide on which finite number of factors would be documented for transcripts of CANBEC. The codes followed by the transcribers for the intra-discoursal features (such as length of silence or interruptions) were provided by Cambridge University Press. These codes were essentially the same as those used in CANCODE, and they allow for CANBEC to form part of the Cambridge International Corpus (CIC), and to be used in CIC Tools, the software package developed by Cambridge University Press. While allowing for a certain level of prosodic information, this falls somewhat below that of a strict conversation-analysis approach to transcription, and as such some information on suprasegmental features (such as intonation) is lacking. It also means that applying certain insights from Gumperz's (1982) notion of contextualization cues becomes somewhat unworkable.

While having prescribed codes avoided debate about which codes to use, there were issues of application. Many of the meetings in CANBEC involve multiparty talk, which has the advantage of providing rich data for research (as many empirical studies focus on the dyad), but creates the problems of 'identifying different voices and disambiguating overlaps' (Bargiela-Chiappini and Harris, 1996). Extract 1.7 illustrates these two problems.

(1.7)

> *Internal meeting*
> Relationship of speakers: peer
> Purpose: task-/problem-oriented; planning
> Topic: technical; procedure

> S1: And ex-hosting helps us because er we could cons=+
> S7: [inaudible]+
> S1: +we could potentially consolidate. So yeah.
> S7: +[inaudible]
> SM: So that's why I say we get a [inaudible] full of these [inaudible] and throw them to a a as= a a LAN= local LAN.
> S1: Yeah.
> SM: And actually I'm happy to get everybody Unix machine on on on the front you know.

S1:   Yeah.
SM: On a desk top.
S1:   Yeah.
SM: And then no keyboard no nothing. And then=
S1:   But we'd need a broadcast LAN that that still has kind of routing from broadcast to multicast.
S2?: Well you you put it on the same segment as the server and you know+
S1:   Okay.
S2?: +er= and then we're restricted to= down to ex-hosting.

Here we can see that the transcriber found it very difficult to distinguish between the speakers, and although it was at times possible to make a reasonable guess (for example, S2?), sometimes it was not possible to speculate at all, except for the gender (for example, SM, indicating an unidentifiable male speaker). When more than one speaker spoke at the same time, the usual result was that at least one participant's contribution to the discourse was recorded as being inaudible, and as such was lost. Further issues related to the practicalities of transcribing the data included the quality of the recording itself and the experience and ability of the transcriber.

Once the recording had been transcribed, the sensitive job of anonymization could be started. Hudson and Finell (2000: 1), two of the original team from the CANCODE project, define anonymization as the 'systematic alteration of the original text with an aim to protect all parties involved: speakers, people referred to, corpus compilers and researchers'. As they immediately acknowledge, however, this is not a sufficient definition when faced with the actual task of anonymizing. This is arguably even more so when confronted with the task of anonymizing a corpus of business discourse, given the confidential and sensitive nature of many conversations and the desire to leave the original dialogue as unchanged as possible.

Following Rock (1999) and Hudson and Finell (2000), as well as instructions directly from Cambridge University Press, it was decided that each text would be manually read through by two different analysts. The names of all speakers were changed for another which had the same number of syllables and was of similar tone (for example *Paul* might become *James*, but not *Jeremiah* or *Raza*). Company names were also all changed to another similar in size and within the same field (for example, *Audi* might become *BMW*). When this was not possible – for example, when there were only two companies within the field of business, or where the company in question was a very well-known market leader – the company name was replaced with [*company name*]. While this option hinders the flow of the text, the primary objective of protecting the identities of those involved was upheld. The same principles were applied to various products, although with specific, lesser-known products more creativity was exercised in replacing names.

Dealing with potentially libellous, illegal or scandalous utterances proved to be much more challenging than dealing with proper nouns. For example, one speaker made a derogatory comment about a specific carmaker. As all texts in CANBEC could potentially be published in some format, such a comment was unacceptable and the name of the carmaker was removed and replaced with [*carmaker's name*]. In a series of meetings, the managing director was criticized by name. However, from the text itself it is not possible to ascertain who is being referred to, therefore merely changing the name of the managing director was deemed sufficient. As a last resort, however, the offending language was replaced with [*inaudible*] (in the original transcript this was transcribed using the code <$G?>). Cambridge University Press also requested that any references to the recording itself or directed at the researcher should be removed. While Hudson and Finell (2000) calculated that approximately 4,500 words of CANCODE could be anonymized per hour, with CANBEC the figure was closer to 3,000 per hour, indicating the comparative complexity of the process for the business corpus.

1.5 Corpus size and generalizability

CANBEC can be seen as either a large corpus or a small corpus, depending on the point of comparison. According to O'Keeffe et al. (2007), written corpora of five million words are small, but a spoken corpus of a million words is large. Several general corpora contain hundreds of millions of words, and are therefore several hundred times larger than CANBEC. Such corpora, for example the British National Corpus (BNC), are made up of largely written data, and unlike CANBEC are not specialized (Flowerdew, 2005; Handford, 2010). As argued in Handford (2010), however, comparing spoken and written corpora only in terms of words is questionable, given the far greater degree of detailed contextual information in spoken corpora – such as allocation of speakers, pauses and interruptions – that even a basic level of transcription communicates. Nevertheless, in terms of number of words, at the time of going to print, CANBEC is considerably larger than any other fully transcribed spoken business corpus.

The range of data sources in CANBEC is also considerable: the corpus comprises data from 23 companies, eight of which are multinational, and, as mentioned above, while most of the speakers in CANBEC are British, it still contains speakers from each continent of the globe. Most significantly, CANBEC is the only corpus, apart from Poncini's corpus of multinational meetings (Poncini, 2004), to contain data of external meetings, and is unique in that this data comes from a range of companies. Therefore, while a larger corpus would of course be desirable, when compared to other spoken business corpora on which ground-breaking research has been based, CANBEC is of considerable size. Nevertheless, when dividing the corpus into sub-corpora, care must be taken not to overgeneralize the findings.

The issue of generalizability and corpora is widely debated. According to Lee (2008: 94) 'the more specialized the discourse, the less you need of it to get a representative corpus and generalizable results'. While CANBEC is undoubtedly a specialized corpus of a genre (Handford, 2010), and compared to other similar corpora relatively large, the genre in question is very widely used internationally. Thus the findings are not presented as a comprehensive, representative, generalizable survey of all types of business meetings around the world. Instead, they provide a valid source of evidence for language use in a fairly wide range of different sorts of meetings that can be compared, built on and questioned in future studies of business meetings and spontaneously occurring spoken business discourse. For further discussion of these and other issues relating to size and corpus design see Sinclair (1991), Biber et al. (1998), McCarthy (1998), Hunston (2002), McEnery et al. (2006), and McCarthy and O'Keeffe (2010).

1.6 Outline of the book

Chapter 2 goes on to give the background to this book and explores several of the themes highlighted at the beginning of this chapter in detail. Section 2.2 of the chapter explicates the methodology employed and its rationale. Chapter 3 is centrally concerned with interpreting the genre of the business meeting, exploring the stages of the meetings, and the discursive practices that weave through the stages and constitute the genre. Chapter 4 initially discusses certain lexico-grammatical theoretical issues, such as collocation, and then moves on to statistical findings of single words. These involve word frequencies and significant keywords, the latter indicating how business-meeting language differs from everyday English, and how internal meetings compare to external meetings. Chapter 5 is also centrally concerned with quantitatively produced items, but in this chapter the focus is on multiword units, or 'clusters'. The relationship between these items and discursive practices is explored in some detail. Interpersonal language categories, including pronouns, backchannels, modal verbs, hedging and vague language, are discussed in Chapter 6 through the analysis of longer extracts. Chapter 7 deals with creativity in business meetings, and in particular how certain key stages of the problem-solving process are discursively achieved. Metaphors and idioms, and the statistically significant items *problem, issue* and *if* are analysed in context. Chapter 8 analyses turn-taking organization across several meetings, involving, as in other preceding chapters, comparisons between meetings according to the relationships of the speakers. Finally, Chapter 9 discusses the implications of these findings for teaching, learning and, in particular, developing teaching materials. Throughout the book, there is an attempt to understand a nebulous and thorny concept: that of 'discursive practices' – what they are, what they do, and how they can be indexed by and shown to give meaning to language.

Notes

1. Watson (2009: 228) talks about the dangers of 'language-centred thinking' and the increasingly linguistic focus taken in studies of organizations: 'when a discourse analysis "approach" is taken to organizations, organizations tend to become discursive phenomena'. This study, although centrally concerned with the study of language in several organizations, is in line with Watson in accepting that organizations comprise more than just talk.
2. CANCODE is a five-million word computerized corpus of spoken English, made up of recordings from a variety of settings in the countries of the United Kingdom and Ireland (see McCarthy, 1998: 9–10 for a fuller explication of the CANCODE corpus).
3. In fact, approximately ten per cent of CANBEC is from business lectures, but for this study they were removed from the corpus. As mentioned earlier, any business communication that was not classifiable as a meeting (such as messages left on answer phones) was also removed.
4. Of course, internal and external meetings can be categorized in several ways (see Handford, 2007). Also, the categorization proposed here may not be suitable for certain inter-organizational relationships, such as types of alliances and joint ventures.

References

Bargiela-Chiappini, F. and Harris, S. (1996) 'Interruptive strategies in British and Italian management meetings', *Text*, **16**, 3, 269–97.

Bargiela-Chiappini, F., Nickerson, C. and Planken, B. (2007) *Business Discourse*, Basingstoke: Palgrave.

Biber, D., Conrad, S. and Reppen, R. (1998) *Corpus Linguistics: Investigating Language Structure and Use*, Cambridge: Cambridge University Press.

Boden, D. (1994) *The Business of Talk: Organizations in Action*, Cambridge: Polity Press.

Boden, D. (1995) 'Agendas and arrangements: Everyday negotiations in meetings', in Firth, A. (ed.) *The Discourse of Negotiation: Studies of Language in the Workplace*, Oxford: Pergamon, 83–99.

Charles, M. (1996) 'Business negotiations: Interdependence between discourse and the business relationship', *English for Specific Purposes*, 15, 19–36.

Charles, M. and Charles, D. (1999) 'Sales negotiations: Bargaining through tactical summaries', in Hewings, M. and Nickerson, C. (eds.) *Business English: Research into Practice*, London: Longman.

Cook, G. (1990) 'Transcribing infinity: Problems of context presentation', *Journal of Pragmatics*, 15, 1–24.

Duranti, A. (1997) 'Universal and culture-specific properties of greetings', *Journal of Linguistic Anthropology*, 7, 63–97.

Farr, F. (2005) *Reflecting on Reflections: A Corpus-Based Analysis of Spoken Post Teaching Practice Interactions in an English Language Teaching Academic Environment*, PhD thesis, University of Limerick (Unpublished).

Flowerdew, L. (2005) 'An integration of corpus-based and genre-based approaches to text analysis in EAP/ESP: Countering criticisms against corpus-based methodologies', *English for Specific Purposes*, 24, 321–32.

Gee. J.P., Hull, G. and Lankshear, C. (1996) *The New Work Order*, London: Allen and Unwin.

Graham, J. (1983) 'Brazilian, Japanese and American business negotiations', *Journal of International Business Studies*, 14, 47–61.

Gumperz, J. (1982) *Discourse Strategies*, Cambridge: Cambridge University Press.

Handford, M. (2007) *The Genre of the Business Meeting: A Corpus-based Study*, PhD thesis, University of Nottingham (Unpublished).

Handford, M. (2010) 'What corpora have to tell us about specialised genres', in McCarthy, M. and O'Keeffe, A. (eds.) *The Routledge Handbook of Corpus Linguistics*, Abingdon: Routledge.

Handford, M. and Koester, A. (2010) '"It's not rocket science": Metaphors and idioms in conflictual business meetings', *Text and Talk*, 30, 27–51.

Holmes, J. and Stubbe, M. (2003) *Power and Politeness in the Workplace*, London: Longman.

Hudson, J. and Finell, A. (2000) *The Anonymisation of CANCODE: General Principles and Guidelines*, School of English Studies, University of Nottingham (Unpublished).

Hunston, S. (2002) *Corpora in Applied Linguistics*, Cambridge: Cambridge University Press.

Jaworski, A. and Coupland, N. (1999) 'Introduction: Perspectives on discourse analysis', in Jaworski, A. and Coupland, N. (eds.) *The Discourse Reader*, London: Routledge, 1–44.

Klein, N. (1999) *No Logo*, London: Flamingo.

Labov, W. (1972) *Sociolinguistic Patterns*, Philadelphia: Philadelphia University Press.

Lee, D. (2008) 'Corpora and discourse analysis: New ways of doing old things', in Bhatia, V., Flowerdew, J. and Jones, R. (eds.) *Advances in Discourse Studies*, Abingdon: Routledge, 86–99.

Maxwell, J. (1992) 'Understanding and validity in qualitative research', *Harvard Educational Review*, 62, 3, 279–300.

McCarthy, M. (1998) *Spoken Language and Applied Linguistics*, Cambridge: Cambridge University Press.

McCarthy, M. and O'Keeffe, A. (eds.) (2010) *The Routledge Handbook of Corpus Linguistics*, Abingdon: Routledge.

McEnery, T., Xiao, R. and Tono, Y. (2006) *Corpus-based Language Studies: An Advanced Resource Book*, London: Routledge.

Mirivel, J. and Tracy, K. (2005) 'Premeeting talk: An organizationally crucial form of talk', *Research on Language and Social Interaction*, 38, 1, 1–34.

Murphy, M. (1998) 'Re-viewing business communication: A response to Carmichael, White-Mills and Rogers, and Krapels and Arnold', *Journal of Business Communication*, 35, 1, 128–37.

O'Keeffe, A., McCarthy, M. and Carter, R. (2007) *From Corpus to Classroom: Language Use and Language Teaching*, Cambridge: Cambridge University Press.

Poncini, G. (2004) *Discursive Strategies in Multicultural Business Meetings*, Peter Lang, Linguistic Insights Series.

Rock, F. (1999) *Policy and Practice in the Anonymisation of Linguistic Data*, Report, Department of Linguistics, University of Birmingham (Unpublished).

Sinclair, J. (1991) *Corpus, Concordance, Collocation*, Oxford: Oxford University Press.

Stubbe, M. (2001) 'From office to production line: Collecting data for the Wellington Language in the Workplace Project', *Language in the Workplace Occasional Papers*, 2.

Swales, J. (1990) *Genre Analysis*, Cambridge: Cambridge University Press.

Watson, T. (2009) 'Sociology, narrative and discourse', in Bargiela-Chiappini, F. (ed.) *The Handbook of Business Discourse*, Edinburgh: Edinburgh University Press, 226–38.

2 Background: Theory and methodology

Many of the features examined in this book have also been studied elsewhere using corpora of discourse from various institutional environments, and have been shown to be extremely useful in establishing the 'fingerprints' of individual genres and discourses. For instance, 'keywords' (statistically significant words in a particular register or genre) (Scott, 1999) have been shown to signal both the core content vocabulary (Tribble, 2002) and interpersonal features (McCarthy and Handford, 2004) in academic and spoken business discourse respectively. Clusters, or multiword units (Wray, 2002), and their related functions have been fruitfully studied in business meetings (McCarthy and Handford, 2004; Handford, 2007; O'Keeffe et al., 2007) and in academic discourse (Biber and Conrad, 1999; Oakey, 2002; Simpson, 2004; O'Keeffe et al., 2007), as has turn-taking (Walsh, 2006; Evison, 2008). Specific interpersonal markers of genre such as vagueness and hedging have been studied in media discourse (O'Keeffe, 2003, 2006), healthcare discourse (Adolphs et al., 2007) and academic discourse (Hyland, 1998; Evison et al., 2007), and metaphors and idioms have been analysed in spoken business discourse (Koester, 2006; Handford, 2007; Handford and Koester, 2010). In each case, these linguistic features have been shown to serve conventionalized purposes within their domains of discourse. Genre itself has received considerable attention in various fields including media discourse (O'Keeffe, 2006), academic discourse (Swales, 1990, 2004; Rose, 1997; Flowerdew, 2002; Hyland, 2004) and professional discourse (Bhatia, 1993, 2004; Tribble, 2002), although the tendency has been to analyse written and not spoken genres, even in corpus studies (see Flowerdew, 2002; Handford, 2010). Relevant here is Teubert's (2007: 60) point that spoken language cannot actually be analysed without first turning it into written language.

One much discussed area in business discourse is that of language use in intercultural communication (see Bargiela-Chiappini et al., 2007; Piller, 2009). Poncini's (2002, 2004) work is pertinent here for several reasons: she is one of the few researchers who looks at language in external meetings, she questions the assumption that intercultural, and particularly international, communication is inherently problematic and heavily influenced by national cultural differences, and she employs quantitative and qualitative approaches to her data. Spencer-Oatey's work on 'rapport management' (2000) is also concerned with how people effectively collaborate and build relationships across cultures, with particular attention to face needs. Other studies that apply discourse analyses to intercultural business communication include work by Yamada (1992) and Scollon and Scollon (2001). An excellent, detailed review of such literature is contained in Bargiela-Chiappini et al. (2007).

While all the above studies are relevant, there are a handful of researchers who have profoundly influenced the study of spoken business discourse. The work of Lampi (1986)/Charles (1996) in uncovering the connections between language and its context in negotiations is seminal – for example, in terms of the different types of business relationship. Boden (1994) and Bargiela-Chiappini and Harris (1997) produced early ground-breaking interdisciplinary work on management meetings. More recently, Holmes and Stubbe (2003) and others working on the multi-faceted LWP (Language in the Workplace, mentioned previously in Chapter 1) corpus in New Zealand continue to produce powerful findings on modality, turn-taking, humour, narrative, conflict and intercultural communication. Nevertheless, it is Koester's (2004, 2006, 2010) work on language features in workplace communication that is most relevant here, through the combination of corpus linguistics, conversation analysis, discourse analysis and genre analysis approaches.

The present study aims to complement this developing body of work. The fact that CANBEC is fully transcribed allows the researcher to systematically search for language patterns in over 60 complete meeting texts, as well as focus in on individual meetings or parts of meetings. The corpus thus permits analysis of lexico-grammatical and textual features across a greater number and wider range of meetings than has previously been possible. By consistently referring to the language in the corpus, we can develop our understanding of the context in which it occurs and which it constitutes. Quantitative searches described here have been conducted using the whole corpus, unless where otherwise stated. When looking at extended extracts, meetings taken from 12 companies in particular out of the total 26 represented in CANBEC have generally been preferred, because of their intrinsic interest, the relative amount of background information available with these companies, and because it allows for the contextual or structural comparison of different aspects of the same meeting across chapters (for example, extracts 3.5 and 8.2). Furthermore, meetings that feature a range of nationalities have also been preferred whenever possible, as in extracts 2.1 and 2.4 examined in this chapter.

According to Candlin and Sarangi (2004), genre studies can be simplistic, and can fail to account for the variety and dynamism present in the reality. One of the central aims of this study is to ascertain both recurrence and dynamism of the language and context that construct the business-meeting genre. This will involve interpretation of the discursive norms of internal and external meetings. Chapter 3 will be largely concerned with questions such as: how does an internal sales meeting between a manager and his or her subordinates compare to an external sales meeting between the manager and a potential client? How does the language differ? What discursive practices do the language items invoke? Are similar turn-taking procedures employed? How do the stages of the meeting compare? How do the meetings begin and end? Do the goals differ? How are identities and relationships constructed? What practices can we infer, and are they the same? How typical are such features when compared to other meetings? The relevant methodological steps will be discussed further in section 2.2 of this chapter. In the following section 2.1, several pertinent theoretical concepts applied in the approach will be outlined.

2.1 Theory

Context

Any analysis of naturally occurring speech needs to clarify what is meant by context: is it the stable set of external factors apparent during the communication, such as the venue, or should it be something more explicitly related to or evident within the unfolding discourse? With respect to the genre of the business meeting, while there are undoubtedly regular, stable factors, the context can be seen to change from utterance to utterance. For example, extract 2.1 shows the very beginning of an internal weekly financial meeting in a multinational bank:

(2.1)

Internal meeting
Relationship of speakers: peer
Purpose: reviewing
Topic: procedure

[door slams]
S1: Oh. [inaudible] You didn't have to slam it.
[laughter]

S1:   All right. Let's get started.
SM:[clears throat]
S1:   One eight three three. Seefare financials.

This extract shows that the interactants' perceptions of what is important or appropriate do not necessarily remain stable through the course of a whole meeting, or even a particular turn. Here we have one turn (Sacks et al., 1974) in three parts, involving several changes in footing (Goffman, 1981), each of which alters the context from informal pre-meeting, to signalling the end of the pre-meeting and announcing the beginning of the formal meeting, to addressing the first topic of the agenda and eliciting feedback. Our understanding of context (and hence genre) needs to reflect this type of dynamism.

A strictly top-down, externally imposed, static understanding of context would not be able to effectively account for the dynamism evident in the shifts observable in extract 2.1, and interpreting the data from such a fixed contextual perspective would mainly involve listing as many situational factors as possible. One argument against a cataloguing of contextual factors is that there are 'indefinitely many potentially relevant aspects of context' (Schegloff, 1992: 110). For instance, describing the identities of the participants in a speech event (for example, the sales manager) is an insufficient and misleading approach to context: we need to show which aspects of each participant's identities become 'procedurally relevant' (ibid.) at a given moment in the interaction. The brief extract 2.1 shows clearly how the chair of this meeting shifts from bantering, to starting the meeting, to focusing on the agenda, and in so doing he orients towards the different identities of 'humorous colleague' and 'professional expert responsible for the efficacy of the meeting'.

As with other genre-based studies (Bhatia, 2004; Ventola, 1987; Swales, 1990; McCarthy, 1998; Koester, 2006), the challenge is to recognize what is recurrent and stable while simultaneously recognizing what is dynamic and changeable: while attending to the specific, in the background there is constantly the acknowledgement of the conventional forms, goals, situations, relationships and practices that enable us to recognize a particular genre. Indeed, as Scollon and Scollon (2001: 32) argue, from the point of view of participants, it is the 'shared knowledge of context which is required for successful professional communication'. It logically follows, therefore, that if such knowledge (for example, of setting, roles, agenda) is requisite from the participants' perspective, so it must be for the researcher in order to develop an understanding of the text in question and to account for the 'mutually reflexive relationship' of context and talk, where each dynamically shapes the other (Goodwin and Duranti, 1992: 31). Furthermore, given the potentially infinite nature of context, the possibility that our interpretations might change as a result of considering more of the context necessitates the listener or analyst applying criteria of 'relevance' (Sperber and Wilson, 1996). It is, therefore, part of the job of the discourse analyst to explicate people's socially and culturally varying criteria of relevance, and how they signal such criteria.

Goals

Spoken business discourse, in common with all institutional communication (Heritage, 1997; Sarangi and Roberts, 1999), can be described as goal-driven (Holmes and Stubbe, 2003; Koester, 2006). Indeed, it could be said that the function of an agenda is to provide an outline of the explicit goals of the meeting. Speaker goals can, however, be elusive to the observer (Penman, 1990) for a number of reasons. Participants in a meeting may have multiple goals, some of which may conflict (Tracy and Coupland, 1990); goals may be personal or corporate (Charles, 1996); goals do not necessarily exist prior to the meeting, but may emerge during the course of the communication (Hopper and Drummond, 1990). In addition, as Fairclough (1995: 40) argues, goal-driven models suggest that participants are in conscious control of the discourse to a far greater degree than is probable, a point we will return to below. Another issue concerns professional goals at the local text level and professional goals at the institutional level (Bhatia, 2004). Nevertheless, despite the complexities involved with inferring speaker goals, they have been proposed as the central defining feature of an institutional genre (Swales, 1990; Koester, 2006), and may allow us, at least in part, to account for the variety and dynamism inherent in meetings. A useful distinction in discussions of workplace discourse is that of transactional and interpersonal (or relational) language and goals (Halliday, 1978, 1985; McCarthy, 1998; Coupland, 2000; Holmes, 2000; Spencer-Oatey, 2000; Koester, 2004, 2006; Mirivel and Tracy, 2005).

The business meeting – arguably the most transactional (Boden, 1994) of professional speech events – can feature relational talk to a degree that is surprising both to the analyst and the participants themselves. If we approach the discourse from a speaker-goals and speaker-relations perspective (McCarthy, 2000), then a purely transaction-as-meaning description fails to account for the empirical evidence: speakers in business meetings appear to be deliberately using what is, on one level, interpersonal language, with transactional goals in mind. The sales director (S1) in extract 2.2, who starts talking about football to his client (S2) towards the end of an important sales negotiation, does not do so randomly and without purpose.

(2.2)

External meeting
Relationship of speakers: non-contractually bound
Purpose: buying/selling/promoting a product
Topic: sales

S1: I think next time we'll just get together and we'll we'll thrash it out and then+
S2: Lovely.
S1: +get something together.
S2: Okay.
S1: Okay? Great.
S2: Yeah. That's great. Thanks very much.
S3: Okay. [exhales] (2 seconds) Right.
S1: And I think we've got a football match the week after next [inaudible].

Here, the justification for this apparently off-topic relational move (given by the sales director in the follow-up interview) is the addressing of the transactional goal of making sure his institution makes money, and this is achieved through reminding the client of their companies' mutual relationship. The use of *And* before informing the client about the football game in the final turn is telling, in that there is no semantic link between the ideas of coming to an agreement and playing football. The link is relational and is best understood pragmatically rather than semantically. What he means is: 'we can come to an agreement, and we play football together, because we are in a worthwhile relationship, so let's maintain that relationship'.

Koester states: 'Speakers (also) have goals when engaging in casual conversation, but often these goals are largely relational and not transactional' (2001: 43). However, within the context of business meetings, the correlation between casual conversation and relational goals does not always hold, and care needs to be taken about inappropriately conflating language and goals. The position taken here is close to that of Candlin: 'any given utterance, whether apparently relationally [sic] or transactional in character, can potentially serve both interpersonal and ideational goals' (2000: xviii). That is, relational language (for example, talking about football) can be used to achieve transactional goals such as encouraging the client to remain as such and to buy more from the company (see also Iacobucci, 1990).

This discussion also has relevance to the wider business context. Within the field of marketing, research has been conducted by Iacobucci (1996) and others (Paulin et al., 1997; Paulin et al., 2000; Sharma and Pillai, 2003) to discuss the related notion of relational/transactional approaches in terms of company philosophy or corporate culture. Some companies have a far more relational culture in terms of practice, for example spending time with individual customers and eschewing the use of automated answering machines. Such an approach is intended to persuade existing customers to stay with the company – that is, to accomplish the transactional goals of at least maintaining market share and profits. It is also worth briefly mentioning the potential for conflict between global institutional goals (such as those found in mission statements) and local goals that are formed in the moment-by-moment social interaction (for example, wanting to be liked), and how 'such local goals, usually "trump" such global goals, all things being equal, when there is a conflict' (J. P. Gee, personal communication).

Practices

As mentioned above, there are several issues surrounding a goals approach to discourse – for instance, the temptation to interpret communication as being more consciously driven than is actually the case (Fairclough, 1995). The extent to which naturally occurring speech is consciously produced is a highly complex issue, and has implications for the way we understand and analyse language (ibid.; Gee, 1992; Chafe, 1994, forthcoming). The issue is also of interest to those involved in teaching and training in terms of questions such as whether learners should, or even can, develop a conscious, critical understanding of the communication, or whether the unconscious acquisition of tacit knowledge and appropriate behaviour is sufficient (Gee et al., 1996). This discussion will be returned to in Chapter 9. For our purposes here, a goals approach is combined with an understanding of communication as practice. This means that participants and their institutions undeniably have consciously definable higher-level goals, but when communicating about these goals, they automatically employ relatively ingrained professional and discursive practices to achieve them[1] (see Fairclough, 1995: 40). Emergent goals (Hopper and Drummond, 1990) also occur during the course of the communication (for example, during a meeting, somebody introduces a problem not listed on the agenda), but again these goals will tend to result in particular, conventionalized practices. In other words, the goals describe *what* participants are aiming for (such as the goal of solving the problem in question) and the practices concern *how* the goals are achieved; furthermore, practices may not only achieve goals, but they can also generate goals (Ragan, 1990).

It may be evident that there is considerable potential analytical overlap between practices and strategies. For example, Levinson defines strategies as 'optimal or self-maximizing patterns of behaviour available to participants in particular roles, under the specific constraints of the relevant activity' (1992: 100) and this definition is equally valid for explaining practices.

I will attempt to clarify here how the terms 'strategy' and 'practice' are applied in this study. Firstly, 'strategy' as it is used here should not be confused with the meeting topic 'strategy' outlined in Chapter 1 and the related notion of 'strategy as practice', as proposed in sociological and organizational studies of strategic management (briefly discussed at the beginning of Chapter 7). One difference between strategies and practices, it is argued here, may be a reflection of the researcher's interpretative perspective rather than linguistic content under analysis. Thus, the same language can, in theory, be interpreted as either evidence for practices or for strategies by different analysts, depending on the analysts' respective discourse analytical or pragmatic leaning. The two positions, one prioritizing practices and the other strategies, are briefly outlined here. The later works of Wittgenstein, as well as the social theorists Bourdieu, Foucault, Derrida, Lyotard and Giddens, amongst others, are often cited as influencing those working under a discourse analysis/practice perspective, whereas the influence of the pragmatics philosophers of language, Grice, Austin and Searle, is evident in the work of those analysts who tend towards a more strategic, conscious, intentional interpretation (or description) of participants' actions in texts. For instance, Stubbs (2007: 153), who actually is one of the few corpus linguists to have discussed practices, states that the concept of discourse was 'opened up' for linguists by Grice, Austin and Searle – a claim not likely to be shared by all linguists of the discourse-analysis persuasion. The position taken in this study is to regard practices as the default interpretative mechanism in authentic business-meeting discourse between experienced participants, and strategic language use as something more unusual. The terms 'strategy' and 'strategic' will be used here to imply an intentional choice of how to proceed, whereas practices tend to remain at a more automatic, normative level, as discussed below.

Practices, by definition, tie the communicative event to the wider social context (Fairclough, 1989, 2003; Bhatia, 2004), and therefore allow for greater understanding of the reflexive relationship between language and context. Employing a discourse-as-practice perspective is based on the assumption that 'language and other semiotic forms do not merely reflect entities and relations in social life but actively contribute to their construction and constitution' (Candlin et al., 1999: 323). Business meetings, therefore, partly construct the companies in which they occur, and the reflexive nature of practices explains this (although bearing in mind Watson's (2009) admonition, mentioned in Chapter 1, that linguistic analyses of organizations should not prioritize talk to the exclusion of all other factors). The socially achieved practices of exchanging goods, services or information, or of negotiating, discussing decisions or focusing on procedures, are what go towards constituting the company in question.

A further distinction concerns the way practices explain how much an individual's spoken workplace communication can occur spontaneously or 'automatically', as a result of that person having been apprenticed in particular professional communities (Gee, 1992)[2], whereas, as mentioned above, 'strategies' in this book belong to the realm of conscious intent. Therefore, within a discourse-as-practice account of communication, strategies can still be referred to when explaining the atypical, creative behaviour of expert members (Bazerman, 1994), who can exploit the norms of a genre with specific goals in mind (Bhatia, 2004). Such a distinction is inevitably fuzzy in certain cases; however, it still allows the analyst to make inferences based on authentic data that can then be evaluated by others. This 'automatic' interpretation of practices is explored by Scollon and Scollon (2001: 268), who state that communication tends to arise out of social practice, and that 'we do not really know consciously how we act and communicate; we just do what "comes naturally" in the course of social interactions'. This depends largely on our previous, socially sanctioned experiences in related genres and practices (Gee, 2005).

The corpus as an objective, quantifiable record of 'what comes naturally' can enable the analyst to make inferences about the linguistic manifestation of these practices (Tognini-Bonelli, 2001), as well as the related professional goals. This involves interpreting a selected language item as a critical index of a practice (Ochs, 1996; Silverstein, 2003). That is, certain items can help link the text to its context, and can thus be categorized as critical lexical items. By applying quantitative and qualitative methods (Dörnyei, 2007) to a specialized generic corpus of over 900,000 words to pinpoint such items, it is hoped that a reasonable degree of plausibility can be achieved in inferring certain key meeting-related practices within language. Nevertheless, it is important to emphasize that inferences play a role here, both in allocating certain practices, and in distinguishing between practices and strategies.

To underscore participants' lack of conscious awareness of certain aspects of their communication, when recordees are later shown transcripts of their meetings, a frequent response is 'I had no idea I spoke like that', 'I didn't know I said that' or 'Did we really spend so long talking about football?'. Nevertheless, we are obviously conscious of our communication at some level, and Chafe draws a useful distinction between the immediate conscious focus the interlocutors have on the particular one- or two-second 'intonation unit'[3] (1994: 29) at its moment of production or interpretation (that is, what the speaker is saying at that moment in time) and the peripheral consciousness of 'semi-active information that provides a context' (ibid.) for the intonation unit. This peripheral consciousness on the part of the speaker is concerned with the goal of adequately completing the topic under discussion (what Chafe calls the 'discourse topic', ibid.), and is therefore compatible with the activated practices business people tend to employ to address the goals in question.

While there have been many interpretations and definitions of professional, institutional, discursive, social and cultural practices (Foucault, 1980; Bourdieu, 1977; Giddens, 1984; Fairclough, 1989; Gee, 1990; Stubbs, 1996; Sarangi and Roberts, 1999; Bhatia, 2004, 2008), practices are defined here as shared, sanctioned, recurring, constraining and enabling communicative conventions. These conventions are socially ratified within the specific unfolding context by the powerful participants and the tacit agreement and involvement of the less powerful participants, and are acquired over time through membership of a particular community. By 'powerful', I mean those who are usually institutionally sanctioned to manage the discourse[4]. In this study, the specific context is the genre of the business meeting, each text represents a recording of a meeting in progress, and CANBEC is a collection of such texts. Examples of constitutive practices include: decision-making[5], negotiating, hypothesizing, transferring information, making a client feel valued and delegating responsibility. These will be discussed further in later chapters.

One of the most systematic formulations of practices has been developed by Fairclough (1989, 1995, 2003), employing a critical discourse analysis methodology that takes an ethical, emancipatory stance towards language in society. He defines practices as comparatively established forms of social activity that mediate in complex ways between very general, abstract social structures and very specific, recognizable social events (2003: 23–4). Through practices, certain structural possibilities are controlled while others are excluded. Practices thus, for example, constrain and allow what is possible in the business context. A single external business meeting between a sales manager and a client is an instance of such a social event, whereas 'the new work order of the new capitalism' (Gee et al., 1996: xi), signified by fierce competition, high technology, niche markets and a seemingly empowered yet arguably dispensable workforce is an example of one potentially relevant social structure. An institutional practice that mediates the two could be 'negotiating' and is a way the sales director in extract 2.3 (S1) achieves the goal of selling the product to the client (S2).

(2.3)

> *External meeting*
> Relationship of speakers: non-contractually bound
> Purpose: buying/selling/promoting a product
> Topic: sales

S1: Erm but you know we're prepared to do something like if you say "Well look I'm pretty sure that we're gonna be up to sixteen by by Christmas time or+
S2: Yeah.
S1: +by er April".

How the practice of negotiating is linguistically realized is worthy of attention, to make 'unconscious practices explicit for the purpose of analysis' (Scollon and Scollon, 2001: 268). Here, the sales director is offering an unspecified discount (*we're prepared to do something*) to his client if she can guarantee an increase in business. He creates an attractive conceptual world, a 'shared social space' (Vygotsky, 1987), the realization of which would be favourable to both parties. This is achieved through the use of the cluster *if you say "Well . . ."* which will be explored in more detail in Chapter 7. The issue of vague language (*something*, *by Christmas time or by er April*) is also relevant, as it is a further way that participants can reconstruct and reconceptualize the boundaries of their communication (Evison et al., 2007). Other convergent features include hedges and fillers (*Erm*, *you know*, *like*, *look*, *pretty*), idioms (*be up to*) and the presence of the encouraging, co-constructing backchannel *Yeah*.

Communities of practice

According to Scollon and Scollon (2001), a community of practice develops over time a mutually understandable set of practices, which exists because of some common purpose or goal. Wenger states that there are three crucial dimensions of a community of practice:

- mutual engagement
- a joint negotiated enterprise
- a shared repertoire of negotiable resources accumulated over time (Wenger, 1998: 76)

'Mutual engagement' concerns the regular interaction that members, both novice and expert, have. A joint negotiated enterprise means that, as well as a shared goal, there is also an ongoing process to develop the larger enterprise. 'Negotiable resources' are various routines, including the degree to which interpersonal talk is tolerated, linguistic terminology and even the eating of meals together. A company, or part of a company (such as a logistics department), is a collection of regularly interacting, goal-oriented people who share routines and practices, and can therefore be interpreted as a community of practice. Within the company, or department, or even long-term joint venture, there will be novices who are being apprenticed in adopting the tacit knowledge, practices and values of the community by its expert members (Gee et al., 1996) – for example, by managers.

In answer to the question of how communities, practices, goals, genre and discourse relate, we could say that communities of practice develop suitable genres for the discursive activities in which they are involved – for instance, the business meeting. Meetings embody and provide a platform for various practices that can go on in business, especially management practices. In other words, genres, such as meetings, are the participatory frameworks (Swales, 1990) through which the community can address its goals and develop the enterprise.

It is worth saying a brief word here about discourse communities and communities of practice. While the term 'discourse communities' tends to be associated with lexico-grammar, texts and genres (for instance, Swales, 1990), 'communities of practice' (Wenger, 1998) emphasizes the practices that bind and move the community forward (Bhatia, 2004). This book is an attempt to integrate insights from both, as called for by Bhatia (2004: 149).

Another aspect that makes the business meeting suitable for business, and that is central to an understanding of practices and their communities, is the notion of constraint – for example, in terms of topic, agenda, the chair, time and the relationship between participants. Constraint ensures the meeting unfolds as a meeting should, according to the expectations of the participants. Meetings, through the exercising of power by the chair (Holmes and Stubbe, 2003) and other powerful speakers, can be 'kept on track', or can be finished when deemed appropriate through constraints employed at different levels of the organization. Some companies impose a fixed time limit of, for instance, one hour for meetings; after that time, staff are required to leave the meeting room even if the communication is not finished. Usually, however, only the senior manager or the chair has the power to end the discussion. Subversion and other forms of tension are nevertheless often simultaneously present (ibid.), and such tension can partly be explained from a goals perspective: 'subversion' occurs when the individual's and the organization's goals actively diverge, and the individual consciously, or strategically, queries or subverts the practice in question. A more institutionally sanctioned challenge to existing practices occurs when expert, powerful users of the genre 'exploit generic resources' to respond to novel situations (Bhatia, 2004: 20). Nevertheless, even established members can be censured and even expelled from the community if such exploitation of the genre and its practices is perceived by the powerful in that community to veer too far from its norms (Gee, 1990).

This idea of the tension between the constraining and empowering force of communication is also developed by Sarangi and Roberts, who argue that workers participate in, are restricted by and also create their work environment through practices:

Workplaces are held together by communicative practices ... But workplaces are also sites of social struggle, as certain ways of talking, recording and acting are produced and ordered over time. This regulation of communicative resources, in turn, controls access to the workplace and opportunities within it. (Sarangi and Roberts, 1999: 1)

Through analysing the communicative processes and products of related communities of practice, we can construct a picture of what goes on in different workplaces and among different groups in the same workplace. While previous business-communication research has talked in fairly general terms about the effect different relationships between speakers can have on meeting discourse, this study develops and applies a systematic breakdown of the data in terms of speaker position, power relationships and department, as well as meeting purpose and topic.

Face and politeness

All human interaction has the potential to develop into conflict and confrontation, and politeness is a system of interpersonal strategies, or practices (Watts, 2003), which is intended to minimize that threat (Lakoff, 1990). In work situations, face-threats such as requests, orders, complaints and refusals are an occupational hazard, hence it could be argued that the workplace has a high potential for confrontation. This would help to explain the conclusions of Holmes and Stubbe when they state[6]:

Our analyses indicate that most workplace interactions provide evidence of mutual respect and concern for the feelings or face needs of others, that is, politeness. Politeness is one important reason for modifying the blatant imposition of one's wishes on others. (Holmes and Stubbe, 2003: 7)

This observation is supported by the data in CANBEC. However, rather than politeness being a reason for modifying impositions, it is seen here as a context-sensitive means for softening such impositions, and may indeed be a socially constrained prerequisite (Watts, 2003) of many types of meetings in particular cultures. Bhatia's observation that business activity 'always thrives on building positive relations between various participants' (2004: 15) is relevant here, and because of the considerable evidence supporting this claim in CANBEC, a theme of this book is how this is discursively achieved. Statistically, the two most significant words in business meetings compared to everyday conversation are both interpersonal items (Halliday, 1985): the pronoun *we* and the response token *okay*. When we consider that business is, by definition, primarily concerned with transactions, this is a startling finding. Another finding that reflects the positive preference of business discourse concerns the frequency of *better than* and *worse than*: *better than* is ten times more frequent than *worse than*, which only occurs in relational, off-topic communication.

The notion of face as an academic construct can be traced back to the work of Goffman (1967) and Sacks (1972), but it has received its most systematic (and arguably most criticized – see Matsumoto, 1988; Gu, 1990; Janney and Arndt, 1993; Bargiela-Chiappini, 2003; Watts, 2003) interpretation from a pragmatic perspective from Brown and Levinson (1987). While their approach will not be applied in its entirety here, the notions of 'positive' and 'negative' face are relevant to areas of institutional discourse, including politeness, power, conflict and convergence (Spencer-Oatey, 2000; Handford and Koester, 2010). Social interaction is, according to Brown and Levinson (1987), characterized by each interactant's desire to have his or her own positive and negative face wants met: positive face wants refer to the wants or needs for praise and admiration, and negative face wants to the desire for 'freedom from imposition' (ibid.: 61).

In general, people will not go out of their way to violate one another's face – for example, by strongly criticizing somebody or imposing heavily upon them. When it is deemed necessary to perform a face-threatening act, people will usually attempt to mitigate it. This mitigation is achieved by employing various politeness 'strategies' (Brown and Levinson, 1987), such as being positively polite to your interlocutor by complimenting him or her, or allowing him or her plenty of room to reject an imposition (negative politeness), or wording it in such a way as to appear non-conflictual. Indeed, communication that lacks any such mitigation often signifies strong disagreement.

Nevertheless, it would be incorrect to conclude that spoken business discourse is consistently polite: as Bargiela-Chiappini et al. state, business people are 'inclined to override politeness considerations for the sake of conversational clarity', particularly in international contexts (2007: 195). Furthermore, given that business communication is largely concerned with the discursive negotiation of obligations, the potential for conflict is ever present.

This section has discussed many of the key concepts that underpin this study, and has touched on several items and features that will be explored further in later chapters. In the next section, we will look at how the data have been analysed.

2.2 Methodology

Six steps for analysis

An advantage of many specialized corpora, of which CANBEC would be an example, is that the person who compiled the corpus is often the same person who analyses it (Flowerdew, 2005: 329). This means the compiler/analyst has an understanding of the wider socio-cultural context to which the text belongs, or can contact relevant specialist informants, or, when necessary, act as 'a mediating ethnographic specialist informant to shed light on the corpus' (ibid.). For a large majority of the recordings in CANBEC, I was able to play that role, having developed relationships with individuals in the various companies in order to obtain the recordings, and having been present in the workplaces before, during and after recordings. This allowed for a reasonable level of confidence when interpreting the data, through semi-formal interviews and observation notes, as well as subsequent communication with at least some of the recordees.

In line with other recent corpus-based studies of spoken institutional discourse (see Koester, 2010; Handford, 2010), this book integrates quantitative and qualitative approaches to the analysis of the data. Initially, frequency lists of single words and clusters, as well as statistically significant keywords (Scott, 1999), are produced. Selected items are then interpreted in concordance lines, from which their collocations can be gleaned. What is termed the item's 'discourse prosody', 'the speaker's evaluation of what is being talked about' (Stubbs, 2001b: 449) – that is, the pragmatic stance or connotations signalled by the item in the context – can also be inferred from concordance lines of the item's collocates. Longer extracts featuring these items can then be examined and insights applied from approaches such as conversation analysis, discourse analysis, pragmatics and organization studies to explore the relationship between the text and its social context, the key challenge in the analysis of naturally occurring business talk (Charles, 1996; Bargiela-Chiappini et al., 2007). The advantage of employing quantitative techniques is that it allows for the achievement of a level of objectivity and replicability that is perhaps lacking from much discourse analysis. Notwithstanding this, frequency in language is obviously not a direct reflection of meaning or importance, and unusual communication can be very meaningful.

In order to thoroughly examine the texts, parts of the following approaches and tools are combined: Gee's discourse analytic method (2005), Hallidayan systemic functional linguistics (Halliday, 1985; Martin, 1992), a multiple-goals approach (Tracy and Coupland, 1990), and a contextually informed corpus methodology of the analysis of unfolding speech developed by Carter and McCarthy (Carter and McCarthy, 1995; McCarthy, 1998; O'Keeffe et al., 2007). Gee accessibly clarifies how language and the various levels of the wider social context, including practices, reflexively interact, and multiple-goals and Hallidayan approaches support inferences concerning the language 'choices' speakers display (although, as discussed above, with choices tending to be automatic rather than fully conscious), as well as the interpersonal, textual or ideational functions these choices address. Corpus techniques enable the analyst to quickly and plausibly pinpoint some of the typical language choices, and provide empirical evidence of practices and goals in context (Stubbs, 1996, 2001b; Carter, 2004; Lee, 2008).

An analysis which combines these approaches and tools can begin to account for a range of different agents and factors that generate and are created through the discourse: the institution(s) involved, their specific cultural, social, professional and discursive practices, the participants performing these practices, the relationships between the participants and the communities they form, the institutional, personal and possibly conflicting multiple goals the participants orient to, and the genre that provides a platform for the realization of these factors.

The remainder of this section discusses and demonstrates how the original approach developed here will be used to explore the CANBEC data. Although the book's organization does not unfold exactly in accordance with the framework – outlined in the six steps below – the insights gained from this approach should nevertheless be regularly apparent to the reader throughout the chapters. Even though this approach is laid out as a series of steps, the analysis is cyclical in that there is constant movement back and forth from the text to the context to understand the meanings, goals, practices, identities and structures that the participants construct through their talk (Gee, 2005).

Step 1   Collect and transcribe relevant textual and contextual data.
Step 2   Pinpoint and categorize potentially important linguistic features, such as lexico-grammatical items in the form of single words and clusters.
Step 3   Understand the specific meaning and use of the chosen item in its specific context.
Step 4   Infer the practices and goals that participants orient to through the discourse in which this item occurs.
Step 5   Consider, when possible, which 'Discourses' (Gee, 1992) and social structures are relevant to this discourse. According to Gee, Discourses are 'amalgams of ways of talking, valuing, thinking, believing, interacting, acting' (ibid.: 105) – in other words, they are collections of intertwined practices that various social groups perform.
Step 6   Interpret what communicative activities and socially situated identities are being enacted through these (and other) linguistic features in the data.

Step 1 has already been discussed in detail in Chapter 1. Step 2 involves finding words, clusters, turn-taking behaviour and so on in the corpus that may warrant further investigation. The central concept here is that there are linguistic items and features that play a critical interpretive role in terms of the understanding and development of the meeting context. To avoid the circular danger of saying something is important because the analyst merely intuits it as such

(see Widdowson, 1998), language items and features can be classified
as potentially of interest if:

• they are frequent
• they are statistically significant
• they are stylistically salient or culturally key
• they have been shown to be important in other, related studies.

Items which are frequent or statistically significant can be identified through quantitative analysis using corpus software, whereas
addressing the third and fourth bullet points involves looking for pre-
determined items and features (Stubbs, 2001a; Tribble, 2002), such as
metaphors or turn organization (see Handford and Koester, 2010)[7].
Merely by reading through transcripts, it is also possible to come
across such features by chance. For example, an interesting, although
relatively rare, example of stylistic salience concerns rule-breaking,
which is usually oriented to by the other participants but is not accessible to the analyst using top-down approaches.

Accessing the top two types is usually much more straightforward.
Using corpus software like WordSmith Tools (Scott, 1999) and CIC
Tools in combination with manually reading texts means that finding
such potentially critical items is less subjective than is sometimes the
case in discourse studies (Baker, 2006). For example, as mentioned
above, the most significant keyword by far when the language used
in business meetings in CANBEC is compared to everyday conversation (as represented by the five-million-word CANCODE corpus – see
Chapter 1 for a description) is *we*, whereas words that are associated
with feelings and the family are comparatively much less common in
business meetings. It is also possible to conduct keyword or cluster
searches comparing CANBEC data to corpora of academic speech to
see how the two institutional, goal-driven discourses share certain features and not others (McCarthy and Handford, 2004; O'Keeffe et al.,
2007), or to compare internal-meeting keywords and external-meeting
keywords or clusters, or to look at the keywords or clusters in one
meeting in particular, or one stage of meetings, such as the beginnings.

Given that we are also working with a specialized corpus of genre
(Handford, 2010) of business meetings, which are at least partly
comprised of repeated, recognizable stages or 'moves' (Swales,
1990), the relationship between the language features and the practices and goals they invoke can be examined. Chapter 4 will begin
to explore why *we* is such a popular choice in many types of meetings. A key question here is to what extent the various features are
conventionalized. According to Bargiela-Chiappini et al. (2007: 187),

we can find coherence and order at the moves level, but *not* at the level of linguistic expression. This book, in contrast, is centrally concerned with examining the hypothesis that there are repeated, recurring, recognizable patterns at the lexico-grammatical level, and furthermore that these patterns signify recurrent practices.

A useful tool in the exploration of this language–practice relationship and for conducting steps 3 and 4 is the concordance line. Concordance lines display repeated occurrences of a selected item, and thus potentially allow for the comparison of an item's behaviour in different contexts. To demonstrate this, two sets of concordance lines of the highly significant three-word cluster *you have to* are shown below. Usually the selected item is aligned in corpus software, but cluster words are displayed here in bold and unaligned for ease of reading. Codes contained in transcriber's brackets in the corpus (for example, indicating speaker change) are also absent from the concordance lines.

Concordance lines for **you have to** *in internal manager–subordinate meetings*

No don't close it because you now **you have to** put some attributes for that tag.

Because to change a web page on a server **you have to** have access rights to the directory.

I mean we've always said that **you have to** send it in writing and we've

And in order to do that **you have to** use HTTP. Okay. HTTP protocol that

That's good so erm point actually. Cos then **you have to** go like this and the person will like

being really overworked. Yeah and yeah. Yeah so **you have to** yeah it just er getting inform= Well

you have to go between [laughs] bonus. [laughs] **You have to** go between three and six days afterwards

have to I know but. Yes. The procedure is **you have to** announce it but if you know there are

the next thing in the page. I see. So **you have to** force something to move on. Yeah. to the next

in here which take a bit longer. Uh-huh. Y= **you have to** put a different procedure you know distraction

---

*Concordance lines for **you have to** in external meetings*

voice up and down a bit. Yeah. But **you have to** make a conscious effort to do it if

and I'm ever so sorry about this but erm **you have to** understand there's a new vehicle going through

do. We use the same plug like when **you have to** buy a special. No. It would be the

wanna lose that. [laughs] You're right. What **you have to** put up with George. [laughs] Okay.

agree with you but I don't know what **you have to** do to make them comply. No. That's my point.

some of them. But it might be that **you have to** give them three months' notice. Or in a year's

work to say okay this must be cancelled **you have to** make er a= additional order we have to

can't read my own sometimes. [laughs] Mm. What **you have to** do is get the paper and twist it round

You won't. But but you see. [laughs] What **you have to** understand is we're engineers and we can

you can't go to shop a lot dot co UK stats. And **you have to** have a password to go in from there. Yeah.

The first set of concordance lines, from a sub-corpus of internal, manager–subordinate meetings, unsurprisingly shows the manager directing the staff and giving instructions. The second set of concordance lines from external meetings displays considerable differences when compared to the internal data. There is rarely any sense of obligation in the external meetings (only *you have to make . . .* in the seventh line, but even this is in fact self-referential – that is, the speaker is referring to what her organization has to do), with speakers instead offering non-face-threatening and sometimes general advice (*you have to make a conscious effort, what you have to do is, and you have to have a password*). The cluster is also found in non-transactional exchanges in internal meetings (*What you have to put up with George*) (see Koester, 2004). This difference can also be reflected at the grammatical level, with the cluster sometimes forming part of a cleft clause (*what you have to do is . . .*), thereby focusing attention on the subsequent clause (Carter and McCarthy, 2006). Such an indirect use of the cluster is more than twice as common in external meetings in CANBEC than internal meetings. The cluster also forms parts of longer idiomatic expressions such as *you have to understand* that can serve specific convergent functions (Moon, 1998). These context-specific differences shed light on the issue of practices: whereas the internal manager–subordinate data constitutes the management practice of directing staff, the external data shows a greater concern with the interlocutors' face needs, and with the practice of developing and maintaining relationships. Inter-organizational relationships often require a considerable investment of time and resources, and are also potentially fragile, points which help to explain these recurring differences in practices. A further practice is that of offering a client or potential client non-obligatory advice. These are all issues we will return to at later stages of the book.

Applying the six steps

To further clarify the methodology and concerns of this study, we will look at the first few minutes of a meeting within an international luxury hotel chain in extract 2.4, broken into four stages. After this, steps 3–6 outlined on page 39 will be discussed in more detail. This extract has been chosen because it features several repeated 'interesting' items, such as frequent clusters (*have to, it doesn't matter if, you know*) and positive keywords, for example *we* and *if*. It also features language that is negatively key, or statistically unusual in meetings, for example the 'emotional' expressions like *the score for the division hurts me*. As we shall see, the extract also contains other items and features that can help us interpret the text and its context. All these items are initially pinpointed through step 2. Instantiations of particular steps are noted in brackets.

This manager–subordinate meeting takes place in the company's central London hotel, in the Rooms division (the division responsible for all aspects of service expected by guests). The director of Rooms (S1, male, North American) is talking to the telecommunications manager (S2, male, German), the telecommunications supervisor (Michelle – S3, female, British) and three female telecommunications operators (Somalian, French and Spanish) about the recent disappointing score the telecommunications section of the Rooms division (referred to as PBX) received for its standards-compliance review. He is justifying why it is now necessary for the whole division to follow the standards much more to the letter and what this change will mean in practice. The following, slightly shortened three-minute extract has been broken down into five stages: A: Background to the change; B: A narrative example; C: The point; D: Generalizing the directive; and E: Personalizing the message.

(2.4)

> *Internal meeting*
> Relationship of speakers: manager–subordinate
> Purpose: task-/problem-oriented; giving and receiving information/advice
> Topic: procedure; strategy

S1: So (2 seconds) the standards focus really came into play as a as a company about a year ago. Mr Ford held a meeting in in New York and and Mr Bruce was one of the attendees. And they made a commitment that as a company our goal and our aim has to be
5   to improve our compliance with Central Standards. ... So we've= (1 second) we've committed ourselves that this has to happen. (2 seconds) **A**

In a lot of our= no I shouldn't say that. In some of our hotels ... especially the long serving hotels like London there's employees
10   that have been in their job for a number of years. You know it's not rare fifteen twenty twenty five thirty years in a job (1 second) and an example came up of a PBX operator who works at one of our California hotels ... cos PBX could be a position where a person has for for a while. It's a stable job (1 second) and you know here is a here
15   is an example of an employee who the guests love (2 seconds) is a pleasant enough person. Gets good guest feedback and things but just refuses to use the guest's name. (2 seconds) And you know as a company we're er we're a company that manages with our heart first ... and we're a people company so we always would well ... it's
20   Amy so we'd make an exception. You know she's been here twenty years. It's this it's that. **B**

Well ... I'm here to tell you that ... the company's now saying "Yes we love our employees and we we still provide an excellent work envi-ronment for our employees". But standards are our life. (2 seconds)
25   Standards aren't if you want to= ... if it's convenient for you or when you want to do them. It's= ... this is what we do. It's not an extra job ... it is the job. (2 seconds) **C**

> And it's all of us. If I walk into PBX and answer a telephone ... it doesn't [D]
> say that I don't have to use the guest's name. (1 second) Guest's name
> 30 will be used when known in a natural and discreet manner. (1 second)
> Except for by Kurt Scolari. There is no exceptions+
> S2: Yeah.
> S1: +it doesn't matter if a planning committee member if a res= reser-
> vations agent if Maria if Georgina Powell right now. They have to do
> 35 it. ... If I'm opening car doors at the front door I have to say "Welcome
> to the [company name]". These are our standards. (1 second) Full
> stop. (2 seconds)

> So that's where we in a= as I said. Starting off PBX has always been [E]
> a department that's s= that's done very well with standards. It's= I
> 40 know it's it's for Michelle and Emily the score hurts.
> S3: Yep.
> S1: And I gotta tell you the score for the division hurts me ... and espe-
> cially for the hotel cos I know we're better than that

A: BACKGROUND TO THE CHANGE

In this first stage, the Rooms director is explaining that the decision to fully implement the Central Standards, communicated by
the company chief executive officer (*Mr Ford*) to, among others, the
London hotel manager (*Mr Bruce*). Such intertextual (Bhatia, 2004)
reference to a previous, top-level meeting adds more weight to the
directives which follow.

This first stage contains two instances of the frequent deontic modal
verb *have to* (lines 4 and 6; step 2 of the analysis, as outlined on page 39),
which highlight the importance of this change in policy and the lack
of flexibility the staff are allowed in dealing with it (step 3). There
are further, similar instances in the stages below. According to Swan
(1995), the verb *have to* tends to express obligation in an objective,
official, even external tone, which partly explains why managers often
use it in business meetings. The whole of extract 2.4 is marked by
several strong modal forms, and the underlying message is one of obli-
gated practices that the staff need to adopt (step 4). However, as has
been shown, if we compare the use of *have to* in other meeting contexts, we find that it can be used to achieve different practices (steps
3 and 4). Studying context-specific concordance lines of potentially
critical items enables us to infer practices (Tognini-Bonelli, 2001: 5),
and therefore comparing different context-specific concordance lines

within a particular genre allows us to tentatively infer the practices that reflexively constitute different contexts.

The shifting of agency (step 6) in this extract is also interesting, which we can notice by looking at the subjects of the verbs and some other lexical items. Initially, the decision is made solely at the highest level of the company (lines 3–4: *they made a commitment . . .*), but less than a minute later the director states *So we've* (*1 second*) *We've committed ourselves that this has to happen* (lines 5–6). In reality, the company executives have committed the staff to complying with the standards, but it is the aim of the director as leader to motivate the staff towards acceptance, performance, and even ownership of these changes in their daily professional practices (Gee et al., 1996: 19), aims that are manifested during the unfolding meeting. His linguistic choices reflect and actualize both this goal and his social identity as a senior manager within his work community (step 6). These choices include the use of *So* (line 5; also a top keyword in CANBEC) and *we/ourselves* (line 6): *we* can refer to various differing groups, and here it seems to be inclusive – that is, it includes all the company employees. Interestingly, the re-lexicalization of *commit* (line 6) suggests that the staff have been active in obligating themselves, whereas perhaps a passive form (such as *you have been committed by the management . . .*) would be a more accurate description of reality.

B: A NARRATIVE EXAMPLE

Research into narratives in business talk (step 6) typically highlights how speakers' complex social identities can be negotiated (such as 'manager' and 'friendly person') and how relational goals can be achieved through the use of stories at work (Holmes, 2006). Here, in contrast, we have an extremely on-topic, transactionally oriented story about a worker's behaviour (the worker is referred to in line 20 as *Amy*) that is now professionally unacceptable in the changing environment. This is interesting from an intertextual and interdiscursive perspective. Bhatia succinctly contrasts these two related terms, stating that intertextuality concerns using previous texts in 'conventionalized and somewhat standardized ways' to change the past into the present, whereas:

. . . interdiscursivity refers to more innovative attempts to create hybrid or relatively novel constructs by appropriating or exploiting established conventions or resources associated with other genres. Interdiscursivity thus accounts for a variety of discursive processes, some of which include mixing, embedding, and bending of generic norms in professional practice. (Bhatia, 2008: 175)

In the story, the Rooms director makes intertextual reference to the worker's prior workplace 'texts' (that is, her communication with the customers), thereby making the story relevant to his audience. From an interdiscursive perspective, involving in this case the embedding of one discourse type or genre (in this case a narrative) within another (business meeting), this narrative is of note because the director does not seem to be seeking to achieve any obvious relational goal: it is a very transactional, on-topic story. Furthermore, the storyteller does not feature in the story, acting more as a vessel for the expression of the corporate goals and what they mean in practice to these staff members (step 4).

The purpose of this narrative is to persuade the staff to take on board these changes (step 4). In the first part of this extract there is an interesting mix of very frequent (step 2), convergent language as the director tells the staff about a telephone operator in California: four occurrences of the multifunctional two-word chunk *you know*, the hedges *just, well*, the vague marker *and things* (all of which are statistically significant), ellipsis (*is a pleasant enough person. Gets good guest feedback*), idioms (*make an exception, it's this it's that*) and clichéd business metaphors (*a people company*).

C: THE POINT

Stage C contains a striking shift in footing (Goffman, 1981), content and the director's stance (step 6) following the meta-linguistic performative *Well . . . I'm here to tell you that*. Meta-language is a marker of power in institutional discourse (Thomas, 1984; Koester, 2006) and it would, for instance, be a hazardous challenge to usual business practices and Discourses (step 5) for a subordinate to use this type of language. Following this marked change in footing, the director unambiguously signifies the stance of the company, initially by contrasting two well-trodden, fossilized metaphors: *Yes we love our employees* (lines 22–3), *But standards are our life* (line 24). There soon follows another, much more literal, direct and unequivocal contrast: *This is what we do. It's not an extra job . . . It is the job* (lines 26–7). The strong shift in stance and message is also achieved through a distinct dearth of interpersonal indirectness features, such as hedging and vague items, combined with robust descriptions of the institution's official stance.

Another interesting linguistic aspect is the repetition of *love* (lines 15 and 23). As noted above, such emotional terms are statistically much less frequent in CANBEC than in everyday communication (step 2). This issue is discussed further in relation to stage E. It is also noteworthy that the director changes the subject of the verb (first, the guests love the worker; next, the company loves its staff) without drawing attention to this change, and indeed by structuring the company's love as given information through the use of *Yes* (*Yes we love our employees*), he implies that the participants have already acknowledged this, whereas in fact there has been no such communication.

D: GENERALIZING THE DIRECTIVE

The highly significant business keyword *if* occurs five times in stage D, paradoxically to show the unconditionality of the directive: nobody (including other staff members, such as *Maria* or *Georgina Powell*), except the owner of the hotel chain (*Kurt Scolari*), is exempt from the practice of addressing guests by their names. Once again we see strong deontic modality, plus the significant cluster *it doesn't matter if* (line 33). This cluster is only used in internal meetings by managers – usually, as in this case, as a power marker to their subordinates (step 6). The metaphorical *Full stop* (lines 36–7) is also salient (step 2), as it draws attention to itself as another emphatic marker of the director's company-sanctioned power.

E: PERSONALIZING THE MESSAGE

In this stage, we can see more 'emotional' language, such as *hurts* (lines 40 and 42). As mentioned above, language within this semantic field is markedly unusual in CANBEC (see also Nelson, 2000, for parallel results) and yet the director is an extremely experienced, senior and successful employee within a highly competitive workplace, who we can assume is an expert performer in this genre (Bazerman, 1994). Bhatia (2004: 157) discusses the lexico-grammatical, discoursal and genre-level manipulation by expert members of professional communities to strategically achieve their various goals. This story, the signalling of the concurrence of two staff members present at the meeting (*Michelle and Emily*) and particularly the unusual use of emotive language are arguably such manipulated instances (step 6), and may be intended to persuade the staff at an emotional level of the need for this change towards the standards and to emphasize the importance attached to this message by the director and the company (step 5).

So far in this chapter we have discussed step 2 of the analysis in detail, and looked at how steps 1–6 can be applied to a particular extract. We will now explore in more detail steps 3–6, in particular the relationship between corpus-accessible texts and practices.

Step 3 partly involves applying Gee's notion of 'situated meanings': words do not have general meanings once we start analysing discourse, but instead have 'different specific meanings in different contexts of use . . . the meanings of words are also integrally linked to and vary across different social and cultural groups' (Gee, 2005: 53). Situated meanings demonstrate how language and practices interrelate (ibid.). One such example of situated meanings is that of keywords (Scott, 1999), because consistently reoccurring words can be expected to have an underlying functional cause (Biber, 1988: 13), or, once we start exploring different contexts, causes. This is because '[f]eatures do not randomly co-occur in texts' (ibid.). In CANBEC, one of the most statistically significant words is *if*, and in the specific context discussed on page 48 it is used to reinforce the unconditionality of the company's standards. Later we shall see that, in other meeting contexts, *if* achieves very different practices.

As demonstrated above, once an item has been classified as potentially critical, we can study its collocations and concordance lines; from these we can infer its discourse prosody[8] (Stubbs, 2001b). We can also start considering how it is 'primed' (Hoey, 2005) – for example, at which stage, phase or move of an unfolding stretch of discourse it is primed to occur in the minds of those who participate in meetings (that is, discourse priming). Information concerning discourse prosody and priming can help us make plausible inferences about the practices we are trying to uncover (step 4): such prosodies and primings, it is argued further in Chapter 4, are potential evidence of practices, and certain items can be primed for particular context-specific practices, as in the case of *if*. We will also see in Chapter 7 that *if* can have a negative or a positive discourse prosody, depending on the context. We will return to these issues in greater detail in Chapter 4.

Steps 3 and 4 thus clearly concern the complex relationship between language and practices. While it has been argued that the relationship between certain practices and the text may be difficult to clarify (for example, Bhatia, 2004: 16), the approach taken here draws on corpus-based insights from Tognini-Bonelli (2001: 5) and Stubbs (1996, 2007) concerning the analysis of concordance lines. In short, concordances provide evidence of practices. Concordances of selected items (such as keywords and clusters) taken from a collection of texts which constitute the business-meeting genre, or sub-genres such as manager–subordinate meetings, can provide empirical evidence for the specific item's recurrent collocations, primings and discourse prosodies. We can then begin to make inferences about the business meeting's elusive, normative practices through pinpointing such typical, repeated behaviour across texts and users. As we have seen in the hotel extract, the next step (step 4) is to explore an individual text containing the 'typical' instance of the item in question to further interpret its use[9].

Interpreting recurrent, statistically significant and other selected items as possible indices of practices within a generic framework thus promises to integrate the text with the wider social context in a plausible, repeatable way. The argument that practices can be revealed in the recurrent patterns of a corpus is dependent on a Hallidayan view of the relationship between the (corpus) data and the wider social and cultural context, in that 'repetitions of linguistic patterns in the co-text, revealed by the co-selection of items on the vertical axis of the concordance lines, reflect the context, i.e. the situational and cultural parameters involved in the creation of meaning' (Flowerdew, 2008: 115). In other words, formal patterns repeated across related texts can tell us a lot about context (Halliday, 1994), including traces of practices[10].

As mentioned previously on page 31, these significant items are equivalent to Ochs' notion of a linguistic index, in that they are 'used variably from one situation to another and become conventionally associated with particular situational dimensions such that when that structure is used, the form invokes those situational dimensions' (1996: 411). This quote succinctly demonstrates how the language item in question creates and reflects the context, drawing attention to the stance taken by the speaker[11]. Two key instances discussed by Ochs are epistemic stance, relating to degrees of certainty, and affective stance, concerning the degree of emotion attached to the message. Arguably a further, defining stance in business communication, and in institutional discourse in general, is that of deontic stance, indexing obligation, hence the high frequency and keyness of items like *have to* and *need*.

While steps 3 and 4 are closely related, the emphasis of the fourth step is to look beyond the highlighted item to the surrounding discourse and its context. To do this, it is necessary to move away from word lists and concordance lines, to individual meeting extracts. When carefully reading a single extract, we can also find other patterns and evidence of practices that quantitative analysis fails to uncover.

In conducting steps 5 and 6 of the analysis, we are interpreting the wider social context and its relationship with the language. As such, the following issues can be considered: who is participating in the particular genre (or communicative activity), what communities do they belong to, what identities, relationships, practices and conventions are they invoking or challenging, and what possible ideologies are they recreating through their discourse?

Whereas Fairclough (1989, 2003) talks about abstract social structures, Gee's notion of 'Discourses' – mentioned several times already in this chapter – is perhaps a more accessible, largely equivalent concept (both researchers acknowledge the influence of Foucault). Within each Discourse, new members are apprenticed into tacitly adopting the appropriate norms of the community, and in the workplace it is those who can most ably demonstrate the beliefs and behaviours of the institution's or department's Discourse who tend to get ahead (Gee et al., 1996). Perhaps the most recurrent Discourse in internal business meetings, for example, is the Discourse of being a manager (either with subordinates or peers), and CANBEC provides an unprecedented amount of transcribed data on how this is performed.

One aspect yet to be discussed is the turn-taking in extract 2.4. Merely by looking at the overall turn design, the superior status of S1 is evident: he talks and is allowed to talk for a very long time, without interruption, at the beginning of the meeting. There is also an unusually low degree of backchannelling, which perhaps is caused by the gravity of the topic and the power difference foregrounded by the director's stance. In later stages of the meeting, when there is more discussion, a far higher frequency of backchannels and self-appointed turn-taking is apparent.

The analysis of extract 2.4 has highlighted various linguistic items and features which will be discussed further in later chapters and which are typically used by powerful speakers in business meetings: metaphors, deontic modals, the pronoun *we*, the conjunctions *if* and *so*, as well as hypothesizing, contrasting, repeating and relexicalizing, using metalanguage and narrative. We have also seen that these features both reflect and create the management practices of this workplace, as well as the identities of the managerial staff. The extract is also interesting because of the explicit use of 'new work order' terminology (Gee et al., 1996) such as *goal, aim, compliance* and *commitment*. Such language is intertwined with the Discourses business leaders attempt to create in the workplace: motivated workers who embody company policy, but who are generally not allowed the opportunity to question these goals and aims (ibid.). This issue is returned to in Chapter 6. Although quantitative analyses do not make these terms visible, as they are not statistically significant in the corpus when compared to everyday communication, they are arguably 'culturally' key (Stubbs, 1996: 172) or stylistically salient (Tribble, 2002), in that they play an important role in this discourse.

2.3 Summary

This chapter has explored theory and methodology. Various concepts have been discussed, including context, face and politeness, goals, practices and communities of practice. These will be shown throughout the book to be useful in analysing and understanding the texts. In terms of how the data can be practically interpreted, quantitative corpus techniques and qualitative, discourse-analysis techniques have been combined into a novel methodological framework. By exploiting Gee's (2005) notion of situated meanings, interpretative bridges can be built between recurrent items and features and the context-renewing practices they invoke and reflect. These insights can be related to the social identities of the participants (for example, managers and subordinates) and, when plausible, to the wider Discourses of the genre.

A contextualized corpus like CANBEC allows for the combination of qualitative and quantitative techniques, because individual texts can be manually examined in terms of their uniqueness and coherence, and automated searches can be conducted across a range of related texts. CANBEC can be used to identify potentially critical items within the corpus, and the moments where these items occur. It can also be used to corroborate the interpretations of particular items in context by looking at other examples of those items (in similar and different contexts) as evidence.

The advantage of a corpus over a single text is that patterns become apparent across a range of texts – to bowdlerize Sinclair, who profoundly stated that 'the language looks different when you look at a lot of it at once' (1991: 100), the language of a particular genre looks rather different when you look at a lot of genre-instances at once. With contextual insights, it is also possible to move beyond just saying what patterns there are, to tentatively interpreting what they mean and how that meaning is achieved. The combination of a specialized corpus of institutional speech and the concept of practice should enable a more thorough exploitation of the relationship between corpus and context, and further-reaching inferences about the context, than has perhaps been the case in traditional descriptive approaches to corpus.

Notes

1. See Gee et al. (1996: 22) for a related discussion of how espoused goals and actualized goals in workplaces can differ in practice.
2. In terms of power relationships in a workplace, a normative difference between an expert (for example, a manager) and an apprentice (for example, a newly employed subordinate) in a workplace community is the extent to

which they can, both in terms of aptitude and authorization, successfully and automatically apply and adjust professional practices to recurrent and novel situations. CANBEC repeatedly shows how powerful speakers employ various practices and strategies, whereas those in less powerful positions are more constrained in their language use, both at the lexico-grammatical level and the turn level, but also in terms of interdiscursive aspects (Candlin and Plum, 1999) – for example, using narratives or jokes in meetings.

3. According to Chafe (1994), intonation units are the segments that construct spoken language and can be recognized by various criteria, including pauses, changes in pitch and voice quality. In terms of number of words in spoken English, regulatory intonation units (such as discourse markers) contain on average less than two words, whereas substantive units that carry information contain on average four words.

4. It is also sometimes evident that those in subordinate positions can negotiate the situation, at some risk, and gain more control over the discourse, or contest the power issues. See Ochs (1996) for a related discussion of practices and socialization. See also Foucault (1980).

5. Although the term decision-making is used here, as noted by Boden (1994), it is very difficult to find clear evidence of complete decision-making processes in business discourse. This issue will be returned to in detail in Chapter 7.

6. Although, according to Argyris (1993), certain forms of middle-class politeness and face-saving in talk is detrimental to business.

7. Furthermore, recent developments in critical discourse analysis have also exploited corpora to unearth statistically and culturally key items. For instance, see O'Halloran (2010) for a discussion of corpus-based cultural keywords in media discourse.

8. 'Discourse prosody' is preferred here to 'semantic prosody' (Louw, 1993; see also Sinclair, 1991), because the particular prosody of an item is context dependent. See also Prodromou (2008) on 'pragmatic prosody'.

9. Atypical uses are also interesting, but rather than providing evidence of normative practices, they may be best interpreted from an intentional, strategic perspective (Bhatia, 2004: 157–8).

10. It is important, nevertheless, to remember that such an approach is still dependent on the analyst having a sufficient understanding of the practices themselves and the cultural context in which they occur (see Flowerdew, 2008). An analyst lacking in background knowledge who comes to a specialized corpus 'cold' will not be able to offer many insights into the data beyond superficial description of the surface linguistic features.

11. As noted by Ochs (1996: 432), indexicality is largely equivalent to Gumperz's contextualization cues (1982) and Goffman's notions of footing and frames (1981), as are the 'critical items' discussed here.

References

Adolphs, S., Atkins, S. and Harvey, K. (2007) 'Caught between professional requirements and interpersonal needs: Vague language in health care contexts', in Cutting, J. (ed.) *Vague Language Explored*, Basingstoke: Palgrave.

Argyris, C. (1993) *Knowledge for Action. A Guide to Overcoming Barriers to Organizational Change*, San Francisco: Jossey Bass.

Baker, P. (2006) *Using Corpora in Discourse Analysis*, London: Continuum.

Bargiela-Chiappini, F. (2003) 'Face and politeness: New (insights) for old (concepts)', *Journal of Pragmatics*, 35, 1453–69.

Bargiela-Chiappini, F. and Harris, S. (1997) *Managing Language: The Discourse of Corporate Meetings*, Amsterdam: John Benjamins.

Bargiela-Chiappini, F., Nickerson, C. and Planken, B. (2007) *Business Discourse*, Basingstoke: Palgrave.

Bazerman, C. (1994) 'Systems of genres and the enhancement of social intentions', in Freedman, A. and Medway, P. (eds.) *Genre and New Rhetoric*, London: Taylor and Francis, 79–101.

Bhatia, V. (1993) *Analysing Genre: Language Use in Professional Settings*, Harlow: Longman.

Bhatia, V. (2004) *Worlds of Written Discourse*, London: Continuum.

Bhatia, V. (2008) 'Towards critical genre analysis', in Bhatia, V., Flowerdew, J. and Jones, R. (eds.) *Advances in Discourse Studies*, Abingdon: Routledge, 166–77.

Biber, D. (1988) *Variation Across Speech and Writing*, Cambridge: Cambridge University Press.

Biber, D. and Conrad, S. (1999) 'Lexical bundles in conversation and academic prose', in Hasselgard, H. and Oksefjell, S. (eds.) *Out of Corpora: Studies in Honor of Stig Johansson*, Amsterdam: Rodopi, 181–90.

Boden, D. (1994) *The Business of Talk: Organizations in Action*, Cambridge: Polity Press.

Bourdieu, P. (1977) *Outline of a Theory of Practice*, Cambridge: Cambridge University Press.

Brown, P. and Levinson, S. (1987) *Politeness: Some Universals in Language Usage*, Cambridge: Cambridge University Press.

Candlin, C. (2000) 'Preface', in Coupland, J. (ed.) *Small Talk*, Harlow: Pearson Education.

Candlin, C., Maley, A. and Sutch, H. (1999) 'Industrial instability and the discourse of enterprise bargaining', in Sarangi, S. and Roberts, C. (eds.) *Talk, Work and Institutional Order*, Berlin: Mouton de Gruyter, 323–50.

Candlin, C. and Plum, G. (1999) 'Engaging with challenges of interdiscursivity in academic writing: Researchers, students and tutors', in Candlin, C. and Hyland, K. (eds.) *Writing: Texts, Processes and Practices*, London: Longman, 193–217.

Candlin, C. and Sarangi, S. (2004) 'Preface', in Bhatia, V., *Worlds of Written Discourse*, London: Continuum.

Carter, R. (2004) *Language and Creativity: The Art of Common Talk*, London: Routledge.

Carter, R. and McCarthy, M. (1995) 'Grammar and the spoken language', *Applied Linguistics*, 16, 2, 141–58.

Carter, R. and McCarthy, M. (2006) *Cambridge Grammar of English*, Cambridge: Cambridge University Press.

Chafe, W. (1994) *Discourse, Consciousness and Time*, Chicago: Chicago University Press.

Chafe, W. (forthcoming) 'From thoughts to sounds', in Gee, J. and Handford, M. (eds.) *The Routledge Handbook of Discourse Analysis*, Abingdon: Routledge.

Charles, M. (1996) 'Business negotiations: Interdependence between discourse and the business relationship', *English for Specific Purposes*, 15, 19–36.

Coupland, J. (ed.) (2000) *Small Talk*, Harlow: Pearson Education.

Dörnyei, Z. (2007) *Research Methods in Applied Linguistics*, Oxford: Oxford University Press.

Evison, J. (2008) *Turn-openers in Academic Talk: An Exploration of Discourse Responsibility*, PhD thesis, University of Nottingham (Unpublished).

Evison, J., McCarthy, M. and O'Keeffe, A. (2007) 'Looking out for love and all the rest of it: Vague category markers as shared social space', in Cutting, J. (ed.) *Vague Language Explored*, Basingstoke: Palgrave.

Fairclough, N. (1989) *Language and Power*, London: Longman.

Fairclough, N. (1995) *Critical Discourse Analysis*, London: Longman.

Fairclough, N. (2003) *Analysing Discourse: Textual Analysis for Social Research*, London: Routledge.

Flowerdew, L. (2002) 'Corpus-based analyses in EAP', in Flowerdew, J. (ed.) *Academic Discourse*, London: Longman, 95–114.

Flowerdew, L. (2005) 'An integration of corpus-based and genre-based approaches to text analysis in EAP/ESP: Countering criticisms against corpus-based methodologies', *English for Specific Purposes*, 24, 321–32.

Flowerdew, L. (2008) 'Corpora and context in professional writing', in Bhatia, V., Flowerdew, J. and Jones, R. (eds.) *Advances in Discourse Studies*, Abingdon: Routledge, 115–27.

Foucault, M. (1980) in Gordon, C. (ed.) *Power/Knowledge: Selected Interviews and other Writings 1972–1977 by Michel Foucault*, Brighton: The Harvester Press.

Gee, J.P. (1990) *Social Linguistics and Literacies: Ideology in Discourses*, London: Falmer Press.

Gee, J.P. (1992) *The Social Mind: Language, Ideology and Social Practice*, New York: Bergin and Harvey.

Gee, J.P. (2005) *An Introduction to Discourse Analysis*, Abingdon: Routledge.

Gee. J.P., Hull, G. and Lankshear, C. (1996) *The New Work Order*, London: Allen and Unwin.

Giddens, A. (1984) *The Construction of Society: Outline of a Theory of Structuration*, Cambridge: Cambridge University Press.

Goffman, E. (1967) *Interaction Ritual: Essays on Face-to-face Behaviour*, New York: Anchor Doubleday.

Goffman, E. (1981) *Forms of Talk*, Philadelphia: University of Pennsylvania Press.

Goodwin, C. and Duranti, A. (1992) *Rethinking Context: An Introduction*, Cambridge: Cambridge University Press.

Gu, Y. (1990) 'Politeness phenomena in modern Chinese', *Journal of Pragmatics*, 14, 237–57.

Gumperz, J. (1982) *Discourse Strategies*, Cambridge: Cambridge University Press.

Halliday, M. (1978) *Language as Social Semiotic: The Social Interpretation of Language and Meaning*, London: Edward Arnold.

Halliday, M. (1985) *Spoken and Written Language*, Victoria: Deakin University.

Halliday, M. (1994) *An Introduction to Functional Grammar*, London: Edward Arnold.

Handford, M. (2007) *The Genre of the Business Meeting: A Corpus-based Study*, PhD thesis, University of Nottingham (Unpublished).

Handford, M. (2010) 'What corpora have to tell us about specialised genres', in McCarthy, M. and O'Keeffe, A. (eds.) *The Routledge Handbook of Corpus Linguistics*, Abingdon: Routledge.

Handford, M. and Koester, A. (2010) '"It's not rocket science": Metaphors and idioms in conflictual business meetings', *Text and Talk*, 30, 27–51.

Heritage, J. (1997) 'Conversation analysis and institutional talk', in Silverman, D. (ed.) *Qualitative Research: Theory, Method and Practice*, London: Sage, 161–82.

Hoey, M. (2005) *Lexical Priming*, Abingdon: Routledge.

Holmes, J. (2000) 'Doing collegiality and keeping control at work: Small talk in government departments', in Coupland, J. (ed.) *Small Talk*, Harlow: Pearson Education, 32–61.

Holmes, J. (2006) 'Workplace narratives, professional identity and relational practice', in de Fina, A., Schiffrin, D. and Bamberg, M. (eds.) *Discourse and Identity*, Cambridge: Cambridge University Press, 166–87.

Holmes, J. and Stubbe, M. (2003) *Power and Politeness in the Workplace*, London: Longman.

Hopper, P. and Drummond, K. (1990) 'Emergent goals at a relational turning point: The case of Gordon and Denise', in Tracy, K. and Coupland, N. (eds.) *Multiple Goals in Discourse*, Clevedon: Multilingual Matters, 39–65.

Hyland, K. (1998) 'Persuasion and context: The pragmatics of academic metadiscourse', *Journal of Pragmatics*, 30, 437–55.

Hyland, K. (2004) *Genre and Second Language Writing*, Michigan: University of Michigan Press.

Iacobucci, C. (1990) 'Accounts, formulations and goal attainment strategies in service encounters', in Tracy, K. and Coupland, N. (eds.) *Multiple Goals in Discourse*, Clevedon: Multilingual Matters, 85–99.

Iacobucci, C. (1996) 'Commercial and interpersonal relationships: Using the structure of interpersonal relationships to understand individual-to-individual, individual-to-firm, and firm-to-firm relationships in commerce', *International Journal of Marketing*, 13, 53–72.

Janney, R. and Arndt, H. (1993) 'Universality and relativity in cross-cultural politeness research: A historical perspective', *Multilingua*, 12, 13–50.

Knights, D. and Morgan, G. (1991) 'Corporate strategy, organizations, and subjectivity: A critique', *Organization Studies*, 12, 251–73.

Koester, A. (2001) *Interpersonal Markers in Workplace Genres: Pursuing Transactional and Relational Goals in Office Talk*, PhD thesis, University of Nottingham (Unpublished).

Koester, A. (2004) 'Relational sequences in workplace genres', *Journal of Pragmatics*, 36, 1405–28.

Koester, A. (2006) *Investigating Workplace Discourse*, Abingdon: Routledge.

Koester, A. (2010) *Workplace Discourse*, London: Continuum.

Lakoff, R. (1990) *Talking Power*, Chicago: Chicago University Press.

Lampi, M. (1986) *Linguistic Components of Strategy in Business Negotiations*, Helsinki: Helsinki School of Economics.

Lee, D. (2008) 'Corpora and discourse analysis: New ways of doing old things', in Bhatia, V., Flowerdew, J. and Jones, R. (eds.), *Advances in Discourse Studies*, Abingdon: Routledge, 86–99.

Levinson, S. (1992) 'Activity types and language', in Drew, P. and Heritage, J. (eds.) *Talk at Work*, Cambridge: Cambridge University Press, 66–100.

Louw, B. (1993) 'Irony in the text or insincerity in the writer? The diagnostic potential of semantic prosodies', in Baker, M., Francis, G. and Tognini-Bonelli, E. (eds.) *Text and Technology*, Amsterdam: John Benjamins, 157–76.

Martin, J. (1992) *English Text: System and Structure*, Amsterdam: John Benjamins.

Matsumoto, Y. (1988) 'Reexamination of the universality of face: Politeness phenomena in Japanese', *Journal of Pragmatics*, **12**, 403–26.

McCarthy, M. (1998) *Spoken Language and Applied Linguistics*, Cambridge: Cambridge University Press.

McCarthy, M. (2000) 'Captive audiences: Small talk and close contact service encounters', in Coupland, J. (ed.) *Small Talk*, Harlow: Pearson Education, 84–109.

McCarthy, M. and Handford, M. (2004) '"Invisible to us": A preliminary corpus-based study of spoken business English', in Connor, U. and Upton, T. (eds.) *Discourse in the Professions: Perspectives from Corpus Linguistics*, Amsterdam: John Benjamins, 167–201.

Mirivel, J. and Tracy, K. (2005) 'Premeeting talk: An organizationally crucial form of talk', *Research on Language and Social Interaction*, **38**, 1, 1–34.

Moon, R. (1998) *Fixed Expressions and Idioms in English: A Corpus-based Approach*, Oxford: Oxford University Press.

Nelson, M. (2000) *A Corpus-based Study of Business English and Business English Teaching Materials*, PhD thesis, University of Manchester (Unpublished).

O'Halloran, K. (2010) 'How to use corpus linguistics in the study of media discourse', in McCarthy, M. and O'Keeffe, A. (eds.) *The Routledge Handbook of Corpus Linguistics*, Abingdon: Routledge.

O'Keeffe, A. (2003) '"Like the wise virgins and all that jazz" – using a corpus to examine vague language and shared knowledge', in Connor, U. and Upton, T. (eds.) *Applied Corpus Linguistics: A Multidimensional Perspective*, Amsterdam: Rodopi, 1–20.

O'Keeffe, A. (2006) *Investigating Media Discourse*, Abingdon: Routledge.

O'Keeffe, A., McCarthy, M. and Carter, R. (2007) *From Corpus to Classroom: Language Use and Language Teaching*, Cambridge: Cambridge University Press.

Oakey, D. (2002) 'Formulaic language in English academic writing', in Reppen, R., Fitzmaurice, S. and Biber, D. (eds.) *Using Corpora to Explore Linguistic Variation*, Amsterdam: John Benjamins, 111–29.

Ochs, E. (1996) 'Linguistic resources for socializing humanity', in Gumperz, J. (ed.) *Rethinking Linguistic Relativity*, Cambridge: Cambridge University Press, 407–37.

Paulin, M., Ferguson, R. and Payaud, M. (2000) 'Effectiveness of relational and transactional cultures in commercial banking: Putting client-value into the competing values model', *International Journal of Bank Marketing*, **18**, 7, 328–37.

Paulin, M., Perrien, J. and Ferguson, R. (1997) 'Relational norms and the effectiveness of commercial banking relationships', *International Journal of Service Industry Management*, **8**, 5, 435–52.

Penman, R. (1990) 'Facework and politeness: Multiple goals in courtroom discourse', in Tracy, K. and Coupland, N. (eds.) *Multiple Goals in Discourse*, Clevedon: Multilingual Matters, 15–38.

Piller, I. (2009) 'Intercultural Communication', in Bargiela-Chiappini, F. (ed.) *The Handbook of Business Discourse*, Edinburgh: Edinburgh University Press, 317–29.

Poncini, G. (2002) 'Investigating discourse at business meetings with multicultural participation', *International Review of Applied Linguistics*, **40**, 345–73.

Poncini, G. (2004) *Discursive Strategies in Multicultural Business Meetings*, Peter Lang, Linguistic Insights Series.

Prodromou, L. (2008) *English as a Lingua Franca: A Corpus-based Analysis*, London: Continuum.

Ragan, S. (1990) 'Verbal play and multiple goals in the gynaecological exam interaction', in Tracy, K. and Coupland, N. (eds.) *Multiple Goals in Discourse*, Clevedon: Multilingual Matters, 67–84.

Rose, D. (1997) 'Science, technology and technical literacies', in Christie, F. and Martin, J. R. (eds.) *Genre and Institutions: Social Processes in the Workplace and School*, London: Continuum, 40–72.

Sacks, H. (1972) 'An initial investigation of the usability of conversational data for doing sociology', in Sudnow, D. (ed.) *Studies in Social Interaction*, New York: The Free Press.

Sacks, H., Schegloff, E. A. and Jeffersen, G. (1974) 'A simplest systematics for the organisation of turn-taking for conversation', *Language*, **50**, 4, 696–735.

Sarangi, S. and Roberts, C. (eds.) (1999) *Talk, Work and Institutional Order*, Berlin: Mouton de Gruyter.

Schegloff, E. (1992) 'On talk and its institutional occasions', in Drew, P. and Heritage, J. (eds.) *Talk at Work*, Cambridge: Cambridge University Press, 101–34.

Scollon, R. and Scollon, S. (2001) *Intercultural Communication: A Discourse Approach*, Oxford: Blackwell.

Scott, M. (1999) *WordSmith Tools Version 3*, Oxford: Oxford University Press.

Sharma, A. and Pillai, K. G. (2003) 'The impact of transactional and relational strategies in business markets: An agenda for inquiry', *Industrial Marketing Management*, **32**, 623–6.

Silverstein, M. (2003) 'Indexical order and the dialectics of sociolinguistic life', *Language and Communication*, **23**, 3–4, 193–229.

Simpson, R. C. (2004) 'Stylistic features of academic speech: The role of formulaic expressions', in Connor, U. and Upton, T. (eds.) *Discourse in the Professions: Perspectives from Corpus Linguistics*, Amsterdam: John Benjamins, 37–64.

Sinclair, J. (1991) *Corpus, Concordance, Collocation*, Oxford: Oxford University Press.

Spencer-Oatey, H. (2000) *Culturally Speaking: Managing Rapport through Talk across Cultures*, London: Continuum.

Sperber, D. and Wilson, D. (1996) *Relevance*, Oxford: Blackwell.

Stubbs, M. (1996) *Text and Corpus Analysis*, London: Blackwell.

Stubbs, M. (2001a) 'Texts, corpora and problems of interpretation: A response to Widdowson', *Applied Linguistics*, 22, 2, 149–72.

Stubbs, M. (2001b) 'On inference theories and code theories: Corpus evidence for semantic schemas', *Text*, 21, 3, 437–65.

Stubbs, M. (2007) 'On texts, corpora and models of language', in Hoey, M., Mahlberg, M., Stubbs, M. and Teubert, W. (eds.) *Text, Discourse and Corpora*, London: Continuum, 163–90.

Swales, J. (1990) *Genre Analysis*, Cambridge: Cambridge University Press.

Swales, J. (2004) *Research Genres: Explorations and Applications*, Cambridge: Cambridge University Press.

Swan, M. (1995) *Practical English Usage*, Oxford: Oxford University Press.

Teubert, W. (2007) (with Hoey, M., Mahlberg, M., and Stubbs, M.) *Text, Discourse and Corpora: Theory and Analysis*, London: Continuum.

Thomas, J. (1984) 'Cross-cultural discourse as 'unequal encounter': Towards pragmatic analysis', *Applied Linguistics*, 5, 3, 226–35.

Tognini-Bonelli, E. (2001) *Corpus Linguistics at Work*, Amsterdam: John Benjamins.

Tracy, K. and Coupland, N. (eds.) (1990) *Multiple Goals in Discourse*, Clevedon: Multilingual Matters.

Tribble, C. (2002) 'Corpora and corpus analysis: New windows on academic writing', in Flowerdew, J. (ed.) *Academic Discourse*, London: Longman, 131–49.

Ventola, E. (1987) *The Structure of Social Interaction. A Systemic Approach to the Semiotics of Service Encounters*, London: Frances Pinter.

Vygotsky, L. (1987) in Rieber, R. W. and Carton, A. S. (eds.) *The Collected Works of L. S. Vygotsky*, New York: Plenum Press.

Walsh, S. (2006) *Investigating Classroom Discourse*, London: Routledge.

Watson, T. (2009) 'Sociology, narrative and discourse', in Bargiela-Chiappini, F. (ed.) *The Handbook of Business Discourse*, Edinburgh: Edinburgh University Press, 226–38.

Watts, R. (2003) *Politeness*, Cambridge: Cambridge University Press.

Wenger, E. (1998) *Communities of Practice: Learning, Meaning and Identity*, Cambridge: Cambridge University Press.

Widdowson, H. (1998) 'Review article: The theory and practice of critical discourse analysis', *Applied Linguistics*, 19, 136–51.

Wray, A. (2002) *Formulaic Language and the Lexicon*, Cambridge: Cambridge University Press.

Yamada, H. (1992) *American and Japanese Business Discourse*, Norwood: Ablex.

3 The business-meeting genre: Stages and practices

For the analyst, meetings can seem at first glance to be a messy combination of the recurrent and the dynamic. For example, the meeting may progress through recognizable stages, but the participants may discuss topics that seem to have no relation to the agenda, or may return to topics that had been discussed at length some time earlier. Yet no matter how messy the unfolding discourse may appear, participants seem to know that they are in a meeting and what that means in terms of appropriacy, constraint and predictability. While the particular manifestations of what is acceptable and expected will depend on factors such as national, professional and organizational culture[1], the relative status and relationship of the speakers, and the goals of the communication, meetings nevertheless have structural features that are repeated over different contexts and companies. As with any living genre, however, attempting to tie meetings down to a purely formal or deterministic description will be flawed. This is because participants constantly test the boundaries of the activity they are involved in, both within and across meetings: their goals change, the corporate goals change, the practices employed to address the goals change, and all these factors, over time, can lead to inevitable variations and possible transformations in the genre (Bhatia, 2004) and the wider Discourse (that is, the collections of intertwined practices that various social groups perform – Gee, 1992, and see Chapter 2 of this volume) which it partly constitutes. While the present study is not longitudinal and therefore cannot provide evidence for such changes, it does interpret a wide range of business meetings at the beginning of the 21st century and the features they share.

So far in this book there has been no explicit description of what is meant by the term 'business meeting'. Both internal and external business meetings feature the following elements:

- a set of participants, ranging from dyadic to multiparty
- evidence of an agenda or topic, although this can be formal or informal, planned or spontaneous, written or spoken, fixed or flexible (Holmes and Stubbe, 2003)
- a purpose, reason or goal (Boden, 1994: 84) for the meeting
- specific, constrained turn-taking modes (Boden, 1994: 89),

although turn-taking is also closely linked to the stage of the meeting, the level of formality and the power differences between the speakers (Handford, 2007)
- the influence of institutional, professional and/or national culture
- recognizable beginnings and endings (Bargiela-Chiappini and Harris, 1996)
- degrees of intertextuality (Bhatia, 2004) – for example, references to previous and also subsequent meetings or other events or texts (such as emails and contracts)

A danger with this definition, however, is that it is too broad and may suggest that all types of workplace encounters could be considered meetings. According to Koester (personal communication), the problem revolves around spontaneous encounters: it would be wrong to suggest that all spontaneous encounters are meetings, and yet some meetings are spontaneous. Therefore, spontaneous encounters can be categorized as meetings when they have a clear work-related purpose and topic. This can include relational issues if they are seen as impacting work in some way (for example, reporting to a superior that the employee's relationship with the line manager is affecting his or her performance). Gossiping about one's boss, however, would not count as a meeting.

This chapter presents an in-depth look at the business-meeting genre, focusing on stages and practices as the key genre-defining elements. The chapter begins with an examination of the theoretical background, outlining a model which encapsulates both the repeated features and the dynamism of the genre and which aids understanding of the selection and use of language, before going on to look at the component stages of the business meeting. It will explore how speakers create, acknowledge, participate in and utilize the business-meeting genre through the selection of words and clusters. In section 3.1, an approach to genre that is particularly suited to analysing business communication, developed by Bhatia (2004, 2008) is discussed. This approach explores various layers of practices in genres, and the constitutive role of language. As such, it complements the methodology discussed in Chapter 2 and provides a clear context for selected language items. Section 3.2 explains and exemplifies the 'meeting matrix', which comprises a combination of structural stages and discursive practices. Section 3.3 then applies this matrix to extended dialogues from several internal and external meetings, representing the following relationships: internal manager–subordinate, internal peer, external non-contractually bound and external contractually bound. It is only possible to provide a relatively brief overview of the way participants construct the genre through their language. It should also be remembered that, while this study provides detailed evidence of this language, meetings are in reality multimodal constructs featuring visual and sometimes written communication that the corpus does not contain, but which nevertheless occurred.

3.1 Applying Bhatia's multi-perspective model of discourse to business meetings

According to Bhatia (2004), the study of *written* genres has dia-chronically progressed from close textual analysis, which looked at the surface-level aspects of the text, towards more recent analysis of the genre's relationship with the wider social context, specifically the reflexive relationship between genres and social practices. The analysis of *spoken* discourse, he argues (ibid.: 12) has moved in roughly the opposite direction. Fully transcribed, specialized corpora of spoken genres, such as CANBEC, are relatively recent, and thus it is only recently that a focus on surface aspects of the text, and the shape of the interaction as a whole, has been possible (Flowerdew, 2005; Handford, 2010).

The approaches outlined by Bhatia, ranging from textual analysis to analysis of the social context, are roughly compatible with three different approaches to the study of genre (see also Hyon, 1996). Firstly, the 'genre-as-text' approach, analysing the different discursive goal-oriented stages a genre typically embodies, has been developed by those working in Hallidayan Systemic Functional Linguistics (SFL) (Hasan, 1985; Martin, 1992; Martin and Rose, 2008). Secondly, the work of Swales exploring the importance of communicative purpose and discourse communities in defining genres has been extremely influential, particularly in the field of English for Specific Purposes (Swales, 1990, 2004), but also in institutional communication (Bhatia, 1993; Koester, 2006). A third approach to genre has questioned the textual rigidity which the SFL approach imposes, arguing that genres are highly dynamic and creative, meaning that their form is unpredictable, and that they should be defined in terms of the rhetorical and social action they are intended to achieve (Miller, 1984; Bazerman, 1994; Berkenkotter and Huckin, 1995). For a fuller exploration of these approaches, and their relevance to corpus linguistics, see Handford (2010).

Bhatia's model is applied to written professional and institutional genres (such as reports), although it is also applicable, he argues, to other forms of discourse. The model is holistic and 'multi-perspective', in that it combines textual and social approaches to allow analysis from various points of view: language as text, language as genre, language as professional practice and language as social practice (Candlin and Sarangi, 2004: xv). It should therefore be clear that Bhatia's model of genre analysis is compatible with the methodology outlined in Chapter 2. This chapter now shows how specific practices and their linguistic manifestation create the business-meeting genre.

The analysis of language as text involves exploring lexico-grammatical and other text-internal features, such as functional aspects of discourse and text organization. According to Bhatia (2004: 20), this level of analysis has tended not to make reference to the context, focusing instead on the co-text. Several studies of larger corpora would fall into this bracket (Flowerdew, 2005). Language or discourse as genre, on the other hand, involves reference to the context in order to understand not only text construction but also how the language both reflects and creates the practices that invoke the genre, the social identities of the participants and the communities of practice.

Understanding practices: An example of professional practices

In Chapter 2, the term 'practices' was discussed and it was noted that there are potentially several layers of context that can be interpreted as practices – for instance, very general social practices and much more specific, local discursive practices. Discursive practices can be located in the text and are explored in detail in this study, whereas social practices can be seen as working at a more general level of context. Examples of social practices include classroom teaching, conducting medical consultations and management practices. A further possible distinction is drawn by Bhatia (2004) between professional practices and social practices. He argues that this is a useful way of understanding the different layers of knowledge and context required to perform effectively in the genre itself. For the purposes of this study, professional practices can be distinguished from social practices inasmuch as they extend our understanding of how genres are employed to allow the activation of professional knowledge. Social practices, on the other hand, involve a broader, sometimes longitudinal, take on context, including aspects such as the changing identities of the interlocutors and the pros and cons or even 'evolution' of particular genres (Berkenkotter, 2008: 20; see also Chapter 2 of Koester, 2010).

To understand professional practices, ethnographic data in the form of field notes and interviews is often necessary (Bhatia, 2008).

For example, one external meeting in CANBEC is between managers from the logistics departments of two multinational pharmaceutical companies – one the client and the other the manufacturer of the client's pharmaceuticals – who are planning the opening of a new production plant in Germany. Part of the meeting will be analysed in section 3.3 (see extract 3.10) and elsewhere in this book. In order to understand the professional practices and knowledge necessary for effective participation in logistics meetings, the chair was interviewed on several occasions. He explained that employees need both process knowledge and content knowledge. Process knowledge involves being aware of how the supply chain process is set up and the commensurate practices (that is, the professional practices) that achieve this process: from receiving a forecast (the customer ordering a certain number of packs by a certain date), to entering it on the database, to ordering, testing and transporting the necessary materials, to producing and then packaging and releasing the product. Also relevant is an understanding of the four stages of project management (initiate, plan, execute/control and close). Content knowledge, on the other hand, means knowing the particular products that the (client) company makes, who they distribute to, and understanding 'where this meeting fits in with the larger picture'.

This last aspect of content knowledge – understanding where the meeting fits in – deserves further explanation. These logistics meetings are planned and executed using the SIPOC formula (suppliers, input, process, output, customers – see www.isixsigma.com), a tool used by work teams to clarify how a process-improvement project can be conducted efficiently before the actual work starts. Figure 3.1 shows the anonymized outline of the meeting, which the chair uses to plan and organize meetings, communicated to all participants in advance. The IPO (input, process, output) points are intended to ensure efficient and focused meetings: the input encourages participants to consider what they are bringing to the meeting, the process concerns issues such as the frequency of the meeting, and the output focuses attention on the expectations[2].

A consideration of the points contained in figure 3.1 shows how the meeting fits into the larger picture of previous and subsequent meetings and other actions, and as such is of interest from an intertextual perspective (Bhatia, 2004). In addition, intertextuality is evident when considering 'genre chains' (Swales, 2004) – that is, where genres fit in chronologically with other genres. The following seven points provide a description of the preparatory cycle for this meeting, taken from an interview with the chair:

1 Review minutes from the previous meeting.
2 Decide what actions are appropriate and what cannot be dealt with at this point.
3 Email, and if necessary discuss, results from the previous meeting with relevant senior staff who were not present.
4 Conduct internal pre-meetings with those who are going to be present at the next meeting: talk about what needs to be discussed at the next meeting, and how decisions and proposals can be successfully presented to the other company.
5 Draw up and send out agenda for next meeting with any relevant documents.
6 Conduct next monthly meeting.
7 Write up and send out minutes of the meeting.

These ethnographic insights help paint a clear idea of how professional knowledge and practices relate to the individual meeting in question. Such information can also shed light on what is meant by 'expertise': a new employee may have process knowledge gained in a previous company (professional expertise), but would probably lack the content knowledge of procedures specific to the new organization (content expertise). To be regarded as an expert performer (Bazerman, 1994) in a genre in a particular community, we could argue that both types of expertise are required.

Figure 3.1   IPO in logistics meetings

Input	Process	Output
Actions from last meeting	Monthly meeting on [DATE]	Confidence everyone is focused on the right priorities/direction
Department issues last month	Participants: [NAME]; [NAME]	
Updates for closure of current month's key metrics	Be prepared, proactive, report by exception [i.e. only focus on outstanding/unusual issues]	Understanding on pain points [i.e. bottlenecks or issues in the supply chain process] last/this month
Updates on key projects/ items		
	Celebrate successes	Confirm communication to departments/ individuals
		Confirmed action list

Practices and language

To briefly return to Bhatia's model and the issue of practices and language: Bhatia stresses that the textual, professional and social perspectives of his model interact, and that for applied linguists in particular this allows for a thorough exploration of the text itself, 'often using social context as the explanation for the analysis of lexico-grammatical and discoursal resources' (2004: 21). For example, as described in Chapter 2, practices can be inferred through identifying critical lexico-grammatical items within the corpus which act as pointers, or indices (Ochs, 1996), of the genre, and which can be explained in terms of the social identities and community of the speakers, their relationships with the other participants, and the goals they are navigating.

Bhatia's model is relevant here, because it elucidates the relationship between different aspects of texts (such as meeting transcripts in CANBEC) and their contexts, and how the data can be analysed as genres. This is important because, as Bhatia states, 'it is through genres that professional objectives are achieved, and it is through shared generic knowledge that professional solidarity is maintained' (2004: 21). Genres thus allow participants to serve two core, intertwined goals of business: attending to relationships and transacting appointed or negotiable goods, services or information. In the words of the logistics manager introduced on page 64, people 'need to be aware of what they are bringing to the meeting'.

As noted previously, Bhatia distinguishes between professional and social practices. A further distinction can be drawn between these practices and their associated discursive practices (Candlin et al., 1999; Bhatia, 2008). Discursive practices signify recurrent patterns of linguistic behaviour that are decipherable in transcripts of business meetings[3]. Bhatia (2008: 172) argues that discursive practices can form 'an integral part' of the professional practice in question and exploring them allows an understanding of the 'nature, function and execution' of the business-embedded professional practice.

Much of this study is concerned with inferring and exploring the goal-related discursive practices evident in CANBEC's meetings and their linguistic manifestation. Some examples of discursive practices commonly used by managers which will be discussed below include starting the decision-making process and bringing the discussion back on track. An example given previously of a professional practice is setting up the supply chain process, and a social practice in business could be actively performing the role of a (logistics) manager over time (abbreviated to 'being a (logistics) manager' in figure 3.2). As such, social practices – and to a lesser extent professional practices – are more difficult to locate in meeting transcripts when compared to discursive practices. Nevertheless, overall the topic of a meeting may explicitly reflect the professional practice, whereas the discursive practice often relates to particular stages and actions within the meeting itself. Figure 3.2 shows the relationship between the different levels of practices and language, and each level of practice can be seen as an integral part of the next, higher level: discursive practices are an integral part of professional practices, and professional practices are an integral part of social practices. An utterance from the chair of the logistics meeting indexes these practices, showing how they are realized in text. The utterance most clearly and directly reflects and invokes the discursive practice of clarifying some aspects of concern. As the context widens, moving from professional to social practice, the relationship between the text and the context also becomes more complex.

Figure 3.2   *The relationship between practices, text and context*

3.2 The meeting matrix

As mentioned at the beginning of this chapter, one of the key challenges in accounting for the business-meeting genre is to plausibly combine the dynamic, sometimes novel aspects of communication with the recurrent routines that make a business meeting immediately recognizable. This combination involves, to a large degree, goals and structure. An over-emphasis on goals can make it difficult to pin down a genre, whereas focusing too much on the structure, particularly in the form of stages, can lead to a temptation to fit the data into that structural description, instead of allowing the structure to reflect the data. A case in point is decision-making, categorized as a genre by Koester (2006). As shown by Boden (1994) and Handford (2007; see also Chapter 7), decision-making can be far less clear-cut and incremental than is often assumed. Therefore, strictly adhering to the communicative goal of the encounter as a label for the genre can mean that the analyst may be unable to say much about the genre's structural elements. The beginnings and endings of meetings, like other genres, should, however, be clearly recognizable in the text, because 'speakers need to know just what sort of language event they are involved in' (McCarthy, 1998: 62). Furthermore, by prioritizing communicative purpose, other important contextual factors, such as the relationship of the speakers or companies, may have to be downplayed to a large extent. It would be expected, for example, that an internal manager–subordinate planning meeting would be quite different from an external non-contractually bound planning meeting on many levels, despite both meetings sharing the purpose of planning. Notwithstanding this, as mentioned above, focusing purely on the structural elements of an encounter can lead to the analyst ignoring communication that does not seem to fit within that idealized structure.

Previous research on the genre of the business meeting has proposed three-stage meeting structures (Bargiela-Chiappini and Harris, 1997; Holmes and Stubbe, 2003). The first stage is opening the meeting, the second involves the discussion of the agenda, and the third is the closing of the meeting. In the matrix outlined here, these three stages are also interpreted as obligatory elements of a business meeting, but are subsumed within a broader framework that accounts for the intertextual and dynamic nature of meetings. This structural aspect of the genre is outlined in figure 3.3. The three stages which are obligatory for all meetings are labelled stages 1–3, the preceding stages called pre-1 and pre-2, and the post-meeting effects labelled as stage 4. In this section, a combination of these six

Figure 3.3   Structural aspects of the business meeting

> Stage pre-2: Meeting preparation
> Stage pre-1: Pre-meeting
> > Transition move
> **Stage 1: Opening of meeting**
> > Transition move
> **Stage 2: Discussion of the agenda**
> > Transition move
> **Stage 3: Closing of meeting**
> Stage 4: Post-meeting effects

structural stages, plus three transition moves ('moves' defined here as functional elements which can occur within a speaker turn or across turns) and four goal-related practice categories are proposed as a 'meeting matrix' to account for the meeting genre. The model should account for both the novel as well as the predictable, although, as noted below, not all meetings will follow all stages of this matrix. Nevertheless, it is a useful heuristic, or metaphor (Swales, 2004), and by studying some of the linguistic items which index these structures and practices (Ochs, 1996), we can see how business people *do* meetings through language.

Meeting structure: Openings and closings

Before examining the particular stages that meetings can move through, it is worth briefly mentioning what has been discussed in the literature concerning the openings and closings of meetings. Business meetings lend themselves to genre categorization, because they tend to have relatively clear beginnings and endings (Bargiela-Chiappini and Harris, 1996, although see Koester, 2006: 35 and Koester, 2010). These stages may involve highly conventionalized practices and give rise to formulaic language (Bargiela-Chiappini and Harris, 1996), such as this instantiation of bringing the meeting to a close: *Okay? Er anything else?* Boden states that even the most informal workplace meetings have 'noticeable and analysable openings and closings' (1994: 87). While this position is largely borne out in CANBEC, it is also necessary to reiterate that there are various degrees of messiness at these stages of meetings, particularly in relation to small talk and agenda-related talk. For example, participants can appear to open a meeting by discussing an item from the agenda, then switch back to a relational topic and then return to the agenda and begin the meeting again (see extract 6.1, pages 152–3). Furthermore, meetings tend to be highly intertextual (Bhatia, 2004), with standardized references to other meetings and other texts (such as faxes or phone calls), and separating meetings often involves more of a spatio-temporal than topic distinction.

Bargiela-Chiappini and Harris (1997: 209–11) report that, in their British meeting data on which they based their generic model, there was a clear distinction between the pre-meeting and the opening stage, with the former involving much phatic communication and the latter being the prerogative of the chair. A similar pattern was also described at the ending of meetings. CANBEC data indicates that in both uni-national (British) and multinational meetings, the reality is more complex. For example, where the chair does not exercise his or her power overtly, the beginning of the meeting and the shift from small talk to the meeting topic is far more recursive. As such, we can say that meetings often have 'fuzzy boundaries'. The occurrence of small talk can be very fluid throughout the meeting and is not confined to the pre-meeting stage. Sometimes there is no pre-meeting stage. Similar results to these have also been reported from the Language in the Workplace (LWP) project (Holmes, 2000; Holmes and Stubbe, 2003). Such findings question a rigid reliance on a three-part structural model of meetings and, because of this, a more complex model of meetings is proposed here.

Meeting structure: The six stages

STAGE PRE-2: MEETING PREPARATION

On one level, this stage is optional, as some meetings occur spontaneously[4]. The stage involves any preceding work done which is directly relevant to the meeting in question. This may include previous meetings dealing with the same issues, sending out the agenda, and any previous decisions made concerning the meeting by the concerned parties and which will be discussed in this meeting. Like the final stage (stage 4), this stage is qualitatively different from the other stages in that it may not be accessible in the corpus transcripts, but it is fundamental to the meeting process. This stage tends to be finished some time (for example, an hour, a day or a month) before the next stage, but provides intertextual (Bhatia, 2004) links to the present meeting. Extract 3.1 shows how the managing director (S6 in the extract) postpones the discussion of using promotional DVDs or CDs until the next meeting, to which the present meeting can thus be regarded as a precursor.

(3.1)

Internal meeting
Relationship of speakers: peer
Purpose: reviewing
Topic: procedure

S2: Even DVD quality you can get about an hour and three quarters on.
S6: We'll have a chat about it next time [inaudible].
S7: Okay.

STAGE PRE-1: PRE-MEETING

At this stage, some of the participants may discuss the topic or some aspect related to the meeting just before the meeting actually starts, or pay attention to the face needs of participants (or possibly even their own face needs) through small talk (Holmes, 2000). This interaction may be between members of the same company, or members from different companies. In terms of topic, Mirivel and Tracy (2005: 1) say 'pre-meeting talk' can include 'work talk, meeting preparatory talk and shop talk' as well as small talk, where 'work talk' involves some topic related to the job, 'meeting preparatory talk' is specifically about some aspect of the meeting (such as a point on the agenda or the refreshments), and 'shop talk' would be akin to work-related gossip. Once again, this stage is optional. In regular internal manager–subordinate communication, this stage is often bypassed.

Transition move: Cuff and Sharrock (1985: 154) state that '[t]he fact that a meeting is about to start is made visible to potential participants', for example, the transition move in extract 3.2 from a presentation-based meeting in a merchant bank:

(3.2)

Internal meeting
Relationship of speakers: peer
Purpose: planning
Topic: strategy

S2: Okay. We may as well= we may as well start. (2 seconds) So …

STAGE 1: OPENING OF MEETING

This stage is necessary. The meeting begins when a quorum of participants is present and then the issue or issues to be discussed are highlighted, often in terms of an intertextual item such as an agenda, proposal or email. If this is the first external meeting between the companies or the participants, then the issue(s) to be discussed will be explicitly outlined and agreed upon at this stage (see extract 7.8 on page 202). If the meetings are more frequent and/or regular, then such references may be less explicit. Usually this stage is signalled by the chair or senior manager, but this is not necessarily the case, particularly in some external meetings.

In external meetings, it is noticeable that stages pre-1 and 1 may be rather fluid. Even when the meeting seems to have formally started, there may be some return to small talk. This seems to be the case when the meeting may not have begun as intended (as in extract 6.1 on pages 152–3) or the participants may be getting ahead of themselves too early in terms of either the agenda or the fine detail of the first point. The chair usually directs this.

In regular internal meetings this stage may be little more than perfunctory – for example, in weekly dyadic intra-departmental manager–subordinate meetings. In extract 3.3, the technical manager opens the meeting with his subordinate thus:

(3.3)

Internal meeting
Relationship of speakers: manager–subordinate
Purpose: reviewing
Topic: technical

S1:   Right. Okay. So current technical problems?

There is no small talk or explicit addressing of face issues, signalling that the expectation is for the established, efficient transfer of information. In peer meetings, in contrast, we may see a similar situation to that of many external meetings, with clear attention being paid to face.

Transition move: Bargiela-Chiappini and Harris (1997: 210) state that this move 'signals the beginning of the discussion, when the Group (as opposed to the Chair) is allowed and encouraged to play a more active role', as in extract 3.4. This move is sometimes bypassed.

(3.4)

> *Internal meeting*
> Relationship of speakers: manager–subordinate
> Purpose: task-/problem-oriented; giving and receiving information/advice
> Topic: procedure; strategy

S2: I have stated the service problem ... erm ... what I'd like to do is now if maybe ... if you can kind of work in groups or perhaps two or three of you on the ... on the flip chart.

STAGE 2: DISCUSSION OF THE AGENDA/TOPIC

This stage is necessary and can be broken down into several 'phases', or may be made up of only one phase. In institutional discourse, 'clusters of activity' (Heritage, 1997: 167), or phases, can be recognized in overall structural organization, each of which involves the 'pursuit of a specific sub-goal' in talk which is task-focused and usually centres on a specific topic from the official agenda. In terms of logistics meetings, the chair of the pharmaceutical meeting discussed throughout this chapter stated that typical topics might include reviewing previously agreed actions, or checking whether all the customers' orders were fulfilled on time. Each of these topics can discursively constitute a 'phase' of a meeting.

In terms of how a phase may be organized over turns, Holmes and Stubbe's (2003: 68) linear/spiral distinction is relevant, because contextual factors will affect the particular patterning for that phase of the meeting (for example, the relationship of speakers, meeting purpose and topic). In dyadic manager–subordinate meetings, the phase or phases will usually involve addressing a series of points from the agenda in a linear pattern and the phases themselves will progress methodically. This will be reflected in the clearly organized turn-taking, often in question and answer patterns. Internal peer meetings (among managers), which are often concerned with decisions and problem-solving, may be more spiral or cyclical in terms of turn-taking, with frequent topic shift and topics and issues being abandoned and returned to after several turns. The same cyclical patterning can be observed over whole phases in these meetings. Such issues will be explored further in Chapter 8.

Not all meetings have the stage 2 phase structures outlined above. Negotiations, for example, which can form several meetings, a single meeting or a phase or phases of an individual meeting (as discussed in Chapter 1) follow a different pattern. Graham (1983) outlines four related phases of negotiations, also observed in CANBEC data across whole meetings, each of which builds on the previous phase:

1 Non-task sounding
2 Task-related exchange of information
3 Persuasion
4 Concessions and agreement

The first phase involves small talk and building rapport. The second is concerned with positioning and communicating about needs. The third involves participants trying to lead the others to accept their position and intentions and, in the fourth phase, there is movement towards agreement. Unlike, for example, an internal manager–subordinate review meeting where the order of phases could probably be rearranged without any considerable loss in the coherence of the meeting (because such meetings are often concerned with reviewing distinct points on the agenda), it would not be possible to reorder negotiation phases.

Stage 2 forms the definitive bulk of each meeting, so the data which will be examined in detail in section 3.3, and in following chapters, is mainly taken from this central stage of different meetings.

Transition move: 'The Chair's dominant role is re-established, and the Group's role proportionally restricted' (Bargiela-Chiappini and Harris, 1997: 210), as in the utterance by the chair towards the end of the meeting in extract 3.5. Once again, the occurrence of this move is dependent on the type of meeting.

(3.5)

> *Internal meeting*
> Relationship of speakers: peer
> Purpose: planning; reviewing
> Topic: sales; logistics

S1:   Yes. That's it. Can we have a chat the three of us through [inaudible].

STAGE 3: CLOSING OF MEETING

This is a necessary stage and can be sudden or circuitous. In regular meetings, this will tend to occur quite quickly, especially in manager–subordinate meetings as in extract 3.6. Here, S1 is the chair and S4 is a sales executive.

(3.6)

> *Internal meeting*
> Relationship of speakers: manager–subordinate
> Purpose: reviewing
> Topic: sales

S4: Well I've been told it is but+
S1: Yeah.
S4: +y= you never know.
(4 seconds)
S1: Very very [inaudible]. Facts and then decisions. (1 second) Okay folks (3 seconds) [inaudible] looking looking a bit more cheerful which is good. (1 second) Thank you.
(13 seconds of various incoherent murmurings and rustle of papers)
[speakers separate]

The chair, in a fairly typical series of moves in a multiparty manager–subordinate meeting, addresses the group with *Okay folks*, makes a (positive) evaluation (*looking a bit more cheerful*) and thanks his subordinates. The use of silence between these moves is also common. In many external meetings, and in internal meetings involving peers, this stage is often more drawn out, as the beginnings of such meetings also tend to be, with more phatic communication and attention to face being woven into the final transactional turns. However, as Chapters 7 and 8 will show, this is not always the case.

STAGE 4: POST-MEETING EFFECTS

This stage concerns the effects and repercussions of the meeting, such as another meeting at a later date, a change (not) implemented following the meeting, or a nullification of the relationship between two companies. This stage acknowledges that it is important to recognize that the end of the meeting in question does not entail the end of the topics, themes or issues related to that meeting. As with stage pre-2, this stage accounts for a level of sequential intertextuality that is not apparent in three-part meeting structures.

This section has built on and suggested alterations to previous research findings concerning the three stages of business meetings discussed at the beginning of the section. The overall structure proposed here is an abstraction which participants may orient towards but may also subvert and the next section will explore how participants ratify, bring into being and manoeuvre within and across these stages through a range of discursive practices.

Discursive practices in meetings

As noted at the beginning of this chapter, the structure of meetings can seem messy. This is not to say that participants are not purposeful in what they are doing – in fact, the apparent messiness observed in authentic data can be explained with reference to recurrent practices being applied to novel situations, as well as to creative strategies that experienced speakers purposefully employ (see Bhatia, 2004). Speakers want to achieve their personal and corporate goals and, in order to achieve these goals, they activate various discursive practices which will be explored here. These practices and the language that constitutes them can actualize the specific structural elements of the genre (that is, the stages, phases and moves outlined previously), such as the instantiation of closing the meeting, but they can also blur such boundaries. As demonstrated in Chapter 2 (extract 2.2), a sales manager may discuss a football game during the closing stage of a meeting with a client, which was shown to be goal-driven behaviour, but his utterance does not neatly fit into a simple abstraction of the meeting structure.

It is obvious that participants in meetings do far more than merely perform the structural stages listed in figure 3.3 on page 69. To account for the unusual as well as the usual in business meetings, some notion of dynamism needs to be included in the meeting matrix. The description will otherwise be at best a rigid idealization of the reality, bearing varying degrees of similarity to the empirical data (Candlin and Sarangi, 2004). It is also crucial that the model demonstrates how the participants orient towards the genre and that it is not merely an analyst's construction. Because of this, the six-stage structure is combined here with the four strands of linguistic behaviour which McCarthy (1998: 33) proposes are found in spontaneous spoken genres: expectations, formulations, recollections and instantiations. Although these strands are not specific to business discourse, they provide a scaffold for meeting-specific discursive practices.

In table 3.1, several of these practices have been categorized according to McCarthy's four strands, including, for example, Holmes and Stubbe's ways of 'managing interaction in meetings' (2003: 71–8), namely 'setting the agenda', 'summarizing progress', 'keeping the discussion on track' and 'reaching a decision'. These examples show that expectations signal the kind of activity the speakers are involved in and the use of the resources of the genre in question (for example, the

Table 3.1   Examples of discursive practices in business meetings

Expectations	setting the agenda
	opening the meeting
Formulations	summarizing progress
	summarizing information
	seeking clarification
	checking shared understanding
	emphasizing shared understanding
Recollections	orienting to past events
	orienting to related events
	orienting to recurrent events
Instantiations	operationalizing topic shift
	bringing discussion 'on track'
	taking discussion 'off track'
	cutting speaker off
	making an aside
	reaching a decision
	blocking a decision
	postponing a decision
	requesting future meeting
	bringing topic to a close
	bringing meeting to a close

agenda). Recollections mark the present context as a recurrent one, and formulations mark the point which the present, ongoing activity has reached[5]. Instantiations are simultaneously the most difficult of the four practices to pinpoint and the most important in the creation of genres (McCarthy, 1998: 37). They enable the speaker to alter or manage the direction of the discourse within the genre while it is in progress and, as such, are the most frequent and essential method by which participants recreate genres (McCarthy, 1998). They may be transactionally or relationally oriented, or both, and they account for the fluidity that is a defining feature of genre in general (ibid.: 37). Some of these examples of the four categories of discursive practice tend to regularly appear in certain stages of meetings – for example, the instantiation 'bringing a meeting to a close' (stage 3) or the expectation 'opening the meeting' (stage 1). Some of the others are clearly related to phases of a discussion (that is, stage 2) – for example, the formulations 'summarizing progress' and 'checking shared understanding', or the instantiations 'keeping discussion on track' and 'reaching a decision'. Section 3.3 will explore the location of certain discursive practices in the data and see how they constitute the business-meeting genre.

These recurrent, reflexive practices provide evidence that the interlocutors in a given genre are aware that they are participating in the genre and are bringing that genre into existence through the very act of participation. Underlying this is the tenet that participants in all genres are not primarily concerned with the recreation of the genre in question, but rather are concerned with achieving their goals. They create and recreate the genre in question through the pursuit of their goals. As Swales argues, '[e]stablished members of discourse communities employ genres to realize communicatively the goals of their communities' (1990: 52), the point being that they do not employ communication to realize specific genres.

It may be evident that the discursive practices described here are equivalent to certain discourse strategies in interactional sociolinguistics. As Gumperz states in a passage that could have been written to describe what many managers do, 'we induce others to participate in conversational encounters by evoking expectations about what is to come and symbolically alluding to shared values and obligations' (1982: 206). Furthermore, Gumperz's discourse strategies are automatic, context-specific, below the level of conscious awareness, tied to tacitly shared goals and constitute particular social relationships (ibid.). They therefore closely share attributes with the notion of practices explored here. As discussed already in Chapter 2, however, the term 'strategies' in this book refers to the intentional choice of how to procede and is usually associated with the social actions of powerful, expert users.

3.3 Applying the meeting matrix

While table 3.1 is not an exhaustive list, it serves to demonstrate that a close reading of the data, combined with ethnographic insights, has allowed interpretation of the interlocutors' communicative behaviour. This section now explores the linguistic indexing of practices (Ochs, 1996) in stage 2 of several internal and external meetings. Within internal communication, manager–subordinate and peer meetings are examined, as are contractually bound and non-contractually bound meetings in external discourse. It should be reiterated that the meeting matrix proposed here subsumes both external and internal meetings. That is, internal and external meetings are parts of the holistic 'meeting genre' and are not intended to be seen as separate genres.

Internal meetings: Manager–subordinate

Extract 3.7 is from stage 2 (the discussion stage) of an internal sales meeting at a UK-based foam manufacturer. S1 is the managing director/chair of the meeting and the other speakers are sales staff. The extract occurs towards the end of a relational sequence about credit cards, during which the managing director/chair is joking about dishonest websites that purport to offer a service, but in truth fraudulently receive payments from unsuspecting 'customers'. This sequence occurs towards the end of a long phase of the meeting which has been focusing on how problems with the company's foam exercise mats can be prevented. As such, the sequence is a problem-solving interlude in a regular meeting that is overtly concerned with planning and reviewing.

(3.7)

> *Internal meeting*
> Relationship of speakers: manager–subordinate
> Purpose: planning; reviewing
> Topic: sales

S1:   Send your credit card details. Whoopee there's another one.
[short laughter]
S2:   No most of 'em are information sites I think where you can't find their address rather than you [inaudible].
5   S3:   Eddie's hol= holiday appeal.
[short burst of laughter]
S1:   Yeah. (1 second) Okay Jimmy on these mats. Get the updated get the e= or= get Brian to give us final costs for the heavy-duty stuff.
S4:   Uh huh.
10   S1:   Non edge sealed. (4 seconds) And then we need to I mean can you give Barnsley a ring Phil? Or i= you know. [inaudible] do them whenever and say "Look how are those mats performing?"
S2:   Yeah yeah yeah.
(3 seconds)
15   S1:   We we we've gotta keep= we've gotta get off the fence here.

The extract features several discursive practices including the end of one instantiation and the beginning of another. The relational sequence involves the managing director taking the discussion 'off track', before he takes it back 'on track' in his second turn shown in the extract (line 7) through the silence and keyword discourse marker *Okay* (this is one of the top two keywords in CANBEC, along with *we*). The vocative *Jimmy* and the metastatement *on (these mats)* explicitly clarify who is being addressed and what the topic is, and could be evidence of a formulation. The use of the imperative *Get* in this turn might be a bald directive, or could more feasibly, given the clustering of interpersonal (Halliday, 1994) features in this extract – such as repetitions, hesitations, the hedges *I mean* (line 10), *you know* (line 11), the vague language *stuff* (line 8) and *whenever* (lines 11–12), and the deontic modal verbs *need* (line 10) and *can* (line 10) – be interpreted as ellipsis (possibly with a modalized request such as *Can you get . . .* being the unelided form). Further instructions are then given to *Phil* (S2), with the managing director shifting the footing (Goffman, 1981) and concluding the sequence more forcefully with this cluster of evaluative, overtly managerial interpersonal features (line 15): the strong modal of obligation *gotta,* the pronoun *we,* the creative metaphor *get off the fence* (the fossilized form being 'sit on the fence') and the emphatic deictic marker *here. We've gotta get off the fence here* indicates the rationale for the preceding directives: the sales team needs to be more proactive. A very common use of metaphorical language, as this instance demonstrates, is to make evaluative comments less face-threatening (Carter, 2004; see also Chapter 7). The choice of the pronoun *we* by the managing director is also interesting given that, even though he is the speaker, he is probably not including himself as an agent of the action expressed in *We've gotta get off the fence.* However, by using *we* rather than *you*, he again downplays the potential face-threat of the directive. He thus seeks to heighten the sense of collaboration, even though it may not actually exist in practical terms. This is a use of *we* also noted by Poncini (2002). In terms of language and practice, metaphorical and idiomatic language often occurs at the end of a sequence, as it does here, to summarize and assess the previous points (Drew and Holt, 1998). As such, the metaphor *get off the fence* could also be interpreted as a summarizing formulation. We will revisit metaphorical language in Chapter 7.

The timing of this instantiation (bringing the discussion back on track) through the directives and evaluation has arguably more force, because sequentially it is immediately preceded by a relational interlude. The sudden topic shift to a highly transactional frame is in stark contrast to the light-hearted mood of the discourse a few seconds previous to this, which raises the possibility of relational language being used tactically to further transactional goals.

Extract 3.7 is made up of discursive practices that are recognizable in stage 2 of other internal and external meetings, such as bringing the discussion back on track, as well as certain practices that are more typical in stage 2 of manager–subordinate meetings, such as issuing directives. The extract also exhibits discursive features which are less common for a manager–subordinate meeting, such as cyclical turn-taking (Holmes and Stubbe, 2003), with the topic being returned to following an unrelated topic, combined with a large amount of small talk in the discussion stage. This is partly a result of the problem-solving that occurs in this meeting and partly of the style of communication favoured by this manager. In this and other meetings, a high degree of relational communication, both at the sequence (Koester, 2004) and at the topic (McCarthy, 2000) level are evident in his speech.

Many regular manager–subordinate meetings typically feature continuously on-topic, linear turn structure (discussed further in Chapter 8), especially in dyadic encounters, and are often concerned with reviewing and planning, as in extract 3.8. Here, the seamless transition from one topic to the next in stage 2 is marked through the use of *Er okay. Right* by the manager (S1).

(3.8)

Internal meeting
Relationship of speakers: manager–subordinate
Purpose: reviewing; planning
Topic: technical

S1: Erm [sucks lips] but I'll mail his CV and then what I'll do is I'll I'll say to people well those who can make use of him make your pitch to me. Erm there is a project that I'll talk to you about that I might want to get him involved with. Er.
S2: Cool.
(2 seconds)
S1: Er I'll talk= take it in in any other business. Er okay. Right. Current and future work?
S2: Proje= er analogue.
S1: Mhm.
S2: Erm it's ongoing. Er we'll get that sorted in the next er week or so.
S1: Right.

A considerable part of managing involves checking and ensuring that staff are doing what they should, and such a linear, incremental communicative approach allows for the succinct, efficient addressing of these goals. Were the manager to employ a more cyclical turn structure to reviewing, through starting one topic and then returning to a previous one before reaching closure on the topic in hand, it might be both time-consuming and confusing.

Internal meetings: Peer

Extract 3.9 is from stage 2 of a peer meeting at the same foam-manufacturing company as the manager–subordinate meeting in extract 3.7. This extract shows how the chair (S1, who is also the chair in extract 3.7) operationalizes topic shift (line 4) and then attempts to drive the peer-group towards making the decision.

(3.9)

> *Internal meeting*
> Relationship of speakers: peer
> Purpose: planning
> Topic: strategy

      S1: Bloody government departments are a pain.
      (2 seconds)
      S2: [exhales loudly]
5   S1: Right. We'll have to review this when Derek comes in anyhow but I mean we've gotta get all our ducks in a row on what we're doing and what happens next week and so on. So+
      S2: Yeah.
      S1: +okay right we'll [inaudible] that. But essentially w= the IPPC and the t= t= t= planning permission a= with the nods and winks we've
10   had from the planners (1 second) what I wanna do is get that ruddy cheque sent today+
      S2: Yeah.
      S1: +or get that order placed. And the cheque y= the cheques in the pos= just the ultimate er.
15   S2: Yeah but they won't be interested in proceeding it till they have a cheque so there's no point+
      S1: Yeah there's no= yeah there's no point [inaudible].
      S2: +[inaudible] unless unless there is one.
20   S1: No. Absolutely. But there. Yes there will be a cheque in the post. Yeah if we do it.
      S2: Just bear it in mind that we need to make that decision before one o'clock.
      S1: Indeed.

At the beginning of this extract, the chair makes a negative evaluation of government departments, thus concluding the previous topic, before initiating the next phase of the meeting. This phase is concerned with reaching a consensus about a new joint business venture, which initially involves sending a large cheque to their future partner. What is interesting is how the chair clearly states his preference in terms of a desirable action (lines 10–11), but his colleagues raise possible problems with his proposal through recollections. They make reference to previously gained information – for example, S2 says *Yeah but they won't be interested in proceeding it till they have a cheque* (meaning that the future partner will not carry out the order without payment in advance), which has direct relevance to the decision of whether they place the order or send the cheque. Such a categorical, unhedged reaction would seem unlikely in a manager–subordinate relationship, as would the cautioning recollection by S3 in lines 21–2 *Just bear it in mind that we need to make that decision before one o'clock* (the one-o'clock deadline exists because of banking hours). Such 'powerful' behaviour frequently occurs in internal peer meetings, even when, as in this case, the chair is also the managing director. Interrupting the chair is also more likely to happen in peer than in manager–subordinate meetings, particularly in such decision-focused sequences. Furthermore, the practice of decision-making is more common in peer than manager–subordinate internal meetings.

So far this section has explored various practices in internal meetings; it will now turn to examining practices in external meetings.

External meetings: Contractually bound

Extract 3.10 is taken from the meeting between the two large pharmaceutical companies introduced in section 3.1 of this chapter. The extract is from the third discussion phase of stage 2 of the meeting (that is, the third point on the agenda), discussing how to organize deliveries of the pharmaceutical orders within the database. The chair from the client pharmaceutical company (S1) is addressing what he sees as the biggest problem, classifiable as an issue of contested, emerging (Bjørkeng et al., 2009) professional practice, in the companies' current working relationship: the manufacturing company (represented by S3 in extract 3.10) is proposing not allowing the client company to change or combine their order at short notice, even when the order change is relatively small. In a post-meeting interview, S1 from the client company stated that he suspected the problem was caused by the inflexibility of the communication within the manufacturing company. The participants have been discussing the issue for approximately ten minutes already and seem no nearer an agreement.

(3.10)

External meeting
Relationship of speakers: contractually bound
Purpose: reviewing; planning
Topic: logistics; production

S1: But but but that what you're saying there differs from what you said to begin with because what you're saying there is it depends on production capacity and I totally agree. We might say= we might not be talking about the difference between eight hundred packs and two thousand which is very very small. We might be talking about [inhales] eight thousand packs and twenty thousand and in which case you're saying "Look+

S3: Yeah.

S1: +you know that additional twelve thousand packs is ano= is an extra day's work".

S3: Yeah.

S1: And I can imagine why you're saying "No".

S3: Yeah.

S1: "We're not prepared to firm that up". So I think we've got to look at production capacities.

S3: Yeah.

S1: We've got to look at component availability. But I'm worried when I hear (2 seconds) we ha= we we can't logistically increase one order by er from eight hundred to two thousand which I would have thought would be two minutes' work and cancel two orders that might be five minutes' work. I might be exaggerating the timescales but that really worries me if we're doing that because we've got a list of twenty two orders where we're saying bring forward increase quantity you know put date back. If you're saying we haven't got the staff or we haven't got the systems that can cope with that I think we've got a resource issue. (1 second) Or a systems or way of working issue.

S3: Yeah.

S1: Because what we're gonna hear is we're gonna put all these requ= there are gonna be requests that come through to to combine orders to whatever. If we haven't got things in place there we're gonna we're gonna put this list together and you're just gonna say (2.5 seconds) rejected. Rejected.

S3: Yeah.

S1: Rejected. Rejected. Rejected. And=

(1.5 seconds)

S3: Rupert I will tell you [inaudible] our er [inaudible] we should talk about the routine process and the routine process should not go ahead with this way of working. We talk we don't talk about ten materials we talk about six hundred material numbers.

40

One of the main types of formulations are summaries. Charles and Charles (1999: 77) distinguish between 'procedural' summaries (referenced to the agenda and usually occurring at the end of a certain phase, showing for everyone's benefit the progress made so far), 'topical' summaries (related to a specific item on the agenda, and occurring just after a discussion on that topic) and 'tactical' summaries (referenced to the hidden agenda of the party in question, and allowing the speaker to 'wrestle for tactical control', putting his or her 'own gloss on events' (ibid.)). While 'procedural' and 'topical' summaries are common in all meetings, 'tactical' summaries tend to occur predominantly in negotiation meetings (ibid.) and arguably in the negotiation phases of other meetings.

The first turn in extract 3.10 by S1 contains a formulation: he clarifies what he sees as a contradiction in S3's argument, and then chooses which line of argument he agrees with, *and I totally agree* (line 3). This seems to bear a strong similarity to a 'tactical' summary, although the term 'tactically clarifying' is preferred here: the difference between a summary and a clarifier is arguably that, whereas a summary is a *semantic* category based on the meanings in the text, a clarifier is a *pragmatic* category because it attempts, at least apparently, to interpret the speaker's intended meaning. By developing this interpretation of the other company's position, S1 is addressing his 'hidden agenda', which does indeed allow him to negotiate tactical control of the discourse (Charles and Charles, 1999: 77).

S1 then instantiates a shift in the discourse through the use of certain rhetorical devices, such as the strong deontic modal *we've got to look at* (line 14), exaggeration (acknowledged by *I might be exaggerating the timescales* in line 21), the unusually personal *I'm worried* and *that really worries me* (lines 17 and 22) and the aggressive repetition of *rejected* (beginning line 33) in an attempt to persuade the manufacturing company to accept his interpretation and proposed course of action.

The chunk *If you're saying we* (line 24) could also be seen as evidence of an instantiation, because through placing the responsibility for the intractable problem with the manufacturing company, S1 is again trying to coerce S3 into coming to a decision which will benefit the client company. S3 does not directly respond to his line of argument, but instead returns to the issue of routine working (*routine process*, line 38), which he had begun to discuss at the very opening of this phase of the meeting.

This extract thus demonstrates the apparent messiness and cyclical nature of decision-focused processes and their constitutive practices. The extract is also interesting, because the speakers are wrestling over the implementation of professional practices that will dictate the organizational norms for the duration of this long-term collaboration. The somewhat forceful behaviour of S1 can also shed light on the range of actions that embody the social practice of being a senior manager, and has parallels with extract 2.4 from the hotel meeting which was discussed in Chapter 2, even though the relationship between the speakers is different. This extract therefore shows how different layers and stages of practices can be pinpointed and inferred in communication.

External meetings: Non-contractually bound

Extract 3.11 is from a sales negotiation meeting between the managing director (S2) and the marketing manager (S3) of an industrial-machinery manufacturer, and the sales person from a magazine publisher (S1). This extract occurs approximately three-quarters of the way through the meeting, and is from the beginning of the persuasion phase of the negotiation (Graham, 1983). The sales person (S1) is trying to persuade the buyer (represented by S2 and S3) to sign a one-year contract which involves a bigger package and a greater financial outlay than they have previously paid. Up until this meeting, the industrial-machinery manufacturer has dealt with the publisher on an ad hoc basis.

(3.11)

External meeting
Relationship of speakers: non-contractually bound
Purpose: buying/selling/promoting a product; negotiating
Topic: sales

S1: What I was thinking is if and you spent two thousand two hundred and fifty pounds with us. [inhales] I mean what what I was thinking is if I could do you (2 seconds) erm (4 seconds) see [sighs] I don't know if you could sort of planning on going up to around about sort of three thousand pounds (1 second) with us. Cos what I was thinking about doing is is doing like (2 seconds) a little package deal and doing you six insertions of any one …

5

S2: And that includes one in the= one in the directory.
S1: One in the guide. On in the guide to the coalfields (1.5 seconds) and
10   then I'll do you another five of your choice out of Coal PLC. (2 seconds)
        So all right you're you're upping your budget by two hundred and
        thirty quid over t' year. But you're getting an extra two adverts to try
        and help you out. Er well obviously+
S2: Mm.
15 S1: +we're getting a commitment from you for the full year (1 second) er
        in agreement.
    (6 seconds)
S2: What are= what your feelings are Kevin? I mean it's you you're the+
S3: Yeah.
20 S2: +you're the marketing bod.
S3: Yeah.
S2: [laughs] [inaudible] (2 seconds) You feel that that if= if we do this
        this'll be the only th= place we advertise won't it.
    (1 second)
25 S3: Yeah.
S1: Mm.
S3: Yeah.
    (3 seconds)
S2: See we've already= we've already paid for the website. The website
30   has cost us three fifty.
S3: Yeah.
S2: So we've got that there anyway.

It is possible to break this exchange into two parts: the sales pitch
(lines 1–16) and the response (lines 18–32). The two are separated by
an extremely long silence of six seconds, during which time the buyers
are considering the proposal. In meetings in CANBEC, talk tends to
be continuous, and silences are very rarely longer than three or four
seconds[6]. It is interesting that the sales person does not attempt to fill
the silence, and this could be a tactical approach to force a response
from the buyer, given that silence can be employed to fulfil a variety of
speech acts (Saville-Troike, 1985; Jaworski, 1993).

The use of *if* in this extract is also of note, with the sales person
employing it in his first turn in the extract to hedge his proposal,
combined with other indirect forms such as *what I was thinking is if
I could* (lines 2–3), *I don't know if you could sort of* (lines 3–4). By
down-toning the force of his offer, he is addressing the negative face
needs of his interlocutors. He also admits that they will have to pay
more, but then concentrates on the benefits by saying *So all right . . .
But you're getting . . .* (lines 11–12). He also positions his argument

so that it is the buyer who will benefit, and who is in a needy condition: *to try and help you out* (lines 12–13). All of these factors combined indicate that this is an instantiation: he introduces the topic of the package and tactically combines negative politeness strategies with positive and necessary benefits in order to encourage the industrial-machinery manufacturer to decide to invest.

Following the six-second silence, the buyers respond with an indirect negotiating move (lines 18–32): by talking to his colleague *Kevin* (S3) directly, interpreting his reticence and tactically clarifying their position (through the formulation *You feel that that if= if we do this this'll be the only th= place we advertise won't it* and the subsequent discussion of the website) the managing director is tactically exerting pressure on the seller to make a better deal because the manufacturer's budget is tight and they already have a website which covers some of their advertising needs.

This response could also be described as an 'account' (Levinson, 1983: 306). Accounts, which can involve an excuse or a justification, are used in negotiations 'as linguistic objects that seek to effect substantive change' (Firth, 1995: 201) – for example, to instantiate a problem-solving phase (ibid.: 212). The above response by the managing director is probably a justification of the marketing manager's silence on one level, but may also be a tactic to gain a better position in the negotiation. Firth states that accounts allow the negotiation to progress from a conflictual situation to one where there is agreement, and that they are achieved sequentially over turns: 'an account is not randomly produced in the negotiation . . . [but] is sensitive to contextual contingencies, not least discourse sequencing and the perceived 'stance' of the other party' (ibid.: 205). This account in extract 3.11 is evidence of goal-driven behaviour, as the negotiator employs an account when it is perceived to diffuse disagreement without damaging his position.

3.4 Summary

This chapter has examined a major theme of this book, that being the systematic identification of the business-meeting genre. The combination of an overall structure which describes the repeated, if sometimes fuzzy, stages of meetings,with linguistically realized discursive practices that constitute the goal-driven activities of the participants in their communities, can help account for the dynamism and recurrence of this genre.

An important issue regarding the relationship and status of the speakers concerns whether the enacting of discursive practices is the prerogative of powerful speakers. Often the answer seems to be affirmative (see Holmes and Stubbe, 2003: 71), especially at certain stages (for example, the expectation of opening the meeting), but factors such as the topic can influence whether less-powerful speakers are enabled to invoke certain discursive practices. In Chapter 8 (extract 8.2), we will see how, in the manager–subordinate meeting from which extract 3.7 is also taken, the subordinate staff can come to a decision very much as managers do in peer meetings – that is, collaboratively. Such a collaborative instantiation demonstrates that the practices are not purely the domain of the most powerful speakers, or single speakers, but can be jointly constructed by members of communities whose roles are far more dynamic than their official status would suggest. On a more general level, as was discussed in Chapter 2, practices need the cooperation of senior and subordinate participants in order to be realized. In addition, the contestation and negotiation of power by less-powerful speakers is evident in many meetings.

Another area explored in this chapter was the tactical nature of many practices. Building on the work of Charles and Charles (1999) and Firth (1995), it discussed the employment of particular instantiations, formulations and accounts to address the speakers' company goals and improve their bargaining position when negotiating. This is a topic that would warrant further study.

On a final note, the probabilistic (as opposed to deterministic) nature of genres and their linguistic realization should be mentioned. Certain lexico-grammatical features and various practices are commonly found in business meetings, but it should not be deduced from this that they will always be found in that particular type of meeting. Notwithstanding this qualification, it is possible to link various categories and features that are proposed and analysed in this book. For instance, many recurrent, critical lexico-grammatical units can be categorized in terms of their discursive practice – the chunks *in other words* and *so I think*, which can be used to summarize, provide two examples of this. Summarizing is an example of the practice of formulations, which are a key part of the genre of the meeting and therefore provide strong evidence for participants actively 'doing' the genre. In this way, the discursive practices bridge the words in the text and the meeting itself, explaining how the words reflect and create the meeting in a meaningful, recognizable way. As has been shown in this chapter, many discursive practices are achieved over turns, not simply by a single lexico-grammatical item. In Chapters 4 and 5, several critical words and clusters will be exposed which participants use when indexing practices, and which thus provide a more 'bottom-up' perspective on many of the contextual aspects discussed in this chapter.

Notes

1. See Chapter 5 of Pan et al. (1998) for a discussion of cultural differences in perception of what is appropriate and successful in meetings.
2. When asked to clarify the absence of the SIPOC suppliers and customers from the meeting outline, the chair stated that it was unnecessary to mention that the suppliers give the input and the customers receive the output information, as such 'supplier/customer information was obvious' to the participants.
3. Discursive practices can share labels with functions, for instance 'summarizing'. Whereas functions are a textual category and closely related to the notion of intentional strategies explored in Chapter 2, discursive practices, as practices, can be seen as forming part of the wider 'socio-cultural context' (Fairclough, 2003; Bhatia, 2004), albeit at a more local level of context that is relatively close to the text. Discursive practices and functions will be discussed further in Chapter 5.
4. While this stage is optional on one level, on a more abstract level all meetings build on previous meetings and related communicative events.
5. See also Hutchby and Wooffitt (2008) for a detailed discussion of formulations in conversation analysis. For a fuller discussion of McCarthy's strands, see Handford (2007).
6. Reflecting the fact that most speakers in the corpus are British; Japanese speakers, for instance, may be more comfortable with longer silences (Yamada, 1992; see also Saville-Troike, 1985).

References

Bargiela-Chiappini, F. and Harris, S. (1996) 'Interruptive strategies in British and Italian management meetings', *Text*, **16**, 3, 269–97.

Bargiela-Chiappini, F. and Harris, S. (1997) *Managing Language: The Discourse of Corporate Meetings*, Amsterdam: John Benjamins.

Bazerman, C. (1994) 'Systems of genres and the enhancement of social intentions', in Freedman, A. and Medway, P. (eds.) *Genre and New Rhetoric*, London: Taylor and Francis, 79–101.

Berkenkotter, C. (2008) 'Genre evolution? The case for a diachronic perspective', in Bhatia, V., Flowerdew, J. and Jones, R. (eds.) *Advances in Discourse Studies*, Abingdon: Routledge, 178–91.

Berkenkotter, C. and Huckin, T. (1995) 'Rethinking genre from a sociocognitive perspective', *Written Communication*, **10**, 475–509.

Bhatia, V. (1993) *Analysing Genre: Language Use in Professional Settings*, Harlow: Longman.

Bhatia, V. (2004) *Worlds of Written Discourse*, London: Continuum.

Bhatia, V. (2008) 'Towards critical genre analysis', in Bhatia, V., Flowerdew, J. and Jones, R. (eds.) *Advances in Discourse Studies*, Abingdon: Routledge, 166–77.

Bjørkeng, K., Clegg, S. and Pitsis, T. (2009) 'Becoming (a) practice', *Management Learning*, **40**, 2, 145–59.

Boden, D. (1994) *The Business of Talk: Organizations in Action*, Cambridge: Polity Press.

Candlin, C., Maley, A. and Sutch, H. (1999) 'Industrial instability and the discourse of enterprise bargaining', in Sarangi, S. and Roberts, C. (eds.) *Talk, Work and Institutional Order*, Berlin: Mouton de Gruyter, 323–50.

Candlin, C. and Sarangi, S. (2004) 'Preface', in Bhatia, V., *Worlds of Written Discourse*, London: Continuum.

Carter, R. (2004) *Language and Creativity: The Art of Common Talk*, London: Routledge.

Charles, M. and Charles, D. (1999) 'Sales negotiations: Bargaining through tactical summaries', in Hewings, M. and Nickerson, C. (eds.) *Business English: Research into Practice*, London: Longman.

Cuff, E. and Sharrock, W. (1985) 'Meetings', in van Dijk, T. (ed.) *Handbook of Discourse Analysis*, London: Academic Press, 95–117.

Drew, P. and Holt, E. (1998) 'Figures of speech: Figurative expressions and the management of topic transition in conversation', *Language in Society*, **27**, 495–522.

Fairclough, N. (2003) *Analysing Discourse: Textual Analysis for Social Research*, London: Routledge.

Firth, A. (1995) 'Accounts in negotiation discourse: A single-case analysis', *Journal of Pragmatics*, **23**, 199–226.

Flowerdew, L. (2005) 'An integration of corpus-based and genre-based approaches to text analysis in EAP/ESP: Countering criticisms against corpus-based methodologies', *English for Specific Purposes*, **24**, 321–32.

Gee, J.P. (1992) *The Social Mind: Language, Ideology and Social Practice*, New York: Bergin and Harvey.

Goffman, E. (1981) *Forms of Talk*, Philadelphia: University of Pennsylvania Press.

Graham, J. (1983) 'Brazilian, Japanese and American business negotiations', *Journal of International Business Studies*, **14**, 47–61.

Gumperz, J. (1982) *Discourse Strategies*, Cambridge: Cambridge University Press.

Halliday, M. (1994) *An Introduction to Functional Grammar*, London: Edward Arnold.

Handford, M. (2007) *The Genre of the Business Meeting: A Corpus-based Study*, PhD thesis, University of Nottingham (Unpublished).

Handford, M. (2010) 'What corpora have to tell us about specialised genres', in McCarthy, M. and O'Keeffe, A. (eds.) *The Routledge Handbook of Corpus Linguistics*, Abingdon: Routledge.

Hasan, R. (1985) 'The structure of a text', in Halliday, M. and Hasan, R. (eds.) *Language, Context and Text: Aspects of Language in a Social-Semiotic Perspective*, Cambridge: Cambridge University Press, 52–69.

Heritage, J. (1997) 'Conversation analysis and institutional talk', in Silverman, D. (ed.) *Qualitative Research: Theory, Method and Practice*, London: Sage, 161–82.

Holmes, J. (2000) 'Doing collegiality and keeping control at work: Small talk in government departments', in Coupland, J. (ed.) *Small Talk*, Harlow: Pearson Education, 32–61.

Holmes, J. and Stubbe, M. (2003) *Power and Politeness in the Workplace*, London: Longman.

Hutchby, I. and Wooffitt, R. (2008) *Conversation Analysis* (Second edition), Cambridge: Polity Press.

Hyon, S. (1996) 'Genre in three traditions: Implications for ESL', *TESOL Quarterly*, **30**, 693–722.

Jaworski, A. (1993) *The Power of Silence*, Newbury Park: Sage.

Koester, A. (2004) 'Relational sequences in workplace genres', *Journal of Pragmatics*, **36**, 1405–28.

Koester, A. (2006) *Investigating Workplace Discourse*, Abingdon: Routledge.

Koester, A. (2010) *Workplace Discourse*, London: Continuum.

Levinson, S. (1983) *Pragmatics*, Cambridge: Cambridge University Press.

Martin, J. (1992) *English Text: System and Structure*, Amsterdam: John Benjamins.

Martin, J. and Rose, D. (2008) *Genre Relations: Mapping Culture*, London: Equinox.

McCarthy, M. (1998) *Spoken Language and Applied Linguistics*, Cambridge: Cambridge University Press.

McCarthy, M. (2000) 'Captive audiences: Small talk and close contact service encounters', in Coupland, J. (ed.) *Small Talk*, Harlow: Pearson Education, 84–109.

Miller, C. (1984) 'Genre as social action', *Quarterly Journal of Speech*, **70**, 2, 151–67.

Mirivel, J. and Tracy, K. (2005) 'Premeeting talk: An organizationally crucial form of talk', *Research on Language and Social Interaction*, **38**, 1, 1–34.

Ochs, E. (1996) 'Linguistic resources for socializing humanity', in Gumperz, J. (ed.) *Rethinking Linguistic Relativity*, Cambridge: Cambridge University Press, 407–37.

Pan, Y., Scollon, S. W. and Scollon, R. (1998) *Professional Communication in International Settings*, Oxford: Blackwell.

Poncini, G. (2002) 'Investigating discourse at business meetings with multicultural participation', *International Review of Applied Linguistics*, **40**, 345–73.

Saville-Troike, M. (1985) 'The place of silence in an integrated theory of communication', in Tannen, D. and Saville-Troike, M. (eds.) *Perspectives on Silence*, Norwood: Ablex, 3–18.

Swales, J. (1990) *Genre Analysis*, Cambridge: Cambridge University Press.

Swales, J. (2004) *Research Genres: Explorations and Applications*, Cambridge: Cambridge University Press.

Yamada, H. (1992) *American and Japanese Business Discourse*, Norwood: Ablex.

4 *Significant meeting words: Keywords and concordances*

Chapters 2 and 3 have shown how business meetings are made up of various stages, how different practices can be inferred by looking at the language that is found in such stages, and how certain language items seem to play a particularly important role in meetings as they unfold. Chapters 4 and 5 involve something of a step backwards, in that step 2 of the methodology outlined in Chapter 2 will be activated – that is, to pinpoint and categorize potentially important linguistic features, such as lexico-grammatical items in the form of single words and clusters. However, as discussed in Chapter 2, this is only a preliminary step, and these items need to be explored in more specific contexts to unearth and infer their reflexive practices.

Two programs were used for accessing and compiling the data lists: WordSmith Tools (Scott, 1999) and CIC Tools (the software package developed by Cambridge University Press). The former allows for a top-down method of analysis, whereby the software runs frequency counts and keyword searches of groups of texts or single texts, whereas the latter allows for a more bottom-up approach, where a particular lexical item can be examined as it occurs in different contexts (for example, according to the relationship of speakers, the meeting topic or the nationality of the speaker). Using both programs therefore permits an understanding of frequent and key items in the corpus and allows for insights into the effect of context on their distribution. The effect that the context can have on the occurrence of a particular lexical item is a fascinating area of study, prompting questions such as whether a particular word or chunk behaves differently in different types of meetings. As this chapter involves an automated quantitative study, the extent of the analysis will largely remain at the lexico-grammatical level, but where areas of interest are found these will be further analysed and discussed in the succeeding chapters.

4.1 Institutional language and everyday English

A question frequently asked by researchers, teachers and learners is: 'How does business English differ from everyday communication?' Comparing everyday communication with institutional discourse has attracted interest in many fields, including corpus linguistics (Nelson, 2000; O'Keeffe et al., 2007), corpus and discourse analysis (McCarthy and Handford, 2004), pragmatics (Kasper, 2000) and conversation analysis (Drew and Heritage, 1992a; Heritage, 1997). A widespread argument, particularly in conversation analysis, is that ordinary conversation is the 'benchmark' against which other types of discourse (for example, institutional discourse) can be compared and from which they can be distinguished (Drew and Heritage, 1992b: 19). Such comparisons will, it is argued here, reveal systematic differences in the form of keywords. Three related factors that evidence 'distinctly institutional orientations in talk at work' (ibid.: 25) in comparison to ordinary conversation are:

- orientations to the tasks and functions
- restrictions on kinds of contributions that can be made
- distinctive features of inferences made by participants about how the interaction should progress

The first of these points concerns the goals and practices which constitute the institution (for example, a manager outlining how stakeholders' benefits could be achieved). Discriminatory discourse might be an example of the second category (although there are several instances of this in CANBEC in external meetings). The third might involve the improbability of a lawyer expressing shock or sympathy upon hearing what the client has done, whereas in everyday conversations not offering such reactions 'would be interpreted as disaffiliative' (Drew and Heritage, 1992a: 24). As we will see below, there are many lexico-grammatical items that are either far more or far less frequent in business meetings than in everyday English, which it is argued here can shed light on the institutional orientation of business-meeting discourse.

Heritage (1997) outlines six categories for analysing the institutionality of interaction:

1 Turn-taking organization
2 Overall structural organization of the interaction
3 Sequence organization
4 Turn design
5 Lexical choice
6 Forms of asymmetry

According to Heritage, 'lexical choice is part of turn design; turn design is part of sequence organization; sequence organization is part of overall structural organization' (1997: 179), showing how different linguistic levels of spoken discourse, as opposed to written discourse, are integrated. The first and third categories will be discussed further in Chapter 8, and the second category was explored in Chapter 3. While turn design is touched on here, lexical choice is very much the focus of this chapter and the next. The sixth category concerns forms of social asymmetry in terms of issues such as the relative status and relationship of the interlocutors and their respective institutions (for example, peer communication in intra-organizational meetings, and contractually bound communication in inter-organizational meetings). This asymmetry category pervades all the other categories (ibid.) and therefore provides one categorization (amongst others) through which the data can be explored.

Previous work looking at how the complete CANBEC corpus compares to everyday English and another form of institutional language, namely academic speech, has been conducted, firstly by McCarthy and Handford (2004) on a smaller sample of the data, and more recently on the complete CANBEC corpus by O'Keeffe et al. (2007). Both studies initially conducted frequency and keyword searches, and concluded that spoken business English, while sharing properties with both other discourses (for instance, the tendency towards convergence and non-threatening relationships of everyday talk and the goal-driven, sometimes speculative domain of academic talk), also displays systematic differences. Differences include the particular relationships within and across institutional communities and a distinct 'interaction order' (Sarangi and Roberts, 1999).

This chapter is concerned with pinpointing the frequent and statistically significant critical lexical items within the interaction order of business meetings. The chapter will primarily explore the results of a statistical comparison between the language of business meetings as reflected in the CANBEC corpus and 'everyday language', as represented by a sub-corpus of CANCODE (the Cambridge and Nottingham Corpus of Discourse English). This sub-corpus is the reference corpus, and is made up of the 2.7 million words from the 'socializing' and 'intimate' CANCODE data (SOCINT). The 'socializing' data stem from 'social or cultural activities entered upon by participants but not in professional or intimate settings', whereas the 'intimate' data involve contributions from 'family members or close friends in private, non-professional settings' (McCarthy, 1998: 10). The reference corpus does not include the remaining 'pedagogical', 'professional' or 'transactional' categories from CANCODE. This is because these three categories share much in common with business meetings, in that they are all examples of institutional and overtly 'transactional' discourse; therefore, strictly speaking, they are not instances of everyday English. SOCINT, however, is arguably the largest, most representative corpus to date of what could be considered ordinary conversational English.

4.2 Lexico-grammatical theoretical considerations

The following section provides a brief overview of some of the issues and concepts relevant to an understanding of the relationship between lexis and grammar, and how the relationship between the two can be interpreted as being much closer than traditional approaches would allow. This is relevant to the present study, because it can help bring about an understanding of why certain language is in the corpus, and how this language relates to and creates the contextual constraints and opportunities in business meetings.

The open-choice principle and the idiom principle

Traditional approaches to lexis and grammar have viewed them as separate entities (Carter and McCarthy, 2006). Grammar is thus seen as consisting of patterns which are generative, in that they provide the framework of language, while grammatically and semantically appropriate vocabulary can be inserted into these patterns. Words have synonyms, for example, that can be inserted without changing the overall meaning of the text. It is through this 'slot and filler' (Cook, 1998) approach that meaning is constructed. Dictionaries and grammars have been designed on this paradigm, as have various English language teaching materials. In its strongest form, grammar and meaning are seen as autonomous; that is, the syntagmatic and paradigmatic axes are independent of each other (Chomsky, 1957).

This approach has been termed by Sinclair the 'open-choice principle' (1991: 109), which he contrasts with the 'idiom principle'. He argues (1996: 82) that, while the former exhibits a 'terminological tendency', in that words have a fixed meaning in reference to the world, the latter exhibits a 'phraseological tendency': words tend to go together to form phrases, and make meanings by their combinations. Idioms, fixed and semi-fixed phrases and collocations are evidence of the idiom principle and account for much naturally occurring language. On the other hand, examples of the open-choice principle are relatively uncommon (Sinclair, ibid.) and only occur when describing something rare. Because of this rarity, the word would not have formed any collocations with other words or phrases. The essence of the Sinclair argument is that words follow and create patterns. A word, once it appears in a text, has been affected by and in turn affects the other words and structures around it. This entails that form and meaning share a degree of interdependence that cannot be accounted for in the traditional 'slot and filler' approach.

In a paper that strongly supports this interpretation of language and provides empirical evidence based on their findings from the Bank of English corpus, Hunston et al. state that 'all words can be described in terms of patterns . . . [and] words which share patterns also share meanings' (1997: 209). Although Hunston et al. are discussing specific types of lexico-grammatical patterns (such as 'verb by -*ing*'), we can say that, in general, lexico-grammatical patterns can have varying degrees of rigidity, from fully fixed expressions like *at the end of the day*, to semi-fixed multiword clusters, such as *if you say, "Well . . . "*, to collocations between single word forms (like *business* and *partner*).

Nelson (2000) argues that, in the context of business English, there is much evidence of such constraints at the collocational level. A parallel position is proposed by Alejo and McGinity (1997), who argue that, when we choose vocabulary, we 'use the idiom principle, that is, we severely limit the choice of what comes next. This tendency is very important where business English is concerned, for in this discipline concordance and collocation are considerably limited' (Alejo and McGinity, 1997: 216). Nelson (2000) and Alejo and McGinity (1997) therefore conclude that one of the characteristics of business English may be the constraints of collocations. That is, certain collocations will be highly unlikely in a business context, whereas others may be far more frequent than in other registers or genres.

Collocation and the idiom principle (Sinclair, 1991), however, only allow for interpretations of discourse up to the textual level and by themselves cannot account for all restrictions in language use. What this means is that, while the idiom principle can help account for lexical choices at the collocational and colligational[1] level, more contextual insights need to be applied if the fact that there is considerable lexical constraint in authentic language use is to be accounted for. Applying concepts such as discourse prosody, discourse priming, genre, power, discursive and professional practice, and community of practice allows for the operationalization of this context, and for the appreciation of constraint as a factor at all levels of interpretation. When considering instances of the idiom principle in their discourse context, Gee's assertion that 'language has meaning only in and through social practices' (2005: 8) seems highly pertinent. Practices constrain what language is likely to occur in a given context and strongly influence how the members of the community in question will interpret that language.

Related to this is the issue of synonymy. While work by Biber et al. (1998: 100) shows how 'the actual patterns of use (of apparent synonyms) are strikingly different', in CANBEC items that appear synonymous at the semantic, collocational and even colligational levels display marked differences at the contextual level. Indeed, Chapter 2 showed how one cluster, *you have to*, can have different meanings depending on the context in which it is used and the practices it constitutes. Similarly, in Chapter 1, forms of the lemma *negotiate* were shown to be quite different in internal and external meetings.

Discourse prosody, priming and practices

As mentioned in Chapter 2, two concepts that will help unearth the pragmatic and discursive constraints and behaviour of particular items and thus the practices they index are discourse prosody (Stubbs, 2001) and Hoey's notion of priming (2005). Discourse prosody expresses something close to the function of the item, is attitudinal, falls on the pragmatic side of the semantic–pragmatic continuum and links meaning to purpose within a particular context (Sinclair, 1996; Stubbs, 2001). Baker states that discourse prosody makes it possible to find patterns between the language and particular discourses and communities, and that keywords and concordance lines can help unearth these patterns (2006: 87). Priming – that is, how words and clusters become mentally 'loaded with the contexts and co-texts in which they occur' (Hoey, 2005: 8) through repeated use in certain contexts – explains how participants in particular communities tend to reproduce appropriate language; the right words in the right places, as it were. Hoey shows that priming can explain not only collocations and discourse prosody, but also where items tend to occur in a stretch of discourse – that is, discourse priming: 'every word is characteristically primed for a range of genre, domain and situationally-specific features' (2005: 165). By extension, priming should also explain how discursive practices and the language that constitutes them become normalized through recurrence in the genres of particular communities, which we could term 'primed practices'. Priming is thus a potentially powerful concept for explaining how practices are acquired and sheds light on the process by which new and apprentice members of mature communities of practice develop expertise in that community. Chapters 4 and 5 are centrally concerned with unearthing which words and clusters are 'primed' for use in business meetings, and from there it is possible to begin to infer their reflexive practices.

4.3 Word frequencies

The aim of a word-frequency comparison is to see which words occur most frequently in one type of text. These items can then be compared with another list from a different corpus to see whether they occur more or less frequently. In this way, the beginnings of a very tentative picture of the corpus in question can be built and note taken of some suggestive patterns that can be further explored.

This section looks at the most frequent words in CANBEC and the most frequent words in the reference corpus of everyday speech, SOCINT, initially in rank-order lists. The frequency column in table 4.1 gives the total number of occurrences in the corpus and the percentage refers to the proportion of the corpus the item in question represents. For example, *the* occurs 32,032 times in CANBEC and it accounts for 3.76 per cent of all the words in CANBEC.

The most striking initial feature between the two lists in table 4.1 is their similarity, which offers some credence to St John's (1996) concern that significant lexico-grammatical differences between everyday English and business English may not be decipherable.

Table 4.1   Word frequencies in meetings and everyday conversation

CANBEC meetings frequency list				SOCINT frequency list			
#	Word	Freq.	%	#	Word	Freq.	%
1	the	32,032	3.76	1	I	85,005	3.16
2	and	19,650	2.31	2	the	78,837	2.93
3	to	18,403	2.16	3	and	74,619	2.78
4	I	16,494	1.94	4	you	72,542	2.70
5	a	16,318	1.92	5	it	59,328	2.21
6	you	15,869	1.86	6	yeah	54,976	2.05
7	it	15,553	1.83	7	a	52,843	1.97
8	yeah	14,927	1.75	8	to	49,615	1.85
9	that	14,290	1.68	9	that	40,123	1.49
10	we	12,078	1.42	10	of	34,487	1.28
11	of	11,479	1.35	11	was	31,884	1.19
12	in	9,011	1.06	12	in	31,465	1.17
13	is	8,660	1.02	13	laughs	26,316	0.98
14	er	8,059	0.95	14	oh	26,047	0.97
15	so	7,983	0.94	15	it's	25,934	0.96
16	it's	7,655	0.90	16	know	25,300	0.94
17	but	6,882	0.81	17	mm	24,116	0.90
18	on	6,867	0.81	18	no	22,026	0.82
19	for	6,210	0.73	19	but	21,710	0.81
20	have	5,905	0.69	20	like	21,185	0.79
21	erm	5,731	0.67	21	they	20,608	0.77
22	know	5,697	0.67	22	he	20,416	0.76
23	be	5,541	0.65	23	well	20,172	0.75

Table 4.1 (Continued)

#	Word	Freq.	%	#	Word	Freq.	%
	CANBEC meetings frequency list				**SOCINT frequency list**		
24	they	5,484	0.64	24	is	20,101	0.75
25	if	5,362	0.63	25	er	19,490	0.73
26	do	5,153	0.61	26	so	19,054	0.71
27	well	4,958	0.58	27	on	18,411	0.69
28	that's	4,826	0.57	28	have	18,127	0.67
29	just	4,806	0.56	29	we	17,804	0.66
30	what	4,631	0.54	30	just	17,488	0.65
31	got	4,586	0.54	31	what	17,029	0.63
32	this	4,305	0.51	32	do	16,588	0.62
33	one	4,300	0.51	33	right	15,408	0.57
34	with	4,291	0.50	34	all	15,363	0.57
35	no	4,168	0.49	35	erm	15,138	0.56
36	at	4,091	0.48	36	there	14,943	0.56
37	not	4,029	0.47	37	don't	14,511	0.54
38	right	3,990	0.47	38	got	14,475	0.54
39	all	3,987	0.47	39	for	14,084	0.52
40	was	3,813	0.45	40	she	13,968	0.52
41	there	3,745	0.44	41	this	13,784	0.51
42	think	3,736	0.44	42	that's	13,498	0.50
43	can	3,686	0.43	43	be	13,155	0.49
44	are	3,497	0.41	44	not	13,138	0.49
45	as	3,409	0.40	45	one	12,667	0.47
46	then	3,229	0.38	46	think	11,863	0.44
47	or	3,193	0.38	47	then	11,807	0.44
48	get	3,186	0.37	48	with	11,253	0.42
49	don't	3,151	0.37	49	at	10,901	0.41
50	them	3,080	0.36	50	if	10,756	0.40

Another possible interpretation, to be argued here, is that this initial finding lends weight to Nelson's notion of everyday English being the 'mother' of business English (Nelson, 2000): many of the words used in business are the same as those used in more prosaic situations, but their collocations, prosodies and primings are constrained in contextually recognizable ways, and the practices they constitute are often specific to, or highly typical of, business.

The top 50 words of both the CANBEC and SOCINT lists, and indeed the top 100, are virtually all de-lexicalised words. This can be explained in terms of the idiom principle: the most frequent words in language have virtually no meaning or semantic weight, but do have many collocates, whereas the least frequent words in a language or register have considerable semantic weight, but few collocates. The two lists up to the 150-word point are very similar, and in table 4.1, 44 of the top 50 are the same. Looking further down the list past this artificial cut-off point, it can be seen that, of the six words which do not occur in the CANBEC list, three are found in the top 60 of the SOCINT list.

While the two lists are very similar, a closer examination reveals certain differences in position, particularly in terms of personal pronouns. *She* is rank 40 in SOCINT, but is only rank 176 in CANBEC. Although *he* is also less frequent in CANBEC (rank 22) than in SOCINT (rank 55), the contrast is not so stark. This gender difference is also reflected in the composition of the corpus itself, with 79 per cent of the speakers being men. For research on the area of gender in CANBEC, see Mullany (forthcoming). The top ends of the lists also show differences: whereas *I* is the most frequent word in SOCINT, it does not occur until fourth place in CANBEC. *You* and *we* also occupy different places. Pronouns are one of the most important ways of signalling identity and convergence in business meetings (Poncini, 2002) and will be discussed at various stages of this book.

The pronoun *I* is the most frequent word in SOCINT, but *the* occupies first place in CANBEC, which is unsurprising considering that meetings are most often called to discuss 'things' (that is, nouns). The article *the* is also the most frequent word in academic speech (O'Keeffe et al., 2007: 207). The first noun in CANBEC, *time* (which frequently occurs in clusters, ibid.), does not actually occur until rank 84 (although *one* occurs at 33, it is usually a number). There are more nouns in the top 200 words in CANBEC compared to SOCINT (at a ratio of 10:7), and the types of nouns are also different. Whereas SOCINT includes vague nouns (*things, stuff, people*), the nouns in CANBEC are usually more specific and concrete, as might be expected (*year, week, meeting*).

A quick look at some collocations of *the* shows how these findings can combine at the lexico-grammatical level: the words which most commonly appear immediately after *the* in CANBEC (the R1 position – that is, one place to the right in a concordance line) are *other, same, moment, time, end*; whereas in SOCINT they are *one, time, other, thing* and *way*. The most frequent words occurring two places after *the* in CANBEC (the R2 position) are *of, and, that, one* and *is*; whereas in SOCINT they are *and, I, that, thing* and *you*. The interpersonal pronouns *you* and *I* are again immediately noticeable in SOCINT and noticeably absent in the CANBEC collocations. The collocations also show that, while (often metaphorical) time and place references are an important feature of everyday conversation, they are even more so in meetings. For example, the cluster *at the moment* features 473 times in CANBEC and is the third most frequent three-word cluster, occurring over two and half times more often per million words than in SOCINT. Also, the pattern *the . . . of* is very common in CANBEC, occurring over 900 times. While *of* also collocates strongly with *the* in SOCINT, this particular pattern is over 50 times more frequent in CANBEC. In discussing noun phrases, Carter and McCarthy (2006: 833) show how several clusters featuring *the . . . of* are typical of written language and also regularly feature metaphorical time and place locations, such as *the end of* (the seventh most frequent three-word cluster in CANBEC). This shows how language used in business meetings, while undoubtedly sharing many similarities with everyday talk, features some differences and is in other ways more similar to written language. This similarity with written language – for example, in terms of its higher lexical density and greater prevalence of noun phrases – may partly help explain the widely held assumption that business English is more formal than everyday English.

4.4 Keywords

As discussed in Chapter 2, keywords are those single words (and contractions such as *didn't*) which occur with significantly high frequency in comparison to some norm (Scott, 1999). They are a useful method for characterizing a text or genre (ibid.) and the related notion of lexical choice indicates how speakers relate to and create the specific institutional context (Drew and Heritage, 1992b). As such, keywords are seen as potential critical lexical indexical items of the business-meeting genre and its practices, requiring further interpretation in longer extracts.

As has been argued by Nelson (2000), keywords offer more insight than basic frequency counts, because high-frequency words show considerable overlap between business English and everyday English and may fail to capture crucial differences. Through keyword comparisons, the business lexicon begins to emerge (ibid.; McCarthy and Handford, 2004). As has been powerfully argued by Nelson (2000), business English is distinct from everyday English in that it comprises a limited set of semantic fields which reflect the institutional nature of the business world in terms of activities and relationships. An example is the word *partner*. While it has a range of possible meanings in everyday English including lover, team member ('tennis partner') and fellow criminal ('partner in crime'), if it is used in a business context it has a limited, specific meaning of a person or company with whom another person or company is involved in an organizational relationship.

Negative keywords

In order to understand something, it is often useful to see what it is not – in this case, language that may be relatively untypical in business meetings. This section will briefly explore the top 200 negative keywords – that is, words which are statistically highly unlikely to occur in business meetings when compared to everyday speech. That is not to say they never appear in meetings: extract 2.4 on pages 44–5 showed a manager using emotional language (which tends to be less frequent in the corpus) quite rhetorically.

Table 4.2 displays the top 50 negative keywords in CANBEC, painting a picture of life outside work. Several of the top 200 negative keywords can be easily categorized in terms of grammar and topic. They reflect various aspects of *life* (rank 132) between the bookends of *born* (139) and *died* (179). There are many nouns that relate to *home* (50), such as *family* (53), *mum* (22), *brother* (137), *husband* (184), the physical building, including *house* (30), *bedroom* (167), *garden* (116) and references to *dog* (147) and *cat* (122). All of these are in

Table 4.2   CANBEC top 50 negative keywords

#	Word	#	Word	#	Word
1	oh	18	were	35	though
2	was	19	nice	36	don't
3	she	20	school	37	ooh
4	I	21	didn't	38	had
5	like	22	mum	39	funny
6	mm	23	know	40	little
7	he	24	and	41	love
8	you	25	said	42	your
9	her	26	ah	43	me
10	my	27	used	44	quite
11	really	28	dad	45	night
12	she's	29	lovely	46	when
13	yes	30	house	47	never
14	no	31	it	48	dear
15	did	32	thought	49	his
16	went	33	go	50	home
17	God	34	remember		

the singular, because the speakers often refer to particular objects and entities such as *the cat* in casual conversation. In terms of other nouns, we see those that relate to time at the end of the (work) day, including *night* (45), *tonight* (176), *bed* (67) and *sleep* (95). There are food nouns including *bread* (189), *cheese* (163), *meal* (169) and *wine* (80). There are 'people' nouns, such as *woman* (76), *man* (91), *baby* (130), *boy* (88), and 'education' nouns, like *school* (20), *university* (144), *course* (140) and *teacher* (164). There are several pronouns, as was suggested by the raw frequency lists, including *I* (4), *he* (7), *she* (3) and *it* (31), as well as possessives. Adverbs feature fairly heavily, including *always* (86), *never* (47), *quite* (44) and *really* (11), and several (evaluative) adjectives are present: *weird* (119), *awful* (123), *cool* (155), *tired* (198), *horrible* (97), *good* (84) and *beautiful* (78). There are also several very common verbs including *went* (16), *were* (18), *said* (25), *had* (38), *go* (33), and verbs relating to internal states such as *thought* (32), *know* (23), *knew* (181), *feel* (77) and *felt* (200). There are also two modals: *couldn't* (114) and *must* (81). The appearance of the modal form *must* is highly intriguing: obligation is one of the defining features of the workplace, and *must* is one of the most prototypical modals of obligation (see Chapter 6 for a discussion of linguistic expressions of obligation in CANBEC). Yet this list shows that *must* is statistically far more typical of everyday communication than it is of communication in meetings[2]. Findings like this bring to light the value of (fully transcribed) corpora.

Certain discursive tendencies can be inferred from these grammatical and semantic groupings: the past tense is much more common than the present tense in SOCINT as compared to CANBEC and this suggests that, in business, people talk about the future and present more than they do in everyday life (a hypothesis that is further supported by the occurrence of *will* at rank 20 in the positive-keyword list). Narratives may be more common in everyday communication, which would also help explain this discrepancy in the use of tenses, as well as the occurrence of *like*, which is often used as a marker of reported speech (Carter and McCarthy, 2006), as is *said*. As might be expected, outside of business, people talk a lot about family, friends, their home, food and their evenings. Perhaps less immediately predictable are the adjectives, which are highly evaluative and often negative. The occurrence of certain adverbs may also be surprising, such as *always*, but when considering that many of the words on this list tend towards hyperbole, such as *hate*, *awful* or *loads*, which is often found in everyday communication (Carter, 2004), the relative absence of words such as *always* and *never* in business is perhaps not so surprising. Spoken business English, as a form of institutional discourse, tends towards caution and a relatively high level of formality (McCarthy and Handford, 2004). A high level of emotion in many of the words in the top 200 keywords is also evident; for example, in the adjectives listed above, expletives, and even in the backchannels *oh* and *gosh*, which suggests that these may be inappropriate in many business communities. This is not to suggest, however, that business people never use these in meetings. As demonstrated in Chapter 2 with the hotel manager (extract 2.4, pages 44–5), expert users of a genre can employ unusual strategies (involving the use of emotional language like *hurt me*) for seemingly purposeful effect. Moreover, several of these negatively key items and topics are more common in CANBEC during small-talk sequences, most typically at the beginnings of meetings.

It is possible to speculate that some of the items in the top 200 keywords may not be negatively key in a cultural context other than that of the British Isles (which provided the cultural context for the reference corpus CANCODE). For example, in some other cultures, it is normal to start the business discussion with questions about the well-being of your business partner's family[3], and therefore certain of the family words listed above may not appear on comparative keyword lists from such cultures. Furthermore, some words seem distinctly British, such as *gosh*, and words like *wine* or *cheese* would be less likely in many other cultures. Nevertheless, words relating to some kinds of food and drink, and many of the other semantic groupings outlined above, may be less probable in many business meetings around the world. It is also of note that many of the words on this negative-keyword list are etymologically derived from Anglo-Saxon (for example *home*, *feel*, *did*), whereas many of the positive keywords, which are explored below, are derived from French and/or Latin.

Positive keywords

This section will now examine three positive-keyword lists[4], produced using the log likelihood procedure in WordSmith Tools (Scott, 1999): one for all meetings in CANBEC (table 4.3), one for internal meetings (table 4.4) and one for external meetings (also table 4.4). Table 4.3 shows which single words are statistically much more frequent in the whole business-meeting corpus, compared to SOCINT. The '%' column indicates the percentage of the whole corpus the item represents.

Table 4.3   Positive keywords from all meetings in CANBEC

#	Word	%	#	Word	%	#	Word	%
1	we	1.42	18	if	0.63	35	for	0.73
2	we've	0.32	19	which	0.25	36	us	0.17
3	okay	0.35	20	will	0.21	37	server	0.02
4	we're	0.28	21	customers	0.04	38	so	0.94
5	hmm	0.06	22	per	0.05	39	vehicle	0.02
6	the	3.76	23	price	0.05	40	er	0.95
7	crane	0.05	24	mail	0.03	41	point	0.09
8	customer	0.06	25	business	0.06	42	tyre	0.02
9	lift	0.08	26	lifts	0.03	43	list	0.04
10	need	0.21	27	is	1.02	44	company	0.06
11	cranes	0.04	28	month	0.06	45	information	0.04
12	order	0.07	29	we'll	0.13	46	system	0.03
13	meeting	0.07	30	stock	0.03	47	terms	0.03
14	sales	0.04	31	issue	0.03	48	cellar	0.02
15	thousand	0.09	32	product	0.03	49	two	0.28
16	hundred	0.11	33	cent	0.04	50	to	2.16
17	orders	0.04	34	problem	0.08			

Table 4.4   Positive keywords from internal and external meetings

Internal meetings			External meetings		
#	Word	%	#	Word	%
1	we	1.31	1	we	1.76
2	we've	0.30	2	we've	0.41
3	hmm	0.07	3	the	4.13
4	customer	0.06	4	okay	0.42
5	we're	0.26	5	we're	0.34
6	okay	0.32	6	orders	0.09
7	sales	0.05	7	need	0.28
8	the	3.65	8	order	0.11
9	meeting	0.08	9	company	0.11
10	thousand	0.09	10	customer	0.05
11	need	0.19	11	will	0.26
12	which	0.26	12	product	0.04
13	mail	0.04	13	terms	0.06
14	hundred	0.11	14	hmm	0.03
15	per	0.06	15	markets	0.03
16	price	0.05	16	system	0.06
17	customers	0.04	17	kilos	0.03
18	business	0.07	18	if	0.68

Table 4.4 (Continued)

Internal meetings			External meetings		
#	Word	%	#	Word	%
19	if	0.61	19	process	0.04
20	cent	0.05	20	batch	0.03
21	order	0.05	21	test	0.06
22	issue	0.04	22	bulk	0.03
23	month	0.06	23	for	0.82
24	server	0.02	24	customers	0.04
25	will	0.19	25	stock	0.04
26	problem	0.08	26	hundred	0.11
27	we'll	0.12	27	is	1.08
28	stock	0.03	28	so	1.03
29	is	1.00	29	date	0.05
30	list	0.04	30	stainless	0.02
31	orders	0.03	31	our	0.18
32	step	0.03	32	material	0.04
33	er	0.95	33	supply	0.03
34	install	0.02	34	August	0.04
35	information	0.04	35	can	0.52
36	us	0.16	36	we'll	0.14
37	product	0.02	37	thousand	0.07
38	client	0.02	38	us	0.19
39	contract	0.03	39	packs	0.02
40	January	0.03	40	two	0.32
41	cost	0.04	41	mhm	0.15
42	for	0.70	42	production	0.03
43	support	0.02	43	servers	0.02
44	so	0.91	44	month	0.06
45	database	0.01	45	three	0.23
46	web	0.02	46	guess	0.05
47	service	0.03	47	companies	0.03
48	marketing	0.02	48	based	0.03
49	network	0.02	49	cover	0.04
50	be	0.65	50	capacity	0.02

Compared to the CANBEC frequency list in table 4.1, table 4.3 shows some considerable differences. One of the most noticeable differences is the number of nouns. These keyword nouns are categorized as follows:

- business-specific nouns: *customer, meeting, sales, business*
- nouns with constrained business meaning (i.e. they have a general, wider meaning outside the business context): *service, support, team, stock*

- nouns with industry- or departmental-specific constrained meaning: *web*, *install*
- time nouns: *January, month, moment*
- functional business nouns: *problem, solution, issue, process, point*

As well as nouns, there are also several other interpersonal and grammatical items:

- (semi-)modal verbs: *will, need, can, gonna* (the contracted form of 'going to'), *gotta* (the contracted form of 'got to')
- pronouns: *we, they*
- backchannels: *okay, hmm, yep*
- fillers: *er, erm*
- conjunctions: *so, if, which, whatever*
- determiners: *the, which, whatever*

Many of these single keywords form collocations and clusters, conforming to Sinclair's (1991) idiom principle introduced earlier in this chapter, and will be explored in context in Chapters 6 and 7.

Keywords in internal and external meetings

As discussed in Chapter 1, one of the unique features of CANBEC is the amount and range of internal and external data, allowing for comparisons between both types of meetings at several levels. This section explores how the two types of meetings compare at the single-word level, following keyword searches with reference corpus SOCINT.

Of the top 50 keywords in table 4.4, 23 are the same in both tables, leaving 27 which are different. There are also some interesting contrasts in terms of relative frequency. By seeing which words occur more commonly in internal meetings compared to external meetings in relation to everyday English, it is possible to begin building a picture of how differences between the two types of business meetings manifest themselves linguistically. From there it is possible to begin to explore how items may index certain discursive practices, and also consider whether such practices are shared across both internal and external meetings, or are particular to one type of meeting.

The top keyword in both internal- and external-meeting lists in table 4.3 is *we*. However, *we, we've* and *we're* are more frequent in external meetings than internal meetings, with *we* being almost half a per cent (that is, almost one in every 200 words) more frequent in external meetings. This can be explained by the use of corporate *we*. This includes inclusive corporate *we*, but more importantly exclusive corporate *we*, where one representative of a company is talking about his or her own company and excluding the representatives of the other company in the meeting. In extract 4.1, S1, the managing director of the visiting company, explains to *Baz* (S3), the technical director of the other company, what his company does.

(4.1)

> *External meeting*
> Relationship of speakers: non-contractually bound
> Purpose: giving and receiving information/advice
> Topic: sales; technical

S3: Well well where where are you g= er= I need to understand where you guys fit in.
(2 seconds)
S1: Okay.
SM:(laughs)
S1: Yeah.
S3: In order to know what I'm supposed to be drawing.
S1: Fine. What what Baz what we do=
S3: Yeah.
S1: Erm we're sort of trying to apply a new model to to a new i= to a relatively new industry.

Such a reference is by definition not possible in internal meetings. This additional use of *we* and the concomitant ambiguity involved in interpreting such items reflect the higher degree of complexity – caused by the range of relationships, goals, agendas and often practical logistics – which may be found in inter-organizational (that is, external) meetings (Poncini, 2002).

Differences in the relative frequency of some of the nouns reflect which topics tend to be discussed in internal meetings compared to external meetings: *sales* (rank 7 internal: rank 145 external), *mail* (13:177), *business* (18:88), *information* (35:102) and *client* (rank 38 internal: not in top 200 of external data). It could be claimed that, in external meetings, people often perform the topics that are discussed in internal meetings: that is, rather than talking about sales, people sell or negotiate in external meetings; rather than talking about making a relationship or discussing hypothetically how to deal with an issue, they make relationships, negotiate the issues at hand and attempt to portray their company in a professional light. The concordance lines overleaf show how the collocation *sales people* (the most frequent two-word phrase involving *sales* in both external meetings and internal meetings, excluding *the sales*), combined with deictics such as pronouns, *here* and *came*, reflect these issues:

*Concordance lines for **sales people** in external meetings*

I think you know the **sales people** here are less inclined to barter with the customer.

I'll tell our **sales people**. They'll be very happy. [inaudible] at the moment.

Er and nor would we do if a customer came to us= despite what the **sales people** might tell you+ [laughs]

---

*Concordance lines for **sales people** in internal meetings*

Another key thing we've got for you all to understand er you [inaudible] **sales people** is there's a huge push this coming year for quarter one performance.

is it er in fact going to save any time for the **sales people** or is it going to make their life harder?

But the **sales people** have also= even though we've told them "Under no circumstances must you do this yourself

---

Some other differences in terms of business nouns may be less obvious: *issue* (rank 22 internal: rank 65 external), *problem* (26:94) and *price* (16:90). One obvious explanation is that these words, especially *problem*, have potentially negative connotations, and external meetings often involve more attention to the relational aspects of communication than internal meetings. Such findings suggest that participants are more likely to talk about and label things as *problems* in internal meetings than in external meetings. However, the cluster *not a problem* is almost twice as common in external meetings as it is in internal meetings.

The results of the backchannel *hmm* are also of note. While *hmm* does feature quite highly in external meetings (rank 14), it is relatively more than twice as frequent in internal meetings (rank 3). While these findings show that it is much more common in internal meetings than external meetings, the particular internal relationship has a strong bearing on its frequency, as Chapter 6 will show.

In terms of modal forms, there are some interesting results. The semi-modal deontic verb *need* is actually slightly more key in external meetings (rank 11 internal: rank 7 external), even though it might be expected that discussions of obligation feature more typically in internal meetings. While *we need to* is more frequent in external meetings, *you need to* is far less frequent in external meetings. *Can* is more common in external meetings than internal meetings (rank 126 internal: rank 35 external), as is *will* (rank 25 internal: rank 11 external), although *we'll* is slightly more common in internal meetings. Further down the keyword lists, *gonna* (going to) is at rank 88 in external meetings, but at rank 101 in internal meetings. Perhaps more surprisingly, given that obligation may be more typically associated with internal communication (a topic that will be discussed further in Chapter 6), *gotta* (got to) is at rank 136 in external meetings, but does not feature in the top 200 words in internal meetings at all. In fact, *gotta* and, to a certain extent, *we need to*, are commonly used to refer to actions that the speaker or speaker's company is obliged to do, for example:

*Concordance lines for **gotta** in external meetings*

---

but we **gotta** get approval ... for of the plan before we can bring any raw materials on site.

Erm and I've **gotta** find out about filling out the forms and things to do that.

The keyness of *if* is roughly equivalent in both lists. Another item that can be put in the loose grammatical category of conjunctions (although it can also be an intensifier), *so*, is also equivalent in terms of keyness, featuring at rank 28 on both lists. According to Carter and McCarthy (2006: 143), the most common use of *so* in everyday speech is as a discourse marker, whose function is to summarize or connect. Its keyness reflects how important such discursive practices are in business.

The position of *so* in a speaker turn is also of interest. While the issue of turn-taking will be dealt with in Chapter 8, it is worth saying a few words here about turn design (Heritage, 1997). Drawing on work by Carter and McCarthy (1995, 2006), Chafe (1994), Biber et al. (1999) and Halliday (1994) on spoken grammar, it can be said that speaker turns in naturally occurring, spontaneous discourse can comprise a three-part turn structure consisting of heads, bodies and tails. Bodies contain the propositional or ideational (Halliday, 1994) content of the message and often follow an SVO syntactic pattern

(Carter and McCarthy, 2006; Biber et al., 1999). Heads and tails, found in the turn-initial and turn-final positions respectively, fulfil regulatory (Chafe, 1994) and interpersonal functions (Halliday, 1994), such as demonstrating that the speaker is taking up a turn or that the speaker is actively seeking agreement from the listener. An example is: *So that's about hundred and fifty a month isn't it.* In this turn, *so*, the head, takes the turn-initial position, signalling that the turn contains a summary; *that's about hundred and fifty a month* forms the main body of the message, and the tail, *isn't it*, is in the turn-final position. Recent research in corpus linguistics (Tao, 2003; Evison, 2008) shows that certain items are statistically much more likely to be found in either turn-initial or turn-final positions than other items. Over a quarter of the instances of *so* in CANBEC, for instance, are at the beginning of turns. The random concordance lines below include such examples of *so* occurring in turn-initial (following a speaker code in the transcript, for example S6) and other positions. As might be expected, such instances tend to signify summaries.

*Concordance lines for **so** in CANBEC*

[S6:] **So** they're actually going out. [S5:] Six are going out

[S6:] **So**+ [S5?:] Too low? [S6:] +**so** what you do is you hang on to those until you get your next orders

next week **so** we ought to be actually designing the= [S2:] Yeah. [S1:] Yeah. **So** we we've got that

and sort of [inaudible] et cetera. **So** it really is erm er a minimum cost minimum resource quick fix.

[S1:] Which we've got as well but I've got enough going to plan an agenda agreed with them. [S7:] **So** what's changed is that they are much clearer now about what they can and can't do.

little combo TV video players in one. [S3:] Right **so** they won't. [S2:] No.

[S1:] Well two [inaudible] and getting down and back= **so** you know I [inaudible]= [SM:] [inaudible] don't have to worry about

---

Insights such as these concerning the potential overall structure of speaker turns could be of great benefit to learners of spoken business English and other spoken registers, as it would enable them to see how spoken and written language can be constructed differently, and how certain items may be primed (Hoey, 2005) to occur in certain positions in the turn.

In contrast to *so*, *which* is much more key in internal meetings (rank 73 internal: rank 12 external), of which 57 per cent form non-restrictive relative clauses, compared to 63 per cent for external meetings. Like *so*, between 20 and 30 per cent of the occurrences of *which* are found in the turn-initial position, depending on contextual factors (see also Tao and McCarthy, 2001). When looking at longer keyword lists, the most striking feature of both internal- and external-meeting lists is that most items are business-related nouns; for example, *machine, invoice, packaging*, or items that can be nouns or verbs: *copy, lead, cost* and *check* (in CANBEC, *copy* and *lead* tend to be used as nouns, or as part of noun compounds such as *lead time*, whereas *cost* and *check* occur more commonly as verbs). In terms of hedging and intensifying adverbs there are some differences: *basically* is slightly less key in external meetings (199:170), but *obviously* is more key (103:157). *Effectively* is at rank 76 in external meetings, but does not feature in the internal meetings list.

4.5 Summary

This chapter has been centrally concerned with the question of how the language used in business meetings compares to everyday English. The first part of the chapter was concerned with discussing certain lexico-grammatical, theoretical issues – for instance, Sinclair's (1991) idiom principle and how it can be employed in interpretations of business discourse. To explore the relationship between the text and the context, notions of discourse prosody, priming and practices were suggested as a way to tie findings of the idiom principle – that is, the recurrent, usual words, clusters and idioms that comprise much spoken business English – to the context. In other words, the argument that business meetings comprise language that is constrained, or primed, has been explored, and may help explain how such constraints and primings can illuminate some of the practices running through the corpus.

As a first step to finding language that typifies business meetings when compared to everyday English, word frequency counts were compared between the CANBEC corpus and the SOCINT corpus. These lists were very similar, although there were some differences noted in terms of pronouns and possible grammatical tendencies. Keyword searches were then examined, which allow for a statistically more sensitive understanding of the language in the meeting genre. The first, negative-keyword search, showed words that are less typical in business meetings than in social and intimate communication, such as *home, family, school, garden* and *music*. More surprising was the occurrence of *must* in this list. The CANBEC positive-keyword list (showing words that are much more typical of business meetings compared to everyday communication) contained many types of nouns – for instance, business-specific nouns, including *meeting* and *sales*, as well as more functional business nouns such as *problem* and *issue*. Apart from nouns, there were several modal verbs, such as *need* and *can*. Moreover, the pronoun *we* was statistically the most significant item, and the words *if* and *so*, as well as certain backchannels, were evident among the most typical words in meetings. Internal and external keyword lists were then compared, with almost half of the items on each respective list differing. Even among items which occurred on both lists, such as *we*, significant statistical differences were evident which could be explained with reference to the differing identities speakers signal in internal and external meetings. The lists also suggested that participants talk about different topics in internal and external meetings, and even the same topic can be dealt with in markedly different ways. These are all items and issues that will be explored in greater detail in subsequent chapters. Finally, there was a brief discussion of the design of turns in meetings, and how certain items may be primed to occur in particular positions in a turn. Turn-taking will be discussed in detail in Chapter 8.

In Chapter 5, lists of the most frequent groups of words (or clusters) will be categorized according to discursive practice, with a selection of them being explored in longer extracts. Therefore, this chapter and the next can be seen as providing a lexico-grammatical foundation for the rest of the book.

Notes

1. Colligation can be defined as 'the grammatical company a word keeps and the positions it prefers'; in other words, 'a word's colligations describe what it *typically* does *grammatically*' (Hoey, 2000: 234; author's stress).
2. Although in both meeting and everyday discourse it also has non-deontic meanings, as in lexical clusters such as *I must admit*, and to speculate about the past, as in *you must have said*.
3. In Saudi Arabia, for example, meetings would usually begin with questions about one's family (Alex Gilmore, personal communication; see also Harris and Moran, 2000).
4. Two sets of nouns have been deleted from these keyword lists. Examples of the first set include names of products, people's names and company names. Names of months, however, have not been removed, because they indicate that specific time-frame references are more common in business than in everyday English. The second set of nouns which have been removed

are those which have a general, everyday meaning, but which also have a highly constrained or specific meaning – for example *prop* (as in mechanical prop, discussed at length in a couple of manufacturing meetings), and *rack* (as in computer rack for electronically storing memory). This second set is somewhat fuzzier than the first in that there are many words which would fit this description, but which have been left on the lists. *Servers* are an example. The reasoning here is that words like *servers* are no longer specific to one type of industry despite having a business meaning (in this case IT). Computers are so commonplace now that this word appears in virtually any type of industry or organization. In contrast, the removed words have usually appeared on the lists because of their repeated use in one particular company, and are therefore unrepresentative of the corpus and the embedded practices.

References

Alejo, R. and McGinity, M. (1997) 'Terminological loans and the teaching/learning of technical vocabulary: The use of economic anglicisms in the business classroom', in Piqué, J. and Viera, D.J. (eds.) *Applied Languages: Theory and Practice in ESP*, Valencia: Universidad de Valencia.
Baker, P. (2006) *Using Corpora in Discourse Analysis*, London: Continuum.
Biber, D., Conrad, S. and Reppen, R. (1998) *Corpus Linguistics: Investigating Language Structure and Use*, Cambridge: Cambridge University Press.
Biber, D., Johansson, S., Leech, G., Conrad, S. and Finnegan, E. (1999) *Longman Grammar of Spoken and Written English*, London: Longman.
Carter, R. (2004) *Language and Creativity: The Art of Common Talk*, London: Routledge.
Carter, R. and McCarthy, M. (1995) 'Grammar and the spoken language', *Applied Linguistics*, **16**, 2, 141–58.
Carter, R. and McCarthy, M. (2006) *Cambridge Grammar of English*, Cambridge: Cambridge University Press.
Chafe, W. (1994) *Discourse, Consciousness and Time*, Chicago: Chicago University Press.
Chomsky, N. (1957) *Syntactic Structures*, The Hague: Mouton.
Cook, G. (1998) 'The uses of reality: A reply to Ron Carter', *English Language Teaching Journal*, **1**, 57–63.
Drew, P. and Heritage, J. (eds.) (1992a) *Talk at Work*, Cambridge: Cambridge University Press.
Drew, P. and Heritage, J. (1992b) 'Analysing talk at work: An introduction', in Drew, P. and Heritage, J. (eds.) *Talk at Work*, Cambridge: Cambridge University Press, 3–65.
Evison, J. (2008) *Turn-openers in Academic Talk: An Exploration of Discourse Responsibility*, PhD thesis, University of Nottingham (Unpublished).
Gee, J.P. (2005) *An Introduction to Discourse Analysis*, Abingdon: Routledge.
Halliday, M. (1994) *An Introduction to Functional Grammar*, London: Edward Arnold.

Harris, P. and Moran, R. (2000) *Managing Cultural Differences: Leadership Strategies for a New World of Business*, Houston: Gulf Publishing Company.

Heritage, J. (1997) 'Conversation analysis and institutional talk', in Silverman, D. (ed.) *Qualitative Research: Theory, Method and Practice*, London: Sage, 161–82.

Hoey, M. (2000) 'A world beyond collocation: New perspectives on vocabulary teaching', in Lewis, M. (ed.) *Teaching Collocations*, Hove: Language Teaching Publications.

Hoey, M. (2005) *Lexical Priming*, Abingdon: Routledge.

Hunston, S., Francis, G. and Manning, E. (1997) 'Grammar and vocabulary: Showing the connections', *English Language Teaching Journal*, 3, 208–16.

Kasper, G. (2000) 'Data collection in pragmatics research', in Spencer-Oatey, H. (ed.) *Culturally Speaking: Managing Rapport through Talk across Cultures*, London: Continuum, 316–41.

McCarthy, M. (1998) *Spoken Language and Applied Linguistics*, Cambridge: Cambridge University Press.

McCarthy, M. and Handford, M. (2004) '"Invisible to us": A preliminary corpus-based study of spoken business English', in Connor, U. and Upton, T. (eds.) *Discourse in the Professions: Perspectives from Corpus Linguistics*, Amsterdam: John Benjamins, 167–201.

Mullany, L. (forthcoming) 'Managers performing masculinities in business meetings', in Angouri, J. and Marra, M. (eds) *Constructing Identities at Work*, Basingstoke: Palgrave.

Nelson, M. (2000) *A Corpus-based Study of Business English and Business English Teaching Materials*, PhD thesis, University of Manchester (Unpublished).

O'Keeffe, A., McCarthy, M. and Carter, R. (2007) *From Corpus to Classroom: Language Use and Language Teaching*, Cambridge: Cambridge University Press.

Ochs, E. (1996) 'Linguistic resources for socializing humanity', in Gumperz, J. (ed.) *Rethinking Linguistic Relativity*, Cambridge: Cambridge University Press, 407–37.

Poncini, G. (2002) 'Investigating discourse at business meetings with multicultural participation', *International Review of Applied Linguistics*, 40, 345–73.

Sarangi, S. and Roberts, C. (eds.) (1999) *Talk, Work and Institutional Order*, Berlin: Mouton de Gruyter.

Scott, M. (1999) *WordSmith Tools Version 3*, Oxford: Oxford University Press.

Sinclair, J. (1991) *Corpus, Concordance, Collocation*, Oxford: Oxford University Press.

Sinclair, J. (1996) 'The search for units of meaning', *Textus*, IX, 75–106.

St John, M-J. (1996) 'Business is booming: 1990s business English', *English For Specific Purposes*, 15, 1, 3–18.

Stubbs, M. (2001) 'On inference theories and code theories: Corpus evidence for semantic schemas', *Text*, 21, 3, 437–65.

Tao, H. (2003) 'Turn initiators in spoken English: A corpus-based approach to interaction and grammar', in Leistyna, P. and Meyer, C. (eds.) *Corpus Analysis: Language Structure and Language Use*, Amsterdam: Rodopi, 187–207.

Tao, H. and McCarthy, M. (2001) 'Understanding non-restrictive *which*-clauses in spoken English, which is not an easy thing', *Language Sciences*, **23**, 651–77.

5 Discourse marking and interaction: Clusters and practices

Readers of business literature, such as magazines, textbooks and vocabulary books, might assume that business people regularly use such words as *profit*, *merger* and *shareholder* when doing business. This chapter will show that in reality, single words like *profit* are less frequent than one may think; instead, much business language, like everyday naturally occurring speech (O'Keeffe et al., 2007), is made up of clusters – that is, groups of two or more words that regularly reoccur (for instance, *at the end of the day*). The prevalence of such items provides further evidence for Sinclair's 'idiom principle' (1991), which argues that a considerable amount of language is made up of collocations, including fixed and semi-fixed phrases (discussed in Chapter 4 of this volume). These clusters, it is argued here, fulfil specialized discursive roles, and are repeated in various meetings involving different employees, companies, industries and nationalities.

Nelson's (2000) distinction between the language people use when *doing* business and the language people use when *talking about* business helps to explain this issue. When people talk about business, then it seems reasonable to expect them to use words like *profit* and *shareholder*. An interview in a magazine or a lecture on an MBA programme would be two such genres where speakers talk about business. In a meeting – and this goes for meetings involving colleagues within the same company as well as external meetings – the speakers are doing, as opposed to analysing, business. The language they use is therefore quite different, because their goals and related practices are different. (See Nelson, 2000, for results from keyword comparisons across spoken and written business corpora of people talking about and doing business.) In a business lecture, the primary goal of the lecturer is to educate the audience about some aspect of business. In a business meeting, the primary goal may be to solve problems, make decisions, convey information or negotiate a deal. When this difference in goals is taken into account, the difference in language used becomes obvious. Furthermore, it has serious implications for the definition and learning of 'business English'.

So what language do speakers repeatedly use in business meetings, and why do they do so? Research in corpus linguistics shows that different speakers who take part in similar social activities at different times and in different places often choose to use the same language (Sinclair, 1991; Biber et al., 1999; Wray, 2002; McCarthy and Handford, 2004; O'Keeffe et al., 2007). A close analysis of that language reveals that much of it consists of prefabricated clusters and not just single words tied together by syntax in a rule-governed manner. Sinclair argues that speakers use prefabricated language because of 'the recurrence of similar situations in human affairs . . . a natural tendency to economy of effort [and] . . . the exigencies of real-time conversation' (1991: 11). That is, speakers who find themselves in repeated situations, such as business meetings, save time and effort by uttering recognizable clusters of words which steer the activity in question in recognizable ways. Rather than creating a novel way of expressing a certain function (such as *Excuse me everybody. Can I have your attention. Given that we all have other commitments and the issues we have to address in this meeting are of some importance, I as the chair want us to start discussing the first issue . . .*), it is more usual to say something pithy such as *We should start.* The other participants in the meeting understand what is to be started, who has the power to start it and the reasons for starting, without these being explicitly stated, because they have been in this situation numerous times before.

Sinclair's (1991) rationale for the use of prefabricated clusters is therefore also relevant to the formation, expectations towards and repeated use of discursive practices within a genre. Furthermore, veering away from such expectations may lead to censure by the group (Gee, 1990). Jaspers critically clarifies this relationship between recurrence in discourse and the wider social practices/Discourses that constrain what is acceptable:

. . . those at the top of social hierarchies will applaud reproduction of the world as it is, while those with less influence may often feel ill at ease or apprehensive about leaving the social paths in which they have learned to think, feel and act, so that although social actors are constantly recreating the social world, they will mostly (feel encouraged to) reproduce established discourses. (Jaspers, forthcoming)

This chapter will demonstrate how clusters are a central aspect of the reproduction of established discourses in business meetings.

5.1 Defining clusters

There is a wide range of terms which are roughly synonymous with the word 'cluster', including 'chunks' (Lewis, 1993; De Cock, 2000), 'lexical phrases' (Nattinger and DeCarrico, 1992), 'formulaic sequences' (Wray, 2002) and 'lexical bundles' (Biber et al., 1999).

Other synonyms include 'prefabs', 'multiword units', 'phrases' and sometimes 'idioms'. In this book, the word 'cluster' will be used to mean any fixed or semi-fixed string which reoccurs in different meetings and which can be inferred to potentially index (Ochs, 1996) a discursive practice. Biber et al. (1999) show how clusters are extremely frequent in texts of all kinds, even though many are not 'idiomatic' in the usual sense of being syntactically fixed and semantically opaque. Idiomatic language of that type will be analysed in Chapter 7. For practical purposes, it is necessary to decide on a frequency cut-off point. Biber et al. (1999) propose that clusters can be seen as significant if they reoccur at least ten times per million words across a variety of texts. As the CANBEC meeting corpus is made up of approximately 900,000 words, if a cluster occurs nine times, and in different meetings by different speakers, then it is regarded as statistically significant.

Much naturally occurring language is made up of clusters (some estimates put it as high as 70 per cent). However, traditional approaches to grammar and semantics would dismiss most clusters as they stand, because they are merely phrasal fragments (O'Keeffe et al., 2007: 70) – for instance, *and then* or *we need to*. Such fragments may not be meaningful as they stand and they may be syntactically incomplete, or, in other words, they can be said to be lacking semantic or syntactic 'integrity' (McCarthy and Carter, 2002). Indeed, Pinker, who follows Chomsky's general approach to language, goes so far as to say that such word-chains are 'deeply, fundamentally, the wrong way to think about how human language works' (1994: 93).

An alternative approach to understanding why there are so many recurrent, fragmentary clusters is posited by O'Keeffe et al. (2007). They state that a useful concept is that of 'pragmatic integrity': does the cluster play any interactive role, and 'refer to the speaker–listener world rather than the content- or propositional world' (ibid.: 71)? For example, is it possible to see what the cluster is doing in the discourse in terms of such features as face preservation and politeness, hedging and purposive vagueness, or discourse marking? They argue that it is this pragmatic analysis, rather than a semantic or syntactic analysis, that will explain the ubiquity of clusters in speech. This insight has relevance to the discussion of heads and tails in the context of turn-taking in Chapter 4. Certain clusters (and single words) may be primed (Hoey, 2005) to occur in the turn-initial position as a head (as well as other turn positions), thus indexing certain textual, interactional, cognitive and validational (that is, 'regulatory' – Chafe, 1994) practices. For instance, *I think* often occurs in the turn-initial position and can signal practices such as offering an opinion, disagreeing and hedging.

An example of a cluster that displays pragmatic integrity and that can constitute certain practices is the very frequent (77 occurrences) four-word cluster *I don't know if*. Semantically and syntactically this cluster is incomplete as it stands. Semantically, it is impossible to know what it is the speaker is referring to, and grammatically it seems safe to assume that this is a fragment of a conditional statement, for example, *I don't know if they'll grant us planning permission*, which refers to future time. This form does occasionally occur in CANBEC, but the use of *I don't know if* as a way of hedging suggestions and which can be related to issues of face is far more frequent, as in the following concordance lines:

*Concordance lines for **I don't know if***

Erm well I just haven't heard from that at the moment. **I don't know if** it's possible to chase him up. Er whether it's down to me or [inaudible].

I don't know if if anyone wants to help me but at least one or two of

I mean what what I was thinking is if I could do you (2 seconds) erm (4 seconds) see [sighs] **I don't know if** you could sort of planning on going up to around about sort of three thousand pounds (1 second) with us.

I don't know if it's a positive note now or whatever but [laughs]

One thing that we could do **I don't know if** James has come up with some of them they could do

---

The first concordance line is taken from a manufacturing company meeting, and it appears again in extract 5.1. In this extract, S3 is the sales manager and S2 is the managing director. They are discussing what to do about a non-paying client who will be at a business conference which the sales manager will also be attending.

(5.1)

Internal meeting
Relationship of speakers: manager–subordinate
Purpose: reviewing; planning
Topic: sales

S3: Erm well I just haven't heard from that at the moment. **I don't know if** it's possible to chase him up. Er whether it's down to me or [inaudible].
S2: I would post a message+
S3: [inaudible]

S2: +just to reply+
[laughter]
S2: +in the same conference.

S3, whose client is the tardy payer, suggests that he would be willing to *chase him up*. By using the cluster *I don't know if*, followed by *Er whether it's down to me or*, he hedges the suggestion so that he does not appear to be pushy while looking for encouragement or confirmation from his manager, and shows that he does not want to encroach on another person's area of responsibility. The managing director (S2) takes up his suggestion and offers a course of action, suggesting he should post a message. Carter and McCarthy (2006: 757) discuss the use of other clusters containing *if* as a pragmatic marker of politeness in everyday speech, such as *if you don't mind*. Chapter 7 will discuss *if* in detail.

This current chapter focuses only on those items which display pragmatic integrity, as this will lead to conclusions regarding how speakers and listeners co-construct and reconstruct practices and meetings in different times and places. At present, however, computers cannot distinguish between clusters in terms of semantic, syntactic or pragmatic integrity, or indeed strings of words that either lack integrity (for example, *and to me*) or are merely fragments of longer clusters (such as *end of the*). The software can only produce lists of items that frequently occur. It is therefore the analyst's job to manually make inferences and interpretations about the raw, automatically produced lists.

5.2 Clusters in business research

Sinclair's (1991) idiom principle was discussed in Chapter 4. It was also noted that Nelson (2000) and Alejo and McGinity (1997) argue that one of the characteristics of business English is the constraint of collocations: certain collocations will be highly unlikely in a business context, whereas others may be far more frequent than in other registers or genres. This finding has also been reported in research on other genres. For example, Oakey (2002) reports that certain clusters feature differently in different genres of academic writing (technical, social science and medical).

One of the reasons why clusters are important is that they provide 'fingerprints' of specific registers or genres. In the case of business meetings, they can show that the participants know that they are in a meeting and that they are in the process of creating that meeting through talk. When the chair says *We should start*, the reaction of the other participants shows that he or she is not referring to, for example, a cooking class. While Carter and McCarthy (2004, 2006; McCarthy and Carter, 2002; O'Keeffe et al., 2007) have been at the vanguard in demonstrating the prevalence of such features in everyday speech through their work on CANCODE (The Cambridge and Nottingham Corpus of Discourse English – see Chapter 1), and while the occurrence of certain categories of clusters in various institutional varieties of English has been well documented (Biber et al., 1999; Simpson, 2004; O'Keeffe, 2006; Adolphs et al., 2007), research into clusters in business discourse has been relatively sparse (Nelson, 2000, 2006; McCarthy and Handford, 2004; Handford, 2007; O'Keeffe et al., 2007). This chapter will look at how aspects of the context, such as discursive practices, are indexed (Ochs, 1996) through the use of critical clusters.

Two studies which have extracted cluster lists from CANBEC are McCarthy and Handford (2004) and O'Keeffe et al. (2007), and both briefly discuss the occurrence of the top 20 three-word clusters. The study by McCarthy and Handford (2004) was based on around 250,000 words of data, mainly from meetings, which was, at the time of writing, the total transcribed and anonymized amount of data available. The findings from the study described in O'Keeffe et al. (2007) are based on the complete CANBEC corpus, which, unlike the data used for this book, also includes non-meeting workplace communication, such as office chat, as well as academic business lectures. As mentioned in Chapter 1, given that the focus of this book is the language of meetings, any data which cannot be considered to be a meeting have been removed.

Both of these previous studies conducted triangulation comparisons using two sub-corpora from the CANCODE corpus: a corpus of spoken academic speech, and a corpus of social and intimate communication (SOCINT, which was also used as the reference corpus for retrieving the keywords discussed in Chapter 4). Based on comparisons between these corpora and CANBEC, McCarthy and Handford (2004) and O'Keeffe et al. (2007) argue that the following functions are evident in spoken business English: 'speculating', 'hedging', 'being vague', 'specifying', 'describing change and flux', 'referring to collective goals', 'protecting face' and 'giving directives'. As such, the studies indicate how spoken business discourse compares with both academic speech and everyday talk: spoken business discourse and academic speech are both goal driven and involve a high degree of speculation and hypothesizing, and everyday talk and spoken business discourse feature a lot of attention to relationship-building. These findings will be referred to when relevant, but, in this book, most quantitative comparisons are between the CANBEC meeting data and SOCINT. Furthermore, the aim here is to develop an interpretation of the data which focuses on discursive practice rather than function (although there is considerable, inevitable overlap in terminology and linguistic focus).

Other studies of naturally occurring spoken business English, such as Boden (1994), Firth (1995, 2009), Bargiela-Chiappini and Harris (1997), Holmes and Stubbe (2003), and Poncini (2004) tend to be primarily qualitative in emphasis, and often apply techniques from discourse analysis and conversation analysis to short extracts of data. Such studies (excluding those reported in Poncini, 2004) have not produced quantitative results, and therefore there are no findings on frequent clusters. Indeed, the review of research into business discourse compiled by Bargiela-Chiappini et al. (2007) indicates that many researchers are averse to relying on quantitative linguistic evidence, perhaps for fear of appearing to prescribe 'native-speaker norms' (a concern that clearly has ramifications for the classroom and training room), or because of an ideological bias against quantitative research (see Baker, 2006), or due to a lack of sufficient data. Koester (2004, 2006) is one exception. The quantitative results explored in her work concern selected 'interpersonal markers', such as deontic modal expressions and vague approximators, as well as 'figurative' clusters, including metaphors and certain idioms. This chapter will outline the most frequent clusters in CANBEC, then categorize a selection of them according to the discursive practices which they index, and finally explore the way they behave in naturally occurring extracts of meetings.

Frequent clusters versus key clusters

Chapter 4 argued that keywords (words which occur with significantly high frequency in comparison to some norm – Scott, 1999) are more telling than raw frequency counts, as 'keyness' (ibid.) shows which words and their collocations are more significant in the field of business English compared to everyday English (even though their overall frequency may not be particularly high). This is not to argue that pure frequency is uninformative: if we accept that a genre constrains language choices, and that, within a particular genre, words can have constrained uses or meanings specific to that genre (for example, *partner* as used in business), then frequent single words and frequent clusters in particular should not be assumed to either have the same meaning or, more significantly for this study, the same use in a different context.

This argument is in contrast to that proposed by Simpson (2004), who analyses those clusters in spoken academic discourse (using the MICASE corpus) which occur more frequently than in her reference corpora[1]. She reasons that, by excluding those clusters which are shared across many registers and looking only at those clusters which occur more frequently, a deeper pragmatic understanding of the register under scrutiny can be gained. However, if it is accepted that the frequency of such clusters can be explained by the fact that they are key structuring devices which are genre-sensitive (Oakey, 2002), then their frequency in other genres is somewhat irrelevant. If a cluster occurs frequently in the genre under analysis, then it can help explain that genre. We should not assume that it indexes the same practice in a different genre[2]. Pure frequency lists rather than comparative frequency lists of clusters will therefore be analysed in this study. The reason the same argument is not made concerning single words is that single words do not usually tend to embody the same degree of pragmatic integrity as clusters, and therefore a keyword search is a very useful tool to distinguish potentially important 'critical' items.

5.3 Cluster lists

This section lists the most frequent two-, three-, four-, five- and six-word clusters in CANBEC (as stated in Chapter 4, 'word' here includes single words and contractions, such as *didn't*). The only seven-word cluster that appears frequently is *but at the end of the day* (appearing nine times). All repetitions signalling hesitations (such as *if you if you*) have been removed, although it is acknowledged that these may be of interest from certain conversation-analysis and emergent-grammar perspectives. The frequency column refers to the number of occurrences of the particular item in CANBEC, and the final column shows what percentage of the corpus that item comprises. Because the percentage of four-word clusters and above is either 0.02% or lower, this column has been removed from tables 5.3–5.5.

Table 5.1   Two-word clusters

#	Cluster	Frequency	%
1	you know	3,494	0.41
2	I think	2,675	0.31
3	of the	2,150	0.25
4	I mean	1,983	0.23
5	in the	1,878	0.22

Table 5.1 (Continued)

#	Cluster	Frequency	%
6	on the	1,864	0.22
7	at the	1,437	0.17
8	to be	1,412	0.17
9	I don't	1,387	0.16
10	to do	1,355	0.16
11	if you	1,309	0.15
12	and then	1,237	0.15
13	have to	1,134	0.13
14	we've got	1,100	0.13
15	to the	1,095	0.13
16	for the	1,073	0.13
17	need to	1,043	0.12
18	we can	1,041	0.12
19	it was	946	0.11
20	and the	944	0.11

Table 5.2 Three-word clusters

#	Cluster	Frequency	%
1	I don't know	578	0.07
2	a lot of	478	0.06
3	at the moment	472	0.06
4	we need to	427	0.05
5	I don't think	349	0.04
6	the end of	341	0.04
7	I mean I	245	0.03
8	a bit of	220	0.03
9	and I think	217	0.03
10	be able to	217	0.03
11	in terms of	217	0.03
12	one of the	216	0.03
13	to do it	216	0.03
14	at the end	207	0.02
15	I think it's	207	0.02
16	we have to	207	0.02
17	end of the	206	0.02
18	I think we	185	0.02
19	you know the	181	0.02
20	have a look	174	0.02

Table 5.3   Four-word clusters

#	Cluster	Frequency
1	at the end of	178
2	the end of the	177
3	have a look at	98
4	end of the day	97
5	a bit of a	83
6	I don't know if	77
7	at the same time	68
8	I don' t know what	64
9	to be able to	58
10	two and a half	58
11	a lot of the	53
12	we need to do	51
13	thank you very much	50
14	I don't know whether	49
15	the other thing is	48
16	if we can get	47
17	in terms of the	47
18	I don't know how	44
19	to make sure that	43
20	if you look at	41

Table 5.4   Five-word clusters

#	Cluster	Frequency
1	at the end of the	116
2	the end of the day	88
3	this that and the other	40
4	and this that and the	33
5	do you want me to	32
6	have a look at it	30
7	and a half per cent	27
8	to have a look at	23
9	two and a half per	23
10	you know what I mean	22
11	I think we need to	21
12	the end of the year	20
13	and have a look at	18
14	I mean I don't know	17
15	the end of the month	17
16	at this moment in time	16

Table 5.4 (Continued)

#	Cluster	Frequency
17	I don't know what the	16
18	from our point of view	15
19	from my point of view	15
20	I don't know if you	15

Table 5.5 Six-word clusters

#	Cluster	Frequency
1	at the end of the day	86
2	and this that and the other	33
3	two and a half per cent	23
4	between now and the end of	10
5	a hell of a lot of	9
6	but at the end of the	9
7	do you know what I mean	9

As stated on page 120, a benchmark of ten occurrences per million words was set as a measure of statistical significance. Figure 5.1 shows the total number of clusters of between two and seven words which occur ten times or more per million words: this means that there are only seven six-word clusters which do so, and only one seven-word cluster – mentioned previously as being *but at the end of the day*. As the graph shows, the frequency of these clusters reduces considerably in relation to the number of words in the cluster. While this is partly because there are many frequent two-word clusters (such as *you know* and *I think*) that display semantic and syntactic integrity, a glance at the list shows that many so-called two-word clusters are both semantically and syntactically fragmented: that is, 'they do not constitute complete syntactic elements at phrasal or clausal levels' (McCarthy and Carter, 2002: 42), or they form part of the longer clusters. Examples include *and then*, *sort of* and *of the*. As argued on page 120, however, a cluster being semantically or syntactically incomplete does not entail that it lacks pragmatic integrity[3]. McCarthy and Carter (2002) give *a bit (of a)* as an example: while it is lexically fairly empty, it plays a definite interactional role – that of a downtoner (for example, *a bit of a problem*). *A bit of a* is also very frequent in CANBEC, appearing 83 times. The keyword *problem* will be discussed in more detail in Chapter 7.

Figure 5.1   Number of clusters at or above ten per million words

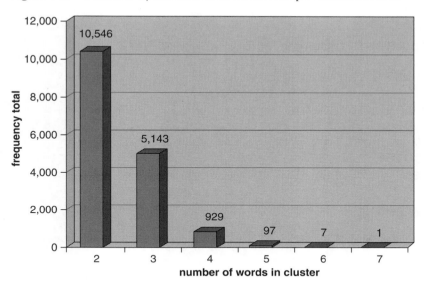

Clusters and single words

The actual frequency of many clusters is higher than that of some very common single words. There are only 44 single words in CANBEC that are more frequent than *you know*, and figure 5.2 compares the frequency of the two-word clusters *you know* and *I think* with four single words from CANBEC. Figure 5.3 compares some longer clusters with the high-frequency word *maybe* and two widely used business-specific words (*profit* and *industry*). These graphs indicate that clusters may well form a central part of linguistic output in business meetings, occurring more frequently than the 'typical' business words. Indeed, according to Wray (2000, 2002), clusters are formulaic, prefabricated sequences which form part of the mental lexicon and can be retrieved automatically without recourse to creative language capability (that is, the part of the brain which deals with grammar). While such views have been vehemently rejected by linguists who advocate the primacy of a creative, grammar-based system (see Pinker, 1994), Wray (1998) has even argued that the use of formulaic, unanalysed clusters may actually have been the earliest forms of human language. Even though corpus linguistics cannot shed light on Wray's fascinating assertions concerning protolanguage, the case for the ubiquity of clusters in various genres of speech is increasingly

Figure 5.2   The frequency of two-word clusters compared to single words

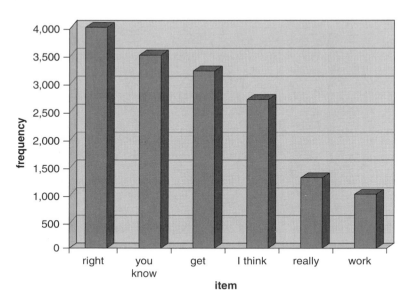

Figure 5.3   The frequency of longer clusters compared to single words

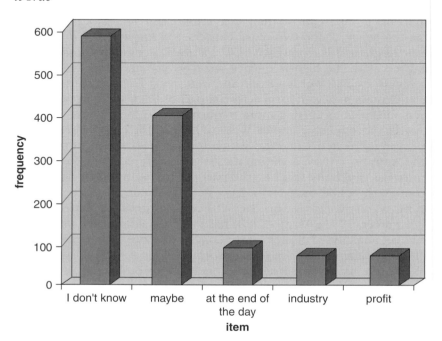

being made. Such findings have far-reaching ramifications for language description, artificial intelligence, and language learning and teaching. However, it is clear that cluster lists, like keyword and frequency lists, can only contribute so much to an understanding of the nature of the discourse under examination, and to gain further insight, qualitative techniques must be applied (McCarthy and Handford, 2004).

5.4 Categorization of clusters

It has been argued that spoken business English shares features with everyday English (Nelson, 2000; McCarthy and Handford, 2004; O'Keeffe et al., 2007) and academic discourse (McCarthy and Handford, 2004; O'Keeffe et al., 2007), whilst also displaying a variety of differences. In both everyday English and spoken business English, interlocutors pay close attention to face needs, and spoken business English and spoken academic English are forms of institutional discourse. As forms of institutional discourse, we can expect similarities in terms of transactional speaker goals, differences in power hierarchy and a level of formality higher than that found in everyday English.

Two studies which have categorized clusters according to function are those of McCarthy and Carter (2002) and Simpson (2004). Whereas McCarthy and Carter analyse clusters in everyday English from the CANCODE corpus, Simpson's study concerns clusters in academic speech from the MICASE corpus. As discussed above, spoken business discourse has been shown to share attributes with both of these registers (McCarthy and Handford, 2004; O'Keeffe et al., 2007). The findings from these two studies will be explored in this section and will provide a platform for the analysis of a selection of the above clusters from CANBEC.

This analysis involves interpreting, when plausible, certain functional categories as instances of discursive practices. As shown in Chapter 3, the same labels can be used to describe the functions and interpret the practices of important language items (for instance, summarizing), and one of the differences between functions and practices involves different concerns with the extent of context. The re-interpretation of selected functions as discursive practices reflects the aim of the present study to move beyond a *description* of the texts (which tends to be concerned with functions and strategies, as discussed in Chapter 3) and their immediate context to allow for an *interpretation* of the wider social context, in terms of how it reflexively enables and constrains the choices of language evident in meetings, and therefore the rights and obligations of the participants in these meetings. This involves exemplifying the link between lexico-grammar and discursive practices, as well as considering wider contextual concerns and their relation to the text, such as the professional practices, social practices and Discourses discussed in Chapter 3. This is not to suggest that functional descriptions of the data are invalid, as they most evidently are valid; the point here is that an analysis focusing on practice permits a greater exploration of the relationship between text and context than a functional analysis allows. Nor is it being implied that functional classifications can simply be replaced at will with classifications based on discursive practice: the latter involve the dual requirements of ethnographic insights combined with textual and contextual evidence that the practices are ratified by the interlocutors, which functional descriptions do not require.

Both McCarthy and Carter (2002) and Simpson (2004) distinguish between discourse-marking functions and interactional functions. In McCarthy and Carter (2002), selected clusters in CANCODE are broken down into the following categories: 'discourse marking', 'protecting face' (involving the use of indirectness and hedges) and 'being vague'. Simpson applies a slightly different framework for categorizing the pragmatic functions. She breaks the items into three main categories: 'primarily discourse-organising functions', 'primarily interactional functions' and 'miscellaneous functions' (2004: 53). In this study, two overall categories have been preferred: primarily discourse-marking practices, and primarily interactional practices. It should be noted that the terms 'interactional' and 'interpersonal' are largely synonymous here, as will be demonstrated in Chapters 6 and 7, where most of these practices are explored in detail. Table 5.6 contains a selection of the discursive practices and the clusters which are inferred to index the practices.

While several specific categories have been taken from the Simpson (2004) and McCarthy and Carter (2002) studies (including 'enumerating/temporal sequencing', 'focusing', 'marking cause and effect' and 'explaining' from the former study, and 'being vague', 'showing shared understanding' and 'being indirect' from the latter), categories from these studies which do not seem particularly relevant to business English (for example, spatial organisers such as *in the book*) have been removed. Moreover, certain very frequent clusters in CANBEC cannot be accommodated in these frameworks, which suggests that the language items are more typical of business meetings (as opposed to everyday English or academic spoken English). These include clusters involving modal forms of obligation and necessity, which form a new category headed 'signalling obligation' in table 5.6. The need for such a category is clear: the frequency of deontic modal verbs reflecting obligation was flagged in the keyword comparisons in Chapter 4, and the stages and phases presented in Chapter 3 showed that the work-related discourses, and meetings in particular, often involve managers and staff discussing responsibilities, tasks and decisions. As there are also a number of clusters relating to 'epistemic modality' (that is, degrees of certainty and possibility), another category is included headed 'signalling (un)certainty'.

Various other categories have been added to table 5.6 – for example, the interactional practice of hypothesizing/speculating. One of the most fascinating words in CANBEC is *if*, and it is found in many clusters. While specific practices involving *if* are discussed in different parts of this book, and relate to a range of issues including politeness, categorically directing staff and problem-solving, *if* is used most often in meetings to index the practice of 'hypothesizing/speculating'. The category 'marking/requesting future communication' has been created, as a number of clusters seem to index this practice – for example, *come back and see us (next week)*. In addition, summarizing/reformulating, clarifying own position, checking/showing shared knowledge/understanding, seeking clarification, and evaluating are also included in the categorization of business-meeting discursive practices. It is inevitable that the more one pores over lists and data, the more subheadings emerge. However, although these categories cannot be comprehensive in terms of accounting for all discursive practices or indeed all pragmatic clusters in meetings, they do provide a thorough interpretation of many of the most pertinent practices as evident from the clusters. Furthermore, a considerable degree of overlap with the discursive practices outlined in Chapter 3 should be immediately evident. Indeed, certain practices roughly correspond across both lists, such as summarizing, requesting future communication and clarifying. Nevertheless, while clusters can suggest what practices are being addressed in specific contexts, it is essential to remember that there are many discursive practices that cannot be so neatly indexed by a phrase containing a few words. Many practices are carried out and realized over longer stretches of dialogue, and sometimes over many turns, as clearly shown in Chapters 3 and 8. It should also be remembered that one cluster of language can fulfil various practices and address multiple goals (but for practical reasons, each cluster is assigned to only the seemingly most usual practice within meetings here). Thus, while there is obvious potential for overlap between the practices proposed in Chapter 3 (table 3.1) and those outlined in table 5.6, the lists have not been integrated more fully at this stage. It is also worth reiterating that the practices in Chapter 3 – which specifically concern how the dynamic, overall structure of meetings is constituted through such practices –

Table 5.6.   Discursive practices indexed by particular clusters

	Practice	Cluster	Frequency
Primarily discourse-marking practices	Focusing	in terms of	217
		the fact that	139
		the problem is	49
		one of the things that	13
	Enumerating/ temporal sequencing	and then	1,237
		for the time being	25
		to begin with	11
		in the first place	14
	Linking	and then	1,237
		but at the same time	9
	Marking cause–effect	the reason why	17
		and that's why	17
	Summarizing/ reformulating	so I think	167
		so I mean	49
		in other words	10
Primarily interactional practices	Clarifying own position	I mean	2,675
		from my point of view	19
		from our point of view	19
		I guess for me	18
		what we're trying to do	17
		that's what I'm saying	14
		I'm not saying that	9
		but what I'm saying	9
	Checking/showing shared knowledge/ understanding	you know	3,494
		you know what I mean	22
		what you're saying is	13
		do you know what I mean	9
	Being vague	the other thing	127
		sort of thing	76
		kind of thing	65
		et cetera	54
		things like that	43
		a lot of	35
		and this that and the other	33

Table 5.6 (Continued)

Practice	Cluster	Frequency
	and so forth	32
	or something like that	25
	a couple of	19
	and everything else	15
	all that sort of stuff	11
	that type of thing	11
	the rest of it	9
Hedging	I think	2,675
	sort of	912
	a bit (of a)	636
	I don't know	578
	I don't think	349
	at the end of the day	86
	from my point of view	19
	from our point of view	19
	to be honest with you	14
	I'll be honest with you	14
	as far as I know	11
	I'll be straight up	10
Signalling obligation	we can	1,091
	we need	680
	we need to	427
	we should	257
	we have to	207
	you need to	152
	you have to	132
	I need to know	12
	I think you should	9
Focusing on decisions	so we can	77
	a problem with	58
	not a problem	42
	we might as well	18
	not an issue	15
Hypothesizing/ speculating	if you	1,309
	if I	284
	so if	254

Table 5.6 (Continued)

	Practice	Cluster	Frequency
Primarily interactional practices (continued)	Evaluating	but if	273
		it might	152
		if we can	128
		it may be that	13
		a waste of time	9
		one of those things	9
		a hell of a lot of	9
		that's the other thing	9
	Seeking clarification	do you mean	18
		what do you think	16
		what do you mean	13
	Explaining/ demonstrating	if you look at	45
		I can tell you	16
		as you can see	10
	Being indirect	but I think	166
		do you want (me)(to)	107
		I don't know if/whether	77
		I don't know what	64
		I don't know how	44
		what do you think	15
		I was just thinking	9
	Signalling (un)certainty	we can	1,041
		you can	919
		you could	341
		we might	112
		we should be able to	12
		we might be able to	11
		we could do that	9
	Marking/ requesting future communication	sit down and	21
		sit down with	13
		come back to me	13
		come back to us	9

were arrived at through genre analysis, whereas this chapter employs corpus-linguistic methods to pinpoint the clusters that index the (sometimes identical) discursive practices. In both chapters, the language items are seen to index the practices. This issue will be taken up again in Chapter 9, when teaching and learning implications are discussed, and the two lists are exploited to develop guidelines for a 'skills' syllabus for L1 and L2 learners of business English.

5.5 Clusters in context

So far this chapter has shown that certain clusters are particularly frequent in business meetings, and that many clusters can be categorized according to the discursive practice which they index. This section will look at particular clusters in extracts from meetings with the aim of gaining a deeper contextual understanding of such features. Three items have been selected – *so I think*, *you need to* and *at the end of the day* – because they frequently appear in the corpus and invoke different practices from the above category list (summarizing, signalling obligation and hedging, respectively). Specific extracts have been chosen because they clarify how the item occurs in context. The background information provided with each extract on the meeting in question and on the participants is especially helpful here.

CLUSTER: *so I think*

Key practice: summarizing	
Occurrence in external meetings:	48
↳*frequency per million words:*	*202*
Occurrence in internal meetings:	119
↳*frequency per million words:*	*176*

So I think is one of the most frequent three-word clusters, and it indexes a variety of discursive practices: for example, to explain, to elaborate, and to disagree. In CANBEC, it is most commonly used to summarize what has been said before. Summarizing is a core management practice, which, although categorized here as a discourse-marking practice, is also highly interactional, and has received attention in the literature on meetings (Charles and Charles, 1999; Holmes and Stubbe, 2003; McCarthy and Handford, 2004). In terms of meeting type, *so I think* occurs more often in external meetings than in internal meetings – particularly in the contractually bound external meetings – and in meetings discussing logistics and production.

It often forms part of what Charles and Charles (1999) term 'tactical summaries' (see page 85), where one of the speakers summarizes some information or part of the discussion in such a way as to add support to his or her position. In extract 5.2, the logistics manager (S1) is arguing why a *case by case* approach is preferable when processing orders. S3 is a representative from the supplier.

(5.2)

> *External meeting*
> Relationship of speakers: contractually bound
> Purpose: reviewing; planning
> Topic: logistics

S1: So there're gonna be a number of spot orders.
S3: Yeah.
S1: Now are they gonna be huge quantities? On the whole not.
S3: Yeah.
S1: Sometimes they're gonna be general export packs as well which obviously will help because you might actually say we've got= we've got a stock of this.
S3: Yeah.
S1: Someone's cancelled an order. We've got some spare. We can actually deliver in in eight weeks as opposed to twelve weeks or something like that.
S3: Yeah.
S1: **So I think** we've gotta take a lot of this on a case by case.

It is interesting to see how S1 builds his argument that these *spot orders* should be dealt with *case by case*. He uses the rhetorical question *Now are they gonna be huge quantities?* which is followed up by the negative answer *On the whole not*, implying that small orders should not be as difficult to deal with as big ones. He then stresses that some of the spot orders could be advantageous to the supplier, because they would be able to shift the stock which an imaginary client has cancelled. (Such creativity in business meetings is very common as a form of persuasion/argument and is explored further in Chapter 7.) Such a situation would be mutually beneficial, because the supplier would not need to store this redundant stock, thereby freeing up storage space, and S1's company would be receiving their order four weeks earlier than usual. Then, to summarize this rhetorical argument for increased flexibility, S1 states *So I think we've gotta take a lot of this on a case by case*. The use of *so I think* allows this summary to be both pithy and persuasive.

CLUSTER: *you need to*

Key practice: signalling obligation

Occurrence in external meetings: 32
🖙 *frequency per million words: 130*
Occurrence in internal meetings: 152
🖙 *frequency per million words: 230*

In terms of frequency, *you need to* is an extremely common three-word cluster in business meetings, occurring 152 times, and as might be expected it is far more common – in fact, it is almost twice as common – in internal meetings compared to external meetings. Within internal meetings, unsurprisingly, *you need to* is far more commonly used by managers in manager–subordinate communication than in any other speaker-relationship category. In terms of topic, the cluster features very highly in assessment reviews – it is more than twice as frequent here than in the next most frequent topic, categorized as 'technical'. It is relatively rare in both internal and external marketing and sales meetings, where issues of face are often treated with sensitivity. When it is used in external sales meetings, it can have a significantly different meaning compared to manager–subordinate communication in the same department.

In Chapter 2, the deontic cluster *you have to* was also analysed, showing how the same cluster can constitute quite different practices, depending on the context: in manager–subordinate meetings, it is used to give directives to staff, whereas in external meetings, it is used to give non-face-threatening advice. This suggests that the context can be more important in dictating the way participants understand and use a cluster than the words themselves. Below are two sets of concordance lines for the similar, very frequent cluster, *you need to*.

Concordance lines for **you need to** *in external meetings*

If **you need to** replace it.

may not be something that **you need to** go ahead with now.

+but **you need to** keep telling people.

how much money do **you need to** do this.

Lau= launch support **you need to** talk to Sarah about.

---

*Concordance lines for **you need to** in manager–subordinate meetings*

this is the information **you need to** home in on.
on the outside of the box **you need to** write (1 second)
So **you need to** make your comments now.
every two= well yeah **you need to** do a stock check every once
The the the only th= but **you need to** make your team aware cos you

Once again, the same patterns appear. The concordances here and in Chapter 2 therefore suggest that different items can have the same meaning, and the same item can have different meanings depending on the context. The importance of context in ascertaining the conventionalized meaning of items is also supported by research in psychology (for example, Gibbs, 1981), and in other studies of workplace communication (Vine, 2009). We will now explore the items in longer extracts.

Extract 5.3 is from an internal manager–subordinate meeting. The technical director (S1) is having a weekly meeting with one of the senior technicians (S2) and is telling him that the administrative procedures need to be figured out and followed more intelligently and carefully by the technician's team. This is achieved through the use of *you need to*.

(5.3)

> *Internal meeting*
> Relationship of speakers: manager–subordinate
> Purpose: reviewing; planning
> Topic: sales

S2: Give me till tomorrow.

S1: No. I can't cos I'm not here tomorrow. Or if I am I'm busy. Erm er **you** either **need to** hide that paperwork somewhere where I can't find it.

S2: Okay.

5 S1: Or better still you= and I'll see you hiding it so I'll know where you've hidden it. **You need to** write up those calls or at least find out where the paperwork's supposed to live.

S2: Yeah yeah.

10 S1: So tell Tom and Rob that's what that that= (2 seconds) I need to be= you know I need to be seen to be policing you.

S2: [inaudible]
S1: You know and **you need to** you n= you're all experienced engineers. **You need to** be policing yourself. **You need to** be getting this paper-work back. And those bits of paperwork should be going back to
15   SPR. That's why it says return to= it used to say "Return to account manager" I think but they all now say "Return to SPR".
S2: Yeah.

You need to, as mentioned previously, is more common in internal than external meetings. Overall, however, perhaps somewhat surprisingly, strong modal forms of obligation (Weiyun He, 1993), such as *need to* and *have gotta* are actually more common in external than internal meetings. This higher occurrence of strong modal forms in external meetings can be partly explained by the notion of what can be termed 'self-directed modality', which is very common in these meetings. An example of self-directed modality is evident in extract 5.3, when S1 states *I need to be seen to be policing you* (line 10). He uses a strong modal form to show what he himself needs to do, or at least be perceived to be doing, in this case as a justification for the improvement in the team's administrative efficiency. This notion of self-directed modality will be further explored in Chapter 6.

As mentioned above, in external meetings, rather than being employed to issue directives, *you need to* is used to make non-binding suggestions. It also occurs in questions involving suggestions. As such, it tends to lack any strong threat to face, and means something like 'if you want to do this it might be a good idea'. This is in contrast to the obligation inherent in the examples from extract 5.3 above. Extract 5.4 is taken from an external non-contractually bound sales meeting, in which the managing director of an IT sales company (S2) is enquiring about various options from the sales managers of an internet server provider (S1 and S3). Here it is clear that the two uses of *you need to* do not involve any face-threat whatsoever, and merely allow the speaker to discuss possible courses of action.

(5.4)

External meeting
Relationship of speakers: non-contractually bound
Purpose: buying/selling/promoting a product
Topic: sales

S1: So it's just= it's l= little things like that to consider as well.
S2: Yeah. I see.

S1:   If **you need to** replace it.

S3:   Erm (2 seconds) and then we're allowing you an extra half but that you know that may not be something that **you need to** go ahead with now.

S2:   Yeah.

CLUSTER: *at the end of the day*

Key practice: hedging

Occurrence in external meetings: 37
✏*frequency per million words: 156*
Occurrence in internal meetings: 49
✏*frequency per million words: 73*

At the end of the day is the most frequent six-word cluster in the corpus. It is also the second most frequent six-word cluster in the CANCODE corpus, where it tends to be used to summarize (McCarthy and Carter, 2002). In business meetings, however, it tends to be used in specific types of meetings and by specific groups of speakers, and often as a hedge. It is more than twice as common in external meetings compared to internal meetings, and it is very rarely used in internal manager–subordinate meetings by either managers or subordinates. Even though it is very frequent in external meetings, it hardly occurs at all in those involving IT or pharmaceutical companies. It is overwhelmingly used in manufacturing companies which, in CANBEC, are very male, and very British. CIC Tools can show speaker birthplace, and it shows this cluster is used overwhelmingly by British English speakers and, to a lesser extent, other Western Europeans (unlike, for example, *you need to*, which is widely used by all nationalities in the corpus). This adds support to Carter's view that 'many of the most fixed of fixed expressions are, of course, culture-bound' (1998: 49).

These findings show that *at the end of the day* is usually used by British men in the manufacturing field when talking to either their professional peers, or to clients and vendors. Within this group of factors there is, then, a certain closeness in terms of nationality, profession, status, gender and, often, age, which may go some way to explaining the preference for this cluster. It is interesting that British male managers in the manufacturing industry choose to use this cluster when communicating with their peers, for example, but not with their subordinates. While it may be used by speakers who have much in common, it is often used in meetings to hedge potentially face-threatening statements. The following two extracts (5.5 and 5.6) are from two consecutive meetings, six months apart, involving a vehicle manufacturer and a hydraulics manufacturer, who are developing a multi-utility vehicle. S1 in both meetings is the sales manager from the hydraulics company. S2 is the project manager from the vehicle manufacturer.

(5.5)

> *External meeting*
> Relationship of speakers: contractually bound
> Purpose: planning; reviewing
> Topic: production; strategy

S1: No way will anybody put any conversions that are up for sale at the motor show because it's one of these grey areas again and I'm just trying to clarify it. So (2 seconds) you know you just must be aware that the homologation boys have the final say if you want.

S2: Mm.

S1: Because **at the end of the day** they're responsible for the legality of the car. (1.5 seconds) So I'm just concerned. I'm concerned because it's a threat to the product and a threat to the project and we just have to acknowledge that.

S2: Yeah.

(5.6)

S1: The production model has to take priority in my opinion because **at the end of the day** that's the thing that we're here to do you know. [inaudible]

S2: We're worried about six cranes here. We ought to be worrying about the six hundred that's going to come.

In both extracts, *at the end of the day* serves to mitigate the force of the message and could feasibly be substituted with any of the other hedging clusters listed in table 5.6. Both instances of the cluster are surrounded by other hedges and indirect expressions, which further serve to lessen the face-threat of the rather strong concerns – in the first extract these are *just* (four instances), *you know* and *if you want*, and in the second, *in my opinion* and *you know*.

5.6 Summary

This chapter has been predicated on the assumption that frequently occurring clusters are important in understanding business discourse, the reason being that they seem to form a central component of real-time speech and fluency (Wray, 2002). They are also important, because they are statistically significant, play specialized pragmatic and discursive roles, and may be a central part of our mental lexicon. Even though they have been shown to play key roles in other institutional and everyday spoken and written genres, they are under-researched in business English.

Moreover, the huge importance of clusters has only really been realized since the advent of computerized corpora. As CANBEC is arguably the most representative corpus of business meetings to date, it makes sense to use it to investigate clusters in this genre. Not only does the corpus show what clusters are frequent, but because of the contextual, ethnographic data compiled before, during and after the recordings, and the insights from expert informants, it is possible to infer the constitutive discursive practices with a reasonable degree of confidence. Working from quantitative findings to qualitative interpretations is thus achievable: objective results can be explored in context. This is a distinct advantage of a corpus of this size and of having a researcher who has considerable contextual knowledge of the data, as well as access to the recordees (Flowerdew, 2005).

A core theme of this book is how the words create the genre, and how the genre constrains the words and their meaning. O'Keeffe et al. argue that 'clusters in the CANBEC business data . . . may show us something of the character of SBE (spoken business English) distinct genres' (2007: 284). This and the previous chapter have taken a big step in clarifying some of the most recurrent features of the business meeting genre; recurrent aspects of a genre allow us and the participants to recognize it as such. Institutionalized clusters with pragmatically specialized meanings that index sets of practices can shed light on the specific conventions of a community of practice; they demonstrate the particular approach to problems and the common communicative tools preferred by the community in question (McCarthy and Handford, 2004). However, this relationship between the lexis used by communities of practice in particular genres is probabilistic, and there is no evidence, nor indeed desire to show, that a deterministic relationship between language and genre exists (see Adolphs, 2002). As discussed in Chapter 3, it is the ability of participants to instantiate change through language that both typifies and problematizes genres (McCarthy, 1998: 37).

The issue of learning and teaching business English will be discussed in Chapter 9, but the findings presented here have obvious ramifications for the business language classroom. Most of the practices discussed here are not new, but such empirical evidence demonstrating the relationship between key discursive practices and the language professional business people use to address them, in real meetings and in real time, is new. As mentioned on page 124, one key issue for the language classroom concerns prescribing 'native-speaker' language norms to the 'non-native-speaker' learner. Within the international business context, it will be argued in Chapter 9 that such a line of reasoning may be misguided for various reasons: a sub-corpus involving meetings where English is used as an international language produces very similar results in terms of clusters and practices (for example, 13 of the top 20 three-word clusters are the same, and the clusters which are specific to international business serve primarily equivalent hedging practices involving *I think*). This adds weight to the argument that the time may be ripe for a reappraisal of the importance given to the L1/L2 distinction within the professional business teaching and training spheres. Moreover, denying learners of business English access to efficient language tools which have been tried and tested in authentic communication on the grounds that they have been used by speakers whose first language is English is akin to demanding that learners reinvent the wheel. I am certainly not suggesting that L1-speaker language should be the norm in international business communication, but nor am I suggesting that English used by British or Australian or Singaporean business people is only suitable for use in those countries and by those speakers. Nickerson raises the important point that 'extensive knowledge of grammar could never compete with 20 years' experience in successfully closing a deal' in business (in Bargiela-Chiappini et al., 2003: 82). This is undoubtedly true, and further shows that the most important issue in business is not language ability, but the experience and ability to dynamically manoeuvre within the communities of practice which business people inhabit. Nevertheless, it may also be true that a working knowledge of specific clusters may allow the business person who lacks either an extensive grammar or 20 years of experience to short-wire the system and be a more effective communicator.

Notes

1. These corpora are: The Corpus of Spoken Professional American English, the Bank of English National Public Radio sub-corpus and the Switchboard Corpus. Simpson (2004: 44) states that 'in order to find which expressions are typical of academic speech in particular, and not just high frequency expressions in any speech genre, I first looked for the expressions which were significantly more frequent in MICASE than in all three of the comparison corpora'. Her reference to 'any speech genre' is somewhat problematic, given that the three corpora are rather specialized and cannot be regarded as representative of, for example, everyday speech (indeed, she herself acknowledges that the rationale for choosing these reference corpora was that they were the only ones available at the time).
2. The point here is that, while a formulaic sequence may be syntactically the same in different genres, it may serve a different purpose in each genre. For example, McCarthy and Carter (2002), in their study of clusters in CANCODE, state that *at the end of the day* performs the discourse-marking function of summarizing, whereas *to be honest with you* performs a hedging function. In CANBEC, however, the two clusters seem to be often largely synonymous, with *at the end of the day* also frequently signalling hedging/indirectness, and being positioned before or after potential face-threatening acts.
3. Indeed, Hopper (1998) argues that, from an emergent-grammar viewpoint, incomplete lexical fragments can help show how meaning is created in real time. This position is coherent with a conversation-analysis perspective of how meaning unfolds in the local context. It also begs the question of whether repetitions in the form of hesitations should be analysed in their own right as pragmatically meaningful clusters. Whilst such analysis is absent here, it is noticeable that clusters containing certain words seem to involve a lot of hesitations, such as *if (you if you)*. One possible explanation is that such clusters may incur potential face-threats, hence the tentativeness of the delivery.

References

Adolphs, S. (2002) 'Genre and spoken discourse: Probabilities and predictions', *Nottingham Linguistic Circular*, **17**, 47–60.
Adolphs, S., Atkins, S. and Harvey, K. (2007) 'Caught between professional requirements and interpersonal needs: Vague language in health care contexts', in Cutting, J. (ed.) *Vague Language Explored*, Basingstoke: Palgrave.
Alejo, R. and McGinity, M. (1997) 'Terminological loans and the teaching/learning of technical vocabulary: The use of economic anglicisms in the business classroom', in Piqué, J. and Viera, D.J. (eds.) *Applied Languages: Theory and Practice in ESP*, Valencia: Universidad de Valencia.
Baker, P. (2006) *Using Corpora in Discourse Analysis*, London: Continuum.

Bargiela-Chiappini, F. and Harris, S. (1997) *Managing Language: The Discourse of Corporate Meetings*, Amsterdam: John Benjamins.
Bargiela-Chiappini, F., Bulow-Moller, A., Nickerson, C., Poncini, G. and Zhu, Y. (2003) 'Five perspectives on intercultural business communication', *Business Communication Quarterly*, **66**, 3, 73–96.
Bargiela-Chiappini, F., Nickerson, C. and Planken, B. (2007) *Business Discourse*, Basingstoke: Palgrave.
Biber, D., Johansson, S., Leech, G., Conrad, S. and Finnegan, E. (1999) *Longman Grammar of Spoken and Written English*, London: Longman.
Boden, D. (1994) *The Business of Talk: Organizations in Action*, Cambridge: Polity Press.
Carter, R. (1998) 'Orders of reality: CANCODE, communication, and culture', *English Language Teaching Journal*, **52**, 1, 43–55.
Carter, R. and McCarthy, M. (2004) 'Talking, creating: Interactional language, creativity and context', *Applied Linguistics*, **25**, 1, 62–88.
Carter, R. and McCarthy, M. (2006) *Cambridge Grammar of English*, Cambridge: Cambridge University Press.
Chafe, W. (1994) *Discourse, Consciousness and Time*, Chicago: Chicago University Press.
Charles, M. and Charles, D. (1999) 'Sales negotiations: Bargaining through tactical summaries', in Hewings, M. and Nickerson, C. (eds.) *Business English: Research into Practice*, London: Longman.
De Cock, S. (2000) 'Repetitive phrasal chunkiness and advanced EFL speech and writing', in Mair, C. and Hundt, M. (eds.) *Corpus Linguistics and Linguistic Theory. Papers from ICAME 20*, Amsterdam: Rodopi, 51–68.
Firth, A. (1995) 'Accounts in negotiation discourse: A single-case analysis', *Journal of Pragmatics*, **23**, 199–226.
Firth, A. (2009) 'Doing not being a foreign language learner: English as a *lingua franca* in the workplace and (some) implications for SLA', *International Review of Applied Linguistics in Language Teaching*, **47**, 1, 127–56.
Flowerdew, L. (2005) 'An integration of corpus-based and genre-based approaches to text analysis in EAP/ESP: Countering criticisms against corpus-based methodologies', *English for Specific Purposes*, **24**, 321–32.
Gee, J.P. (1990) *Social Linguistics and Literacies: Ideology in Discourses*, London: Falmer Press.
Gibbs, R. (1981) 'Your wish is my command: Convention and context in interpreting indirect requests', *Journal of Verbal Learning and Verbal Behavior*, **20**, 431–44.
Handford, M. (2007) *The Genre of the Business Meeting: A Corpus-based Study*, PhD thesis, University of Nottingham (Unpublished).
Hoey, M. (2005) *Lexical Priming*, Abingdon: Routledge.
Holmes, J. and Stubbe, M. (2003) *Power and Politeness in the Workplace*, London: Longman.
Hopper, P. (1998) 'Emergent grammar', in Tomasello, M. (ed.) *The New Psychology of Language*, Hillsdale, NJ: Lawrence Erlbaum Associates, 155–75.

Jaspers, J. (forthcoming) 'Interactional sociolinguistics and discourse analysis', in Gee, J.P. and Handford, M. (eds.) *The Routledge Handbook of Discourse Analysis*, Abingdon: Routledge.

Koester, A. (2004) 'Relational sequences in workplace genres', *Journal of Pragmatics*, **36**, 1405–28.

Koester, A. (2006) *Investigating Workplace Discourse*, Abingdon: Routledge.

Lewis, M. (1993) *The Lexical Approach*, Hove: Language Teaching Publications.

McCarthy, M. (1998) *Spoken Language and Applied Linguistics*, Cambridge: Cambridge University Press.

McCarthy, M. and Carter, R. (2002) 'This that and the other: Multi-word clusters in spoken English as visible patterns of interaction', *Teanga*, **21**, 30–52.

McCarthy, M. and Handford, M. (2004) '"Invisible to us": a preliminary corpus-based study of spoken business English', in Connor, U. and Upton, T. (eds.) *Discourse in the Professions: Perspectives from Corpus Linguistics*, Amsterdam: John Benjamins, 167–201.

Nattinger, J. and DeCarrico, J. (1992) *Lexical Phrases and Language Teaching*, Oxford: Oxford University Press.

Nelson, M. (2000) *A Corpus-based Study of Business English and Business English Teaching Materials*, PhD thesis, University of Manchester (Unpublished).

Nelson, M. (2006) 'Semantic associations in business English: A corpus-based analysis', *English for Specific Purposes*, **25**, 217–34.

O'Keeffe, A. (2006) *Investigating Media Discourse*, Abingdon: Routledge.

O'Keeffe, A., McCarthy, M. and Carter, R. (2007) *From Corpus to Classroom: Language Use and Language Teaching*, Cambridge: Cambridge University Press.

Oakey, D. (2002) 'Formulaic language in English academic writing', in Reppen, R., Fitzmaurice, S. and Biber, D. (eds.) *Using Corpora to Explore Linguistic Variation*, Amsterdam: John Benjamins, 111–29.

Ochs, E. (1996) 'Linguistic resources for socializing humanity', in Gumperz, J. (ed.) *Rethinking Linguistic Relativity*, Cambridge: Cambridge University Press, 407–37.

Pinker, S. (1994) *The Language Instinct*, London: Penguin.

Poncini, G. (2004) *Discursive Strategies in Multicultural Business Meetings*, Peter Lang, Linguistic Insights Series.

Scott, M. (1999) *WordSmith Tools Version 3*, Oxford: Oxford University Press.

Simpson, R.C. (2004) 'Stylistic features of academic speech: The role of formulaic expressions', in Connor, U. and Upton, T. (eds.) *Discourse in the Professions: Perspectives from Corpus Linguistics*, Amsterdam: John Benjamins, 37–64.

Sinclair, J. (1991) *Corpus, Concordance, Collocation*, Oxford: Oxford University Press.

Vine, B. (2009) 'Directives at work: Exploring the contextual complexity of workplace directives', *Journal of Pragmatics*, **41**, 1395–405.

Weiyun He, A. (1993) 'Exploring modality in institutional interactions: Cases from academic counselling encounters', *Text*, **13**, 4, 503–28.

Wray, A. (1998) 'Protolanguage as a holistic system for social interaction', *Language and Communication*, **18**, 47–67.

Wray, A. (2000) 'Formulaic sequences in second language teaching: Principle and practice', *Applied Linguistics*, **21**, 4, 463–89.

Wray, A. (2002) *Formulaic Language and the Lexicon*, Cambridge: Cambridge University Press.

6 *Interpersonal language*

The development, maintenance and sometimes termination of relationships between business people, businesses and their customers has been the subject of much research. For example, at the macro level, 'relationship marketing' explores how companies can maximize lifetime customer value and thus benefit financially from deepening and retaining relationships with customers (McKenna, 1993; Paulin et al., 1997, 2000). There has also been interest in the communication used in negotiations since the 1960s (see Bülow, 2009). At a more textual level, research by Lampi (1986), Charles (1996), Charles and Charles (1999), Holmes (2000, 2006), Spencer-Oatey (2000), Poncini (2002, 2004), Holmes and Stubbe (2003), Koester (2004, 2006, 2010), McCarthy and Handford (2004) and Handford and Koester (2010), amongst others, has analysed how relationships are reflected in and affected by the specific linguistic patterns found in spoken business discourse within particular unfolding encounters, within organizations and across business-to-business communication. Time and again, research indicates how attention paid to business relationships through effective interpersonal communication can enhance the success of the overall enterprise, or the individual within it.

This book has thus far explored how language constitutes meetings from a genre perspective and has examined quantitative results from the CANBEC corpus. While the study is concerned with exploring interpersonal language and practices and how they constrain and enable the discourse, there is a consistent danger of oversimplifying the relationship between them. Iedema (1997), for instance, argues that, in institutional discourse, social relations and their enactment through the dimensions of power and solidarity can be interpreted with reference to the interpersonal language register ('tenor'). In interpreting the language of business meetings, power and solidarity undoubtedly provide a powerful heuristic. However, Iedema, referring to Tannen (1993), also states that 'it is not possible to map power and solidarity unproblematically and categorically onto particular linguistic tokens' (Iedema, 1997: 75), asserting that directness could signal both extreme power as well as a high degree of solidarity. Nevertheless, it is argued here that a cautious categorization can be applied while allowing for an unavoidable, and sometimes tactical, degree of fuzziness.

Chapters 6 and 7 will therefore examine certain categories of items related to the institutional, interpersonal dimensions of power and solidarity, which the previous chapters have indicated may index several recurrent discursive practices in meetings. In particular, several of the groups of clusters and interpersonal discursive practices that were pinpointed in Chapter 5 will be discussed. In this chapter, attention will be paid to the following five interpersonal language categories and the social (solidarity or power-related) dimensions and discursive practices they invoke:

1 Pronouns: signalling the social relationship
2 Backchannels: signalling listener solidarity
3 Vague language: signalling solidarity over knowledge
4 Hedges: negotiating power over knowledge
5 Deontic modality: negotiating power over actions

In Chapter 7, where the focus is on creativity in language use and in problem-solving, the practices of focusing on decisions, hypothesizing and speculating are discussed in detail. Evaluating is also discussed in Chapter 7 at length, and to a lesser extent in this chapter.

This chapter begins by exploring the notions of relational and transactional language, and the main focus of this chapter and Chapter 7 concerns business people's employment of this selection of interpersonal (Halliday, 1985) language features in transactional meeting discourse. While other items could also have been discussed – for example, vocatives or epistemic modal verbs – space constraints mean that some important items cannot be explored in the present study.

This chapter makes several references to a sub-corpus of CANBEC, which was specifically developed to allow closer examinations of interpersonal language. This sub-corpus contains nine meetings in total, covering a range of meeting topics and contexts, and with at least two meetings for each of the four relationship categories (manager–subordinate, peer, external contractually bound and external non-contractually bound. See the Appendix for a full breakdown of the sub-corpus.

6.1 The transactional/relational linguistic distinction

In his analysis of service encounters, McCarthy (2000) distinguishes between four types of talk:

1 Phatic exchanges (greetings, partings)
2 Relational talk (small talk, anecdotes, wider topics of mutual interest)
3 Transactional-plus-relational talk (non-obligatory task evaluations and other comments)
4 Transactional talk (requests, enquiries, instructions)

The distinction is also relevant to business communication in general and business meetings in particular, because instances of each type of talk repeatedly feature in internal and external business meetings. McCarthy notes that, even in transactional talk, participants still 'reinforce the relational context' (ibid.: 104) through interpersonal choices (Halliday, 1985) such as pronouns (for example, communal *we*, rather than *I* or *you*), and Koester (2006, 2010) methodically explores such features in workplace contexts. In business meetings, transactional talk tends to take up most of the language and time (Boden, 1994; Handford, 2007), although interpersonal, relational elements are visible at the lexico-grammatical level, and at the turn and sequence level (Handford, ibid.). In addition, an instance of McCarthy's relational talk – small talk – often occurs at the beginning of meetings, as shown in extract 6.1, which is from the beginning of the five-hour multinational pharmaceutical meeting between the client company and the manufacturer of the client's pharmaceuticals, discussed in Chapter 3. In this meeting, S1 and S2 are from the client company and S3, S4 and S5 are from the manufacturer. While S1, the chair, is British, the other participants in this extract are all German (including S1's colleague, S2).

(6.1)

External meeting
Relationship of speakers: contractually bound
Purpose: planning; reviewing
Topic: logistics; production

S1: [inaudible] communication point of view and I think what you've told us today is that it's not as simple as changing it in logistics and packaging just go on. You've got a lot of [inhales] conversations backwards and forwards.
5 S3: At the moment yes. At the moment yes and and this is the only reason why we have to to change our organization to a= to a master supply organization.
S1: Erm (1.5 seconds) tell me last night.

S3:   Er yes.
10   S1:   A good meal out in Aachen?
      S3:   Yeah. [laughs]
      S1:   Yeah.
      S3:   We go to the same restaurant as we er [inaudible] dinner with Ada
            and and Ton. And=
15   [11 relational turns removed from extract]
      S4?:[laughs]
      S1:   Downs= downstairs or upstairs?
      S3:   Er in the garden.
      S1:   Ah. I haven't been there. Good.
20   S3:   [inaudible]
      S1:   Yeah.
      S4:   Mhm.
      S1:   And great food.
      S3:   Great.
25   S4?:[laughs]
      S3:   Yeah. Yeah.
      S1:   Mm. Yeah. Little bit jealous actually. I had a bowl of cereal last night.
      S5?:[laughs]
      [30 relational turns removed from extract]
30   S1:   Cos you're not a morning person.
      S2?:[laughs]
      S1:   [laughs] I think we should make a start. Helen er was on a telecon-
            ference when erm when I left the office. Erm I I guess for me er same
            sort of er agenda as normal if we can work through the logistics
35   work stream meeting minutes erm picking up the various sections.
            I think there're a few things we we've sort of scribbled at the end
            in terms of e= under= any other business. I'd certainly like to look
            at the technical meeting er minutes. That's part of the agenda in
            terms of the logistics section but there's also the (1 second) section
40   four of the= of the technical meeting minutes er goes through the
            you know how we're moving from the project into the operational
            phase.
      S2?:Yeah.
      S1:   And I think it would be worth just covering some of those.

The seemingly fluid transactional–relational–transactional topic
shift is immediately noticeable in this extract (several relational turns
have been removed from the extract so that it is a manageable reading
length and highlights these topic shifts).

In order to obtain useful background information to help interpret
the decisions made by the chair (S1, who is in charge of the project)

in this meeting, several follow-up interviews were conducted. The meeting begins with a very brief exchange about the *conversations backwards and forwards* (lines 3–4), which, according to the chair, was a euphemistic way of raising what he saw as a big problem in the professional practices of the other company, and threatened to have an adverse effect on the efficiency of the project. The timing of this issue was becoming critical for the project, because it was about to move from the planning to the execution/control stage (related to the professional practice of managing projects in four stages: initiate, plan, execute/control, close). However, the chair also commented in a follow-up interview that he had 'jumped in too fast' in raising this issue in what would be a long meeting, and therefore changed the topic to something more affable. He also cited concern over coming across as 'too heavy-handed', again given the stage of the meeting. Moreover, this meeting was at a reasonably early stage of what would be a long relationship (as the 'execute/control' phase should last several years), and therefore ensuring relationships were sufficiently harmonious was still central to this developing community of practice (Wenger, 1998). These ethnographic insights further reinforce the position discussed in Chapter 2 that the relational/transactional distinction, while often clear in terms of topic and language, is more problematic or osmotic at the level of goals.

As might be expected, the off-topic discussion about the previous night's dinner displays many typically relational features, in addition to the topic itself. Firstly, there is a high degree of laughter and some humour (the chair self-deprecatingly talking about his pitiful dinner compared to the visitors'). While humour is widely regarded as highly culture specific, and therefore something that can cause problems in international business communication (Trompenaars and Hampden-Turner, 1998), here it allows for successful convergence between the German and British participants. This finding has also been replicated in communication between Japanese managers and American factory workers (Sunaoshi, 2005). Moreover, anecdotal laughter, like small talk, is much more likely to feature in CANBEC external and peer internal meetings in the pre-meeting stage than elsewhere. It is comparatively less common in manager–subordinate meetings, where the interaction is often more regulated and densely transactional. It should be briefly mentioned, however, that laughter also occurs in highly conflictual meetings which has no relation to humour. For further research on humour in the workplace, see Holmes (2007) and Koester (2010, Chapter 5). Humour will briefly be revisited in Chapter 7.

Another noteworthy feature of the small talk in extract 6.1 is the degree of situational ellipsis. Situational ellipsis means 'not explicitly referring to people and things that are in the immediate situation'

(Carter and McCarthy, 2006: 181), because the meaning is clear from the context. Examples from extract 6.1 include *A good meal out in Aachen* (line 10), *downstairs or upstairs* (line 17), *Er in the garden* (line 18), *Good* (line 19), *And great food* (line 23) and *Little bit jealous actually* (line 27). As Carter and McCarthy argue, it may be inaccurate to think of ellipsis as 'missing' something: the language is sufficient for the needs of the situation, and it is more formal registers that require supplementary elements. Ellipsis tends to be a feature of informal everyday communication, and, as such, it occurs more commonly in meetings during small talk and phatic exchanges than during agenda-related discussions. In both contexts, a sense of comity is created through the tacit acknowledgement that the whole message does not need to be 'spelled out': the practice of ellipsis reflects and reinforces a shared understanding.

Therefore, in terms of humour, laughter and ellipsis, this relational sequence concerned with dinner is very similar to an everyday conversation, a pattern paralleled in other meetings as well. However, this similarity begins to break down when looking at the practice of controlling the topic, and the related issue of turn-taking. As mentioned above, S1 is the most senior person in the meeting and the chair, and he signals what topic is to be discussed, and for how long. It is also noticeable that he asks all the questions. Were one of the other participants to attempt to wrestle control of the discourse by, for example, changing the direction of the meeting to a more transactional footing, it could be perceived as a threat to the chair's power and could be open to sanction. So, while the extract displays a high level of convergence, this convergence is dependent on the interlocutors following professionally constrained norms which are closely linked to meeting expectations concerning the professional social identities of the interlocutors in this context. The issue of turn-taking and power will be given more attention in Chapter 8. The following section will explore pronouns and their role in constructing identities and relationships in meetings.

6.2 Pronouns

In terms of the interpersonal dimensions discussed in this chapter, pronouns are categorized above as being a central mechanism by which speakers signal the social relationship. Pronouns have been touched on already in Chapter 2 and have been shown to be statistically significant in Chapters 4 and 5. Furthermore, in extract 6.1, there are seven instances of *we*. The ubiquity of *we* in business and other forms of institutional communication has been noted elsewhere in empirical studies (Maynard, 1984; Drew and Heritage, 1992; Fairclough, 2000;

Nelson, 2000; Poncini, 2002, 2004). The pronoun *we* is statistically the top keyword in CANBEC (when compared to a corpus of everyday conversation – see Chapter 4 for keyword lists), and its associated pronominal references *us* and *our* are also significant. *We* is also far more frequent in CANBEC than in academic spoken discourse (O'Keeffe et al., 2007). Of course, this is not to suggest that other pronouns do not feature in business meetings: *you* is roughly as frequent in meetings as *we*, and *I* is also widely used, especially in pragmatic clusters such as *I think* and *I mean* (O'Keeffe et al., 2007). The difference concerns the relative use of pronouns in business meetings when compared to other discourses: whereas *we* is positively key (twice as common in business meetings compared to everyday conversation), *you, I, she* and *he* are all in the top 10 most negatively key items, meaning they are considerably less likely to occur in meetings than in everyday conversation.

In Chapters 2 and 4, the concepts of inclusive and exclusive *we* were touched on. Whereas the former refers to all participants, the latter involves the speaker's group but not the listener's. In institutional discourse, five common referents are invoked by *we*, and they occur in either internal meetings, external meetings, or both[1]:

- inclusive personal, referring to all those present at time of speaking (internal and external)
- exclusive personal, referring to one in-group present (internal and external)
- inclusive corporate, referring to both (or more) companies or departments (external)
- exclusive corporate, referring only to the speaker's company or department (external)
- intra-organizational, referring to all employees within a company (internal)

In extract 6.1, there are several occurrences of *we*. S3, who is the most senior member from the manufacturer (that is, not the client), acknowledges that *we have to to change our organization* (line 6), and this *we* is clearly a corporate exclusive *we*. She then states *We go to the same restaurant* (line 13), which is an exclusive personal usage, as it refers to the three members of the manufacturer who are present at the meeting, and who went for a meal the previous day. The chair (S1) officially begins the meeting with the inclusive, personal *I think we should make a start* (line 32) and *if we can work through* (line 34). He then says *a few things we we've sort of scribbled at the end* (line 36), which is an exclusive personal usage, and then employs the inclusive corporate *we're moving from the project into the operational phase* (lines 41–2).

Thus, in the space of less than a minute, he has signalled three different identities through the same pronoun. Zupnik (1994) found that shifts in the personal deixis are power-enhancing in the context of political discourse: speakers can shift in and out of various roles and display multiple identities in particular situations, thus displaying and enacting their power status. *We* in business English certainly seems to operate with similar flexibility, vagueness and power enhancement.

As mentioned previously, *we* is the top keyword in both internal and external meetings. However, *we*, *we've* and *we're* are relatively more frequent in external meetings than internal meetings, with *we* being almost half a per cent more frequent in external meetings (that is, accounting for almost one in every 200 words). The use of corporate *we* explains this difference. This includes inclusive corporate *we*, but more importantly exclusive corporate *we*, where one representative of a company is talking about his or her own company, but not the other company in the meeting. Such a reference is by definition not possible in internal meetings. Moreover, the exclusive personal *we* is more frequent in external meetings. As in extract 6.1, however, it should be noted that exclusive uses of *we* are not necessarily divergent. Indeed, according to Poncini (2002), exclusive *we* can in some circumstances be used convergently; however, Neu and Graham argue that too many exclusive uses of *we* can reduce buyer satisfaction in negotiations (1995). Furthermore, Poncini (2002) also highlights the ambiguous potential of *we*: it is sometimes impossible to pin down exactly who the referent is, and whether it is used inclusively or exclusively. In such situations, deciding on the referent is left up to the hearer, which can be a highly effective cooperative strategy.

It is worth briefly discussing the relative non-keyness of *you* and *I* compared to *we*. As mentioned previously, these two pronouns occur less frequently in business English than in everyday English. In business, the pronoun *we* is perhaps being used as a replacement for *I* and *you*: *we* instead of *you* acts as a softening device (Holmes and Stubbe, 2003: 38; Handford, 2007), and using *we* instead of *I* can emphasize, for example, collaboration, thereby reducing the emphasis on individual agency.

Another use of *we*, related to the reduction in emphasis on individual agency and specific to business and other forms of professional communication, concerns the corporate *we*. It involves the speaker in foregrounding the identity of the company, rather than their own and other participants' personal identity, often in terms of perception, group agency and collective responsibility (Drew and Heritage, 1992: 30; Bargiela-Chiappini and Harris, 1997: 121). Extract 6.2 provides an example.

(6.2)

External meeting
Relationship of speakers: contractually bound
Purpose: buying/selling/promoting a product
Topic: sales; technical

> S2: We'll put this through our model now+
> S1: Yeah.
> S2: +that we've got it properly.

S2 is actually the managing director of this company, and if *we* is replaced with *I*, then the tone changes:

> S2: I'll put this through my model now+
> S1: Yeah.
> S2: +that I've got it properly.

If she were to use *I*, then the hearer might infer that her company is a very small one (which in fact it is, with fewer than ten employees), and one in which she carries out such jobs personally. By using *we*, the implication is that the action will be conducted within her company, probably not by her, and it will part of an organizational process. The level of communication, and perception of the company, is therefore kept at an organizational level.

Another related use of corporate *we* is not so much to foreground the company's identity, but to lessen that of the individual speaker, and therefore his or her responsibility for the action or decision in question (Drew and Heritage, 1992: 30). Such a use might create an impression of officialdom, in one sense thereby objectifying the decision or course of action in question (Fairclough, 1989). This practice was briefly flagged in Chapter 2, and is evident in extract 6.3, taken from a meeting between a firm's technical director (S2) and one of the technicians. They are discussing possible legal pitfalls caused by changes in the law.

(6.3)

Internal meeting
Relationship of speakers: manager–subordinate
Purpose: planning; reviewing
Topic: technical; procedure

> S2: Yeah ... Erm could we put that ... as a disclaimer somewhere? That if er we have complaints about er ... improper [inaudible]. We reserve the right to (1 second) erm=

This disclaimer – beginning with *We reserve the right to* – informs the other party of the corporate, impersonal nature of the agent organization. Recourse on a personal level thus becomes far more challenging. The preceding *we* is somewhat more ambiguous, as it could refer to the two interlocutors, or the company itself. In fact, in the socially sanctioned act of making such a change, both identities are perhaps being simultaneously invoked.

As these extracts and extract 2.4 (examined in Chapter 2) show, pronouns in business communication are tied closely with discursive and professional practices and knowledge relating to identity, personal and corporate face, responsibility and obfuscating responsibility, action, pushing the company line, and convergence. It is also worth noting that pronouns can be interpreted from a lexico-pragmatic rather than grammatical perspective, in that they form part of several of the most frequent, critical pragmatic clusters in meetings, for instance the most frequent two-word clusters *you know* and *I think*. Insights such as these are of considerable benefit to learners and users of business English, and will be further discussed in Chapter 9.

6.3 Backchannels

Backchannels are 'the short verbal responses made by listeners' which signal they do not wish to take over the turn, but which show they are listening (McCarthy, 1998: 176), and have therefore been categorized at the beginning of this chapter as a key means of signalling listener solidarity. Carter (2004: 8) argues that backchannels in everyday speech are one of the means interlocutors use to dialogically create 'an affective convergence or commonality of viewpoint'. This communicative practice is one of the means interlocutors successfully navigate dialogic speech, and accounts for some striking statistical differences between spoken and written forms of the language. For instance, O'Keeffe et al. (2007: 140) show that *right* is over six times more frequent in everyday speech than in newspaper English.

The top 200 negative keywords (that is, items which are atypical of business meetings), discussed in Chapter 4, include several items that could be used as such affective backchannels, including *lovely, oh, ah, yeah, right, ooh, gosh* and *cool*. It is no doubt immediately evident that several of these items might communicate a degree or type of emotion that could be considered inappropriate in the more formal stages and types of business meetings. This relates to Drew and Heritage's (1992: 25) second factor which distinguishes institutional interactions from ordinary conversation (discussed in Chapter 4) – that is, that there are restrictions in the kinds of contributions to the talk that can be made in institutional settings. Indeed, when such items are used in everyday conversation, they are often used to report speech or comment on other situations, such as *And I thought "Oh"*. Instead, CANBEC evidences a selection of constrained items, which again supports Hoey's (2005) notion that certain items are discursively primed to feature more in certain registers and genres than in others.

The item *yeah* is statistically interesting, because it is the eighth most frequent word in CANBEC, but it is still negatively key (that is, it is even more frequent in everyday conversation). In extract 6.1, it is frequently used as a backchannel. Of course, like several other items on the lists, *yeah* is not only a backchannel, as it can also be a response to a question (as a more frequent, informal equivalent of *yes*), it can signal the speaker taking up the turn and it can be used later in a turn – for instance, in the turn-final position as a response-seeking tail.

In terms of which backchannels are more typical of business meetings, *okay* and *hmm* appear to be significant. However, in the negative-keyword list, the item *mm* appears, which raises the question of whether this is the result of transcription differences – that is, are they in fact the same sound, but transcribed differently by the transcribers for CANCODE (with more instances of *mm*) and the transcribers for CANBEC (which features more instances of *hmm*)? Even if this is so, there are still some interesting findings concerning the somewhat non-committal *hmm* when the internal and external data are compared. It is over twice as frequent in internal meetings, and is approximately three times more common in manager–subordinate meetings than peer meetings. In extract 6.4, the manager (S2) is listening to the subordinate talking about customers renewing contracts.

(6.4)

> *Internal meeting*
> Relationship of speakers: manager–subordinate
> Purpose: planning; giving and receiving information/advice
> Topic: procedure

S1: So if they're only taking out for the quarter like till the end of the year+

S2: **Hmm**.

S1: +and then they're taking out a full year's contract. You would look=
it would look in your database ... your+

S2: **Yeah**.

S1: +database ... that ... they should be up for renewal in (1 second) I dunno October some time next year+

S2: **Hmm**.

S1: +and they wouldn't. They'd then be up for renewal in January two thousand and five.

S2: Oh okay.

As this extract demonstrates, *hmm* tends to be used by the manager in such meetings, as a way of signalling the subordinate to continue without offering any positive or negative evaluation of the talk so far. It is far less commonly employed by subordinates, and as such may be regarded as a potential marker of power. Nevertheless, we should remember that in manager–subordinate meetings which have the purpose of reviewing – which account for a majority of manager–subordinate meetings in CANBEC – managers often ask questions which the subordinates then answer. Therefore, it is natural that managers will backchannel much more while the subordinate is reporting past actions or relaying information. The point here, however, is that they often backchannel using *hmm*.

One reason for the lower frequency of *hmm* in external meetings, given the non-committal tone of *hmm*, concerns the interlocutor's positive face. In a study comparing the use of *hmm* and the response token *sure* across several internal and external meetings in one company (Handford, 2007: 116), *hmm* did not occur at all in the external meetings, whereas *sure* was very common. Furthermore, *sure* was frequently used by the client and not just the vendor, as in extract 6.5, where S2 is the client:

(6.5)

> *External meeting*
> Relationship of speakers: non-contractually bound
> Purpose: buying/selling/promoting a product
> Topic: sales

S1: And then you know we've got a couple of questions to ask you and maybe some= +

S2: **Sure**.

S1: +er you know just a few things for you to think about.

While results across the whole corpus concerning the use of *sure* and *hmm* are not as stark as in this particular company, the overall preference is similar. Whereas *hmm* is typical of internal meetings, *sure* is preferred in external meetings. The obvious explanation for this concerns the 'front stage' nature of external meetings and the concomitant expectation that face will be positively addressed and the relationship will be portrayed as being actively continued. The use of a particular backchannel can also be interpreted as a potential 'footing shift' (Goffman, 1981), allowing speakers to 'take up positions of proximity or distance with respect to the sentiments expressed in an utterance' (Hutchby and Wooffitt, 2008: 146), for instance the use of *Oh okay* by the manager at the end of extract 6.4, signalling his understanding and tacit agreement.

6.4 Vague language

While certain traditional perspectives on language that prioritize the written form may cast vague language and other types of indeterminacy in a negative light, an interpersonal and interactive perspective that considers discursive practices and speaker goals does not. As demonstrated here and in the collection of papers in Cutting (2007), the use of vague language may have little to do with a vague grasp of content or communicative goals.

Channell (1994) argues that, given the commonness of vague language, it should not be regarded as a marginal form, and Koester (2006) states that, within cooperative workplace encounters, vague language, along with hedges, tentative modality and a lack of explicit or metalinguistic performatives, is actually the unmarked norm. It is in conflictual situations, in fact, where a lack of such vagueness can be found (McCarthy and Handford, 2004), and McCarthy and Carter (1997: 417) argue that overly precise language infers a high level of assertion and control on the part of the speaker. This issue will be further discussed in Chapter 8.

There are at least two explanations for using vague language in business communication, which in the context of negotiations relate to competitive ('win–lose') or cooperative ('win–win') strategies respectively. Firstly, it enables the speaker to obfuscate personal or professional stance on or commitment to the issue in question, thus conveying at least part of the responsibility for its interpretation to the listener. Silence can also fulfil a similar function. Secondly, vagueness can address the face needs of the listener(s), working towards a perception of convergence and relaxed, mutual understanding (O'Keeffe, 2003). This section is concerned with the second explanation – that is, how speakers signal solidarity over knowledge – and how it is achieved linguistically in meetings.

Koester (2006: 89) outlines three types of vague language: vague nouns (such as *things*), vague approximators (*about*), and vague category markers (*and things like that*). Chapter 2 showed that vague nouns, such as *things* and *stuff*, and certain approximators, such as *about*, are more typical of everyday conversation than talk in meetings. This section is concerned with Koester's third category – vague category markers – as several examples of these markers appear in the cluster lists in Chapter 5, grouped under the practice 'being vague'. O'Keeffe (2003) states that vague category markers tend to be found in clause-final positions and are often made up of a conjunction and a noun phrase (for example, *and/ or everything else*). Vague category markers are also often used to reflect shared knowledge (ibid.; Evison et al., 2007). Through identifying and manually counting all the vague category markers, it was found that they are, overall, considerably more common in external meetings in the sub-corpus. This is somewhat counter-intuitive, as we could expect there to be more shared knowledge among colleagues from the same company than between workers from different companies. Figure 6.1 shows the density per 1,000 words in the sub-corpus.

Figure 6.1   Density of vague category markers (items per 1,000 words)

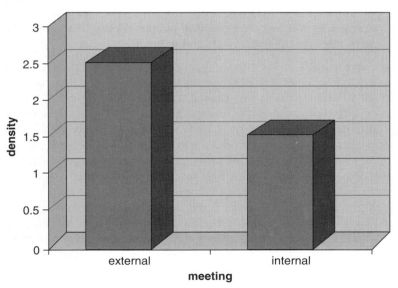

One explanation as to why vague category markers are more frequent in external meetings is that they are used tactically: whereas, in internal meetings, vague category markers reflect assumed shared knowledge, in external meetings, vague category markers can help create an impression of shared knowledge and therefore convergence. This is especially important in non-contractually bound meetings where one or both sides are usually keen to develop a stronger bond between the companies. This accounts for the interesting finding that non-contractually bound external meetings have a higher density of vague category markers than contractually bound meetings. Extract 6.6, a sales negotiation, is the meeting with the highest density in the whole sub-corpus.

(6.6)

> *External meeting*
> Relationship of speakers: non-contractually bound
> Purpose: negotiating
> Topic: sales; marketing

> S1: Because advertising it it's like anything else. At the end of the day you can only= you get so much back from it.
> S2: Mm.
> S1: And if if somebody doesn't want props **or whatever** you know you're not gonna get anything back from it. But it's just that instant you're there you're in it= you're in front of people. It's like [inaudible] you know they take the front covers **and so forth**.

The extract also shows how vague category markers (as well as other vague language including *anything else* and *so much*) can be employed to create a sense of shared understanding – for example, *props or whatever* (the buyer makes hydraulic pit props), seen as essential in negotiations (Bülow, 2009). S1 seems to be saying 'I know your business, we are very familiar, you can trust me, so you should buy more from me'. It is in this sense that the use of vague category markers may be tactical – through attempting to create a sense of 'common ground and familiarity' (Koester, 2006: 91), even when, in truth, the level of shared knowledge is actually relatively low (this is the first visit by this sales person to this company). That this happens across different meetings from different companies suggests it may be a particular discursive practice of external meetings. Vague category markers can also be used to soften requirements or obligations, as in extract 6.7.

(6.7)

> *External meeting*
> Relationship of speakers: contractually bound
> Purpose: planning; reviewing
> Topic: logistics; production

> S1: I don't know whether we should be flagging it in the description
> field so when we do= so it's obvious to everyone. Because I guess
> people people might change and I I g= I guess I I'm keen that the
> knowledge is reta= retained within the erm you know= the visibility
> of the production schedules **or whatever**.

In this extract, the chair is explaining what is required of the supplier. He softens this request by the use of the vague category marker
or whatever, as well as the hedge *I guess* and the marker of shared
knowledge *you know*. Such language use seems typical of contractually bound meetings where the preference is towards cooperation.

While vague category markers are more frequent in external meetings, there is still considerable variation across internal
meetings. The markers are much more common in both peer and
manager–subordinate meetings from within the same department
compared to meetings from different departments, lending weight
to the proposition that, within internal meetings, they reflect shared
knowledge, as within the same department there would be more
shared knowledge than between different departments. This inscruta-
ble utterance from peers in the same department highlights this point:
*It also gets a bit painty **and stuff like that**.*

Before leaving vague language, it is worth briefly discussing the
patterns of particular items. Some, like *et cetera* and *and everything
else*, are much more common in external meetings. *That sort of
thing*, in contrast, typically occurs in internal peer meetings, and is
three times more likely to occur in peer than manager–subordinate
meetings. Interestingly, the lexically linked hedge *sort of* behaves
quite differently (see page 169). *And this that and the other* is the
second highest six-word cluster. It occurs 33 times in the corpus,
which means it is very frequent, especially considering its length
(Biber et al., 1999). Evison et al. (2007) analysed various vague category markers in selected corpora, and found that *this that and the
other* occurred 11 times in a one-million-word corpus of everyday
conversational English, and not at all in a much smaller corpus of
academic speech (both sub-corpora of the CANCODE corpus – see
Chapter 1). It can therefore be said that this cluster appears to be

more frequent in business English than in everyday conversational English. Once again, however, pure frequency figures can be somewhat misleading. As the above figures show, this cluster is used in specific contextual situations: in CANBEC, it is used overwhelmingly by peers, very rarely in external meetings, and never in any type of manager–subordinate meeting. The number of topics is also limited, with the cluster occurring most frequently in (internal) sales and marketing meetings. Possibly most striking of all, however, is the finding that it is only used within two companies, both of which are manufacturing companies. Furthermore, this chunk is used solely by men from Great Britain. We can therefore conclude that *and this that and the other* tends to be used by a small number of clearly defined communities of practice in CANBEC in only a selected set of circumstances: usually in internal meetings between British males, and mainly from the sales and marketing departments of certain manufacturing companies. In the next section, 'hedging', another type of 'fuzzy' language which is pragmatically and sometimes lexically related to vague language, is discussed.

6.5 Hedges

While the first three interpersonal categories explored in this chapter have been primarily concerned with exploring social relations in terms of solidarity, the next two will discuss the negotiation of power, and the related issue of mitigating potential face-threats. As previous chapters have shown, hedges (which lessen the degree of certainty and assertiveness of utterances) are a common feature of business meetings and will be discussed in this section. The word *just*, for example, accounts for over one in every 200 words in CANBEC[2]. Hedges are particularly frequent in the transactional stages of meetings (see Chapter 3), as is evidenced in the following excerpt from extract 6.1 where the meeting coheres:

> S1: [laughs] **I think we should** make a start. Helen **er** was on a teleconference **when erm when** I left the office. **Erm I I guess** for me **er** same **sort of er** agenda as normal **if we can** work through the logistics work stream meeting minutes **erm** picking up the various sections. **I think** there're a **few things we we**'ve **sort of scribbled** at the end in terms of e= **under=** any other business. **I'd certainly like to** look at the technical meeting **er** minutes. That's part of the agenda in terms of the logistics section but there's also the (1 second) section four **of the= of the** technical meeting minutes **er** goes through the **you know** how we're moving from the project into the operational phase.

S2?:Yeah.
S1:   And **I think it would be worth just** covering **some** of those.

The most common forms of hedges in everyday talk, according to O'Keeffe et al. (2007: 175), and which are replicated in this one-minute excerpt, include modal verbs and verbs with modal meaning (*I think, we should, I guess, it would be, I'd like to*), nouns (*things*), adverbs of degree (*certainly*), restrictive adverbs (*just*), stance adverbs (*sort of*), and features of 'onlineness' (that is, the cognitive processing requirements of real-time speech) such as repetitions (*of the of the*) and fillers (*er, erm, you know*). Expressions involving *if* (*if we can*) and certain idiomatic verbs (*scribbled*) could also be added to this list, as they also serve to hedge the force of the message. Several of these multifunctional items are also among the most frequent in CANBEC.

In extract 6.1, the small-talk phase which immediately precedes this opening of the meeting contrasts strongly in that it contains very few hedges. Nearly all of the hedges appear when the chair is outlining the proposed agenda for the day's meeting. This pattern – that interpersonal hedges (unlike boosters) are less common in relational talk, but are more typical of transactional discourse – occurs widely in other meetings as well. This is interesting, because it adds weight to the assertion that these features may mitigate the potential face-threats (Hyland, 1998; Koester, 2006, 2010; Carter and McCarthy, 2006) that are an inevitable feature of the workplace (Holmes and Stubbe, 2003), and are an expected feature of cooperative discourse. The relative ubiquity of hedges in meeting discourse also suggests that they may allow discursive and professional practices to be unearthed.

In order to explore hedges in different types of meetings, the frequencies of two-word clusters were compared. The following six items appeared in the top ten most frequent items in both internal and external meeting sub-corpora: *you know, I think, I mean, sort of, kind of* and *a bit*. The combined frequency of these items is roughly the same across both sub-corpora, accounting for about 1.2 per cent of all words used[3]. This means that these six items plus the hedge *just* make up more than one in every 60 words in CANBEC.

According to Koester (2006, 2010), hedges in internal communication are more commonly found in 'unidirectional' communication, which often involves directives and instructions, than in 'collaborative' communication, which would often feature decision-making. There is considerable overlap between Koester's uni-directional category, which 'involves a discursively dominant speaker telling an addressee *how* to do something or *what* to do' (Koester, 2006: 43), and the manager–subordinate category. Similarly, Koester's collaborative category overlaps to a large extent with peer communication in

CANBEC, as meetings between peers often involve middle or upper managers discussing problems and decisions. It could therefore be expected that the frequency of hedges would be greater in manager–subordinate than in peer communication. This would be plausible, because, as Koester (2010) argues, directives inevitably involve a potential face-threat, and therefore managers in 'white collar' environments (Holmes and Stubbe, 2003), such as in meetings found in CANBEC, may seek to lessen that threat through hedges. However, the results from the CANBEC data are more complex: in terms of raw frequency, these six items are actually more frequent in peer than in manager–subordinate meetings, with *I think* in particular being far more typical of peer meetings. Nevertheless, *I think* can be found in longer clusters and can index several practices, such as summarizing, clarifying, responding, disagreeing and expressing an opinion, some of which are more typical of peer communication. Without prosodic information it is also difficult to infer what certain items like *I think* are doing in the discourse.

These findings show that hedges need to be explored in context, as demonstrated by Koester (2006, 2010) and Farr et al. (2001). The usual solution to this problem is to study concordance lines and distinguish between the items (Hunston, 2002); another solution is to read the whole texts of meetings and interpret the items within them. This latter solution is obviously a far more time-consuming approach. Nevertheless, this approach in theory has the advantage of allowing the researcher to gain a better understanding of how the items are operating in and across the discourse. For example, how much items group together at different stages of a meeting is an important insight, but one that cannot be gained through the use of concordance lines. In order to make inferences about practices, it is necessary to move beyond concordances, as discussed in Chapter 2. The sub-corpus, discussed at the beginning of the chapter, permits such analyses. Although the results are not as generalizable as those from the whole corpus, such an approach still allows for a comprehensive comparison and interpretation of items and features within and across meeting types that would not otherwise be possible. Results were also compared with the whole corpus. This approach allows for the interpretation of critical items which an automated quantitative approach does not highlight, for example the use of metaphors and idioms or certain statistical features of turn-taking. See the Appendix for a full breakdown of the sub-corpus.

The frequency and use of three items – *just*, *kind of* and *sort of* – were analysed using the sub-corpus. These items were chosen because they are, relative to other potential hedges, frequent and easy to

Figure 6.2   Density of hedges (items per 1,000 words)

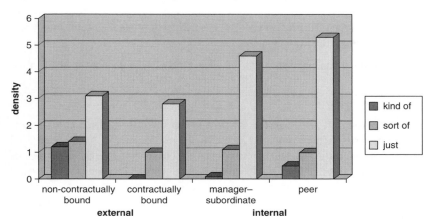

categorize. Moreover, *sort of* and *kind of* seem roughly synonymous, and therefore potentially interesting: items that are apparently synonymous at the semantic level may behave very differently at the contextual level and index quite separate practices. Figure 6.2 shows the relative density (that is, number of instances) of the items per 1,000 words across the sub-corpus according to relationship category.

One of the most striking results is the uneven profile of *kind of*. It only occurs with any frequency in two meetings (an external non-contractually bound meeting and an internal peer meeting), and does not feature at all in five. *Sort of*, in contrast, appears in all meetings except one (a particularly conflictual external contractually bound meeting which featured hardly any hedges at all). *Just*, as might be expected, features in all nine meetings, but is noticeably more typical of internal meetings. These general tendencies are replicated across the wider corpus as well.

The two meetings in which *kind of* occurs very frequently are both concerned with technical ICT (Information and Communication Technologies) issues. Indeed, across the whole corpus, *kind of* is far more typical of such meetings, whether internal or external, occurring up to ten times more in technical ICT meetings than in some HRM (Human Resource Management) meetings. In technical meetings, which obviously contain a high degree of specialized content, it is used to soften the assertiveness of the information being conveyed:

*Concordance lines for **kind of***

It's a bit like Java script but (1 second) it's a **kind of** cross between Java script and Visual Basic

You'll get. It's a basic graphing stat which **kind of** tells you er hit levels and it it's

---

Furthermore, in two external non-contractually bound sales meetings that are both concerned with ICT and feature a high degree of instances of *kind of*, the item tends to cluster towards the end of the meeting, along with other hedges and vague language. This may reflect a practice of finishing such meetings on a collaborative note, through convergence and the downplaying of any impositions and evaluations.

Sort of, in contrast to *kind of*, is up to six times more frequent in HRM and some (internal and external) sales meetings than in technical meetings, and occurs uniformly across all the four main relationship categories (figure 6.2). Furthermore, whereas *kind of* is often used to hedge ideational (Halliday, 1994) content, a close reading of the sub-corpus shows that *sort of* tends to be more overtly interpersonal and interactive, as HRM and many sales meetings tend to be. For instance, it is used to hedge several discursive practices including evaluations, excuses, disagreements and other potential threats to positive face. In terms of negative face-threats, hedges appear when speakers are negotiating some potential imposition, such as directing or suggesting a change to work procedures. The following concordances are taken from peer meetings, and both involve potential negative face-threats: the first is a hedged instruction, and the second involves justifying a proposed change to procedure.

*Concordance lines for **sort of** in peer meetings*

Do you wanna just **sort of** memorize the figures.

So so that it doesn't cos at the minute we're just **sort of** going indefinitely on and on and on and on.

Sort of is also used to negotiate the power differences and social identities of the interlocutors – for instance, in manager–subordinate meetings across the corpus. As such, it can be interpreted in terms of positive face, and is often used by subordinates to their superiors.

The following three concordance lines are uttered by a subordinate to her supervisor in the same top-down appraisal meeting (that is, the manager is appraising the subordinate), the first complimenting and the second and third implicitly criticizing the manager:

*Concordance lines for **sort of** in manager–subordinate meetings*

And I I really thought you were **sort of** like early fifties.

And and there isn't the erm level of **sort of** (1 second) [sighs] (1 second) well I suppose checking.

But then I I'm suspecting= we didn't really talk about it we just had a= [inhales] you just **sort of** took me to one side and said you know "Let's just leave it the way things are".

All of these concordances feature grouping of hedges, indicating how hedges can co-occur not only in terms of the stage of the meeting, but also at the turn level. The repetition of hedges across meetings which feature recurrent practices also supports the argument that hedges are used to mitigate the force of such necessary, but nevertheless potentially face-threatening, practices.

6.6 Deontic modality

Section 6.6 will explore the fifth dimension of social relations, the negotiation of power over actions through deontic modality. Various deontic modal verbs and expressions have been shown on several occasions in this book to be among some of the most statistically significant items in the corpus – an unsurprising finding given that obligation is one of the defining features of work. In extract 6.1, the chair formally begins the meeting, in typical fashion, through the hedged modal of obligation *I think we should make a start*. Chapters 2 and 5 showed how the clusters *you have to* and *you need to* can be employed in different contexts, constituting different practices, and helping to negotiate different social identities and relationships.

This section will look primarily at obligation through the occurrence of certain selected deontic modal and semi-modal verbs including *need (to)*, *should*, *have to* and *must*[4]. These items have been chosen because they are all 'strong' modals of obligation (Weiyun He, 1993; Koester, 2010) and are statistically interesting. Figure 6.3 shows the density per 1,000 words of some of the most interesting items from all meetings in CANBEC. It should also be noted that

Figure 6.3   Frequency of selected deontic modal forms across CANBEC[5]

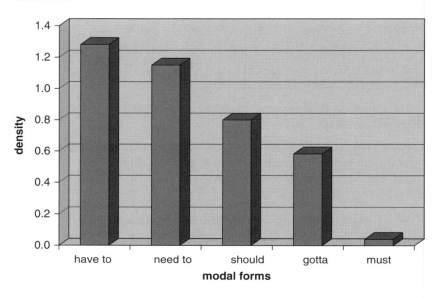

Koester (2006: 77) reports the same order of frequency in her ABOT (American and British Office Talk) corpus, and in the spoken portion of the BNC (British National Corpus).

The discussing, giving, receiving, rejecting and reiterating of directives and requests is a feature of the internal workplace (Holmes and Stubbe, 2003; McCarthy and Handford, 2004; Koester, 2006, 2010), and this section will show how the relationship of the speakers can affect the frequency of such items, their meaning and the conventionalized practices they invoke. This section will also explore the role deontic modal forms play in external as well as internal meetings, further demonstrating the importance of context in understanding language in business meetings.

It has been argued that speakers choose modal items based on their relative status as a participant in the conversation and the perceived truth value of the utterance[6]: the higher these two factors, the stronger the modal form chosen (Weiyun He, 1993). Such an approach suggests two things: there should be more instances of strong modal forms when managers are instructing and directing subordinates, and these forms should be stronger than in meetings involving peers who are discussing the same issues. Furthermore, in external meetings where status is less foregrounded – for example, in non-contractually bound external meetings – there should be fewer instances. In contrast to this assumption, however, these strong modal forms are actually slightly more frequent in external meetings than internal meetings. Within internal meetings, they feature more in manager–subordinate than peer meetings – no doubt due to the high degree of directives in manager–subordinate communication (Koester, 2006, 2010); however, the strength of the modality may not mirror the relative status of the speaker (McCarthy and Handford, 2004).

It is also evident from the data in CANBEC that deontic modals often appear in collaborative, decision-focused communication in both internal and external meetings. In terms of meeting topic, for instance, *need to* is most typical of strategy meetings (at which decisions that have long-term implications for the company or department are made). The three most common deontic modal forms, *need to*, *have to* and *should* (see figure 6.3) are most frequently used in strategy, technical, logistics and procedure meetings, but least frequently in sales and marketing meetings. Overall, *issue* and *problem*, which often index decision-making discussions (as will be shown in Chapter 7), follow a similar pattern. This suggests that both decision-making and directive discourse in sales and marketing are less frequent than in meetings concerned with these other topics.

In understanding why strong modal forms are frequent in external meetings, the inclusive/exclusive distinction is relevant. In the same way that it is possible to refer to one's own company in external meetings through *we*, participants can also direct the strong modal form towards themselves, as shown in Chapter 5. From the external meetings in the sub-corpus, over 75 per cent of all instances of the ubiquitous cluster *we need to* are self-directed. Such self-directed modality is a feature largely specific to external meetings, as only in internal meetings involving clear departmental divisions could the equivalent occur. The extremely high percentage of the self-directed cluster *we need to* (over 90 per cent) in non-contractually bound meetings is interesting. In these types of meetings, it is logical to assume that there is at this stage in the companies' relationship less actual obligation, as the two parties have not formed a binding contract. Such self-directed deontic modality may therefore create a positive impression by showing that the speaker's company is responsible and committed.

As demonstrated with hedges in section 6.5, deontic modal forms also often cluster together. Extract 6.8, taken from the same meeting as extract 6.1, shows how modality is employed to address the speaker's and his company's goals. The notion of identity is relevant here, as the chair (S1) is activating his professional, senior status through the force of his argument and length of his turn, in order to explicitly orient to the required decisions and transactional goals he deems necessary. He initially talks about a report that one of his colleagues, who is presently on holiday, passed on to him for the meeting. He then goes on to highlight the changes that he sees as necessary.

(6.8)

> *External meeting*
> Relationship of speakers: contractually bound
> Purpose: planning; reviewing
> Topic: logistics; production

S1: I guess I can photocopy this but I think w= what's more important is [swallows] we actually discuss this information in terms of what **we need to** do with it. Because you mean f= for instance we're assuming everything's five days so if we built a ninety eight day lead time into our system for the standard five day markets [inhales] we know therefore that your aim is to have everything ready and passed eight days before despatch. So you've got o= o= one day for for getting the despatch ready two days for the invoicing and five days for the distribution.

S3: Yeah.

S1: If we're= if we're looking at some markets that are suddenly now fifteen days obviously what **we want to** do is build that into the firming up lead time. And= but **we also want you to**= have i= (1 second) h= have erm that information upfront. So you know what mar= **you need to** almost flag those markets to say+

S2?: Yeah.

S1: +this is a legalization market+

S2?: Yeah. Yeah.

S1: +and therefore it's not just five days. **We've gotta** have it ready fifteen days before.

S5?: Mm.

The force of the request is built up over the course of the sequence: *we need to – we want to – we want you to – you need to – we gotta have it ready*. Whereas *we need to* refers to both companies and is essentially inclusive, the subsequent degree of obligation becomes progressively stronger and is directed by S1 at the other company, as it is the other company that is obliged to make the changes. Despite the use of *we* in the final *we gotta*, there is no doubt as to where the responsibility lies. This meeting also has six instances of the deontic form of *must*, and as such is very unusual; however, five of these are self-directed towards the manufacturer and are all used by German speakers[7].

Deontic modal forms play a key role in the reflexive constitution of internal meetings, and are widely used in the core management practices of directing and instructing colleagues (both subordinate and peer), and of dealing with problems and decisions. The top three modal forms (*need to*, *have to* and *should*) are all more frequent in manager–subordinate meetings and, unsurprisingly, are used by managers to direct and instruct staff. While other factors (for example, topic) would also affect the degree of obligation, McCarthy and Handford (2004) show that, in different meetings dealing with the same topic within the same company and involving the same managers, the strength of modality may decrease in rough inverse proportion to the difference in status of the participants. In other words, managers in peer meetings often use stronger modal forms than managers talking to subordinates about the same directive.

One type of peer meeting that features a high degree of deontic modal forms is that between peers from different departments. This may be because such meetings typically feature a high incidence of decision-making among the most senior managers in a company or business unit. Colleagues attempt to decide on the most appropriate procedure or strategy for the company or division concerned, and this regularly involves persuasion and claims of necessity. In extract 6.9, the speakers are negotiating the preferable procedure, with each arguing his case. Modality intensifies over interrupted turns, with the chair (S1), who is actually subordinate to S4 in status, finally baldly stating *you gotta work on that code today*.

(6.9)

Internal meeting
Relationship of speakers: peer
Purpose: planning; task-/problem-oriented
Topic: procedure; technical

S1: And if at that point it doesn't work I suggest we postpone the rollout. But if it does work then we continue. And then we don't have to (1.5 seconds) throw something together tonight that may or may not represent the actual production advance.

S4:   Well I mean you're you're not gi= giving me any luxury to er to verify
      the things that this is not= this is the kind of bug I have to work
      around right. So I don't I don't have a luxury to=
S1:   Yeah. You've gotta work on that code today and give us a=
S4:   Just because just because you know er you know the m= machines I
      have I can just you know=

This example suggests that there is a strong relationship between
decision-making and the strength of modals of obligation. This can
be explained from a goals perspective, with decisions being made to
achieve the goals, and strong modals being employed to persuade the
other participants of the efficacy or necessity of the proposed solution
or course of action. This also explains why *we need to* is the default
modal cluster in most meetings, because it achieves all of these aims
with minimal face-threat.

   The negative-keyword list in Chapter 4 shows that *must* is far more
typical of everyday speech than of business meetings in CANBEC,
and figure 6.3 illustrates its comparative infrequency with its
near-synonyms. This is very surprising when we consider that *must*
is a strong modal form of obligation, and obligation tends to be the
feature which distinguishes between work and social life. The explanation offered here concerns the inherently face-threatening nature of
must when used as an other-directed deontic modal verb[8]. McCarthy
and Handford (2004: 181) argue that the comparative difference
in frequency between *need to* and *must* in spoken business English
reveals 'how important preservation of face is, even in a context where
one might expect exigencies, pressure and urgency to be frequent and
paramount'. Indeed, when *must* is used as a deontic modal, it tends to
be either self-directed, as in *I forgot to ring about that I must ring on
Monday about it*, or used in reported speech.

   However, this still does not answer the question of why attending to the face needs of subordinates (and other colleagues) is necessary. Why, in manager-subordinate meetings in CANBEC, is *you must*
never used, but *we need to* occurs over 100 times? Why is *we need to*
more common than *you need to*? One could argue that telling people
what to do is essential at work, so the more direct and unequivocal,
the better. A response to this is offered by McCarthy and Handford:
'Face-protecting and indirect forms for issuing directives are preferred
in order to maintain good interpersonal relations and to promote the
comity, motivation and stability so necessary in business institutions'
(2004: 182).

   A more critical angle is offered by Gee et al.'s (1996) analysis of
modern Discourses found in business. They state: 'workers can no

longer be "ordered" around by "bosses". As partners, they can only be "developed", "coached", and "supported". Hierarchy is gone, egalitarianism is in' (ibid.: 30). They continue: 'the humanistic, democratic reforms are being enacted, not because they create more humanistic, less hierarchical conditions for workers but because they are viewed as the way to create more and/or continuing profit' (ibid.: 125). This link between face and motivation, and the staff 'doing well' for the company is made relevant in extract 6.10. This is the end of the manager–subordinate meeting from the exclusive hotel chain discussed first in extract 2.4 of Chapter 2 (pages 44–5). The meeting has been concerned with agreeing on how to achieve a higher score in the section's appraisal, and the subordinate members of staff (S4 and S5) are telling the manager (S2) how motivating such meetings are.

(6.10)

> *Internal meeting*
> Relationship of speakers: manager–subordinate
> Purpose: task-/problem-oriented; giving and receiving information/advice
> Topic: procedure; strategy

S4: And … Every time I have a meeting for me … I don't know for every-body else but for me it's very motivating. (1 second) I really feel like going back to work and doing well+
S2: That's good to hear.
S4: +and you know.
S2: That's that's what I want+
S4: Yeah.
S2: +really. That's that's d= if= that's what the meetings should have the effect.
S5: Yeah that should [inaudible] afterwards.
S2: You know I was= it's no good sitting here telling everyone off. That's what they did in the past and it didn't work+
S5: Yeah.
S2: +and I knew it's not gonna work but we want to come up with solution but also (2 seconds) you know take the responsibility and stick to the solutions that we [inaudible] now.
S5: Yeah.

The members of staff in this extract profess to being highly motivated by the meeting, and the manager (S2) comments on the previous style of management that tried to motivate through *telling everyone off*. His following evaluation of the change in management style is very much in line with the practices of the 'new work order' (Gee et al.: 1996) – that is, he highlights that staff teams are given the opportunity to find and responsibility for finding solutions to problems, and are thus seemingly empowered (but critically not sufficiently to select or reject the problems, which is the management's role). The staff teams are then expected to consistently implement these solutions and be evaluated by them. In extract 2.4 from the beginning of this meeting, the director's implicit threat concerning job security to junior staff who fail to consistently implement the standards can also be considered a practice of the new work order. How the management threat and the workers' professed enthusiasm are related is open to speculation.

6.7 Summary

Chapter 6 has looked at how interpersonal language is used in transactional and, to a lesser extent, relational discourse. It has explored how pronouns, hedges, vague category markers, deontic modality and backchannels are used in a variety of contexts, and how they can constitute several practices central to business meetings. These include directing subordinates and peers, evaluating, highlighting and dealing with problems and decisions, referring to shared knowledge, negotiating, and developing relationships. The chapter has discussed how these interpersonal items constrain and enable social relations, through the signalling of various dimensions of solidarity and the negotiation of power over knowledge and actions. In so doing, many of the items and themes that arose in Chapters 4 and 5 have been explored in more detail here, through analysis of interpersonal language such as *we*, *hmm*, *I think*, *we need to*, *sort of* and *and that kind of thing*. Furthermore, much interpersonal language can serve transactional goals in business meetings, as discussed in Chapter 2, and therefore care needs to be taken not to conflate goals and language when analysing interpersonal and transactional discourse.

Wenger's (1998) insights into the role of small talk in the development of a community of practice seem relevant here: developing relationships (harmonious or conflictual) through stories, humour and so on is central to developing a community of practice.

Face is a concept which seems highly relevant in explaining linguistic choices in meetings. Vagueness helps to address the face needs of the listeners, but a lack of vagueness can be seen as highly face-threatening or indicative of conflict. Similarly, the choice of deontic modal forms can be explained through reference to face, as certain infrequent verbs (such as *must*) are very face-threatening in the business communities studied here, unlike others, such as *need*. It has been argued here that the linguistic negotiation of obligation is often best understood through reference to face issues.

The speaker relationship, it is argued, can have a particularly constraining influence on the discourse. While some of the results in this chapter were unsurprising (for instance, colleagues in the same department use more vague language than colleagues in different departments), other results were not as expected, such as vague category markers and deontic modality being most frequent in the external, non-contractually bound meetings. A closer analysis of the data revealed that these modal forms tended to be self-directed in such discourse, thus reinforcing the need to explore corpus items in context and not to rely on purely quantitative findings when drawing conclusions. The finding that vagueness as a marker of shared knowledge is actually more frequent in external meetings in CANBEC than internal meetings – and particularly in non-contractually bound external meetings, where there is probably less shared knowledge – suggests that it can be used tactically by company representatives to create a positive, convergent impression. Differences in backchannel use were also noted, with the non-committal *hmm* being preferred in internal manager–subordinate meetings by managers, whereas the more positive *sure* is more common in external meetings. Moreover, as shown at the beginning of the chapter, pronoun use varies considerably in internal and external meetings, not just in terms of pure frequencies, but also in relation to the identities that are invoked. The item *we* was shown to be one of the most important, critical words in business. The profile of hedges is more difficult to summarize, given that, overall, the selected items featured more in internal meetings, but when analysed in specific meetings were sometimes seen to have specific collocations and discourse prosodies, as was the case with *kind of*. Overall, the findings from this chapter, and from Chapter 4, suggest that there is a tendency for external meetings to contain a higher degree of interpersonal language features than internal meetings, indicating the need to nurture such relationships and pay attention to face. Not all external meetings follow this pattern, however, as Chapter 7 will show.

Chapter 7 explores certain aspects of creativity in business meetings through reference to other significant interpersonal features, including the evaluative nouns *problem* and *issue*, the multifunctional *if*, and metaphors and idioms.

Notes

1. Within other, more conflictual types of institutional discourse, there would also be other possible uses of *we* – for example, inclusive peer, non-corporate (the employee's union), which refers to the group's work identity, but usually from a stance which is critical of the institution's management or policy-making body. It is also possible to conceive of an exclusive managerial, corporate *we*, in political contrast to the union *we*. Furthermore, within internal multiparty meetings, exclusive *we* could also be used to contrast the stance of the speaker and one or more of the participants with that of somebody else present.

2. Boosters, or intensifiers, which allow speakers to strengthen evaluation of their comments and develop involvement with their interlocutors (Koester, 2006: 97), are more typical of relational communication in CANBEC. However, hedges can fulfil the same function – as in the chair's comment **Little bit jealous actually** in extract 6.1 – especially when prosodically stressed by the speaker.

3. As previously mentioned, however, raw frequencies allow for a way in to the data, but need to be treated with suspicion, as items can be highly multifunctional. For instance, Chapter 5 showed that *so I think* is commonly used to summarize; however, the two-word frequency lists cannot differentiate between two-word hedges and three-word summaries comprising *I think*. Therefore, deciding whether an item is being used as a hedge or as something else requires a degree of interpretation that corpus software cannot as yet automatically provide.

4. There are other possible modal forms which have not been included here because of their relative infrequency and because of space constraints. *Ought to* occurs slightly over 100 times in the whole corpus, and *had/'d better* fewer than 20. *Want to*, while being a deontic modal, primarily expresses desire or inclination (Koester, 2006: 85), although its use as a modal expressing obligation is briefly explored later in this chapter.

5. The figures in the graph have been calculated following Biber et al. (1998): as not all instances of these modal forms are deontic, a random set of concordance lines is analysed and the percentage of remaining deontic modals is then multiplied by the total in the whole corpus, giving a fraction of the original total. For example, instances of *must* such as *there must be*, *I must admit*, *you must know*, or of *should*, including *we should be able*, *it should last forever shouldn't it* do not involve any notion of obligation, and are not included in the final total. While this inductive method is not 100 per cent accurate, it is sufficient for present purposes and is applied when appropriate throughout the book.

6. Although the notion of truth value of deontic modality seems somewhat questionable.

7. This finding can also be used to encourage learners of business English to confront their stereotypes. When telling learners that Germans use *must* more than other business people in the corpus, my British and Asian students usually respond with a stereotype, such as 'Yes, of course, because Germans

are really direct'. By then explaining to learners that 1) the uses are usually self-referential, and 2) the German equivalent verb *müssen* is less face-threatening than the English *must*, learners can understand that such language use may not be related to the speaker's attitude/personality. Learners can then be encouraged to analyse why they negatively evaluated Germans in this way, when in fact the reason for the use of *must* may be more to do with pragmalinguistic transfer, and why such evaluations may be problematic in international business relationships. The issue of stereotyping will be discussed further in Chapter 9.

8. Apart from the strong face-threat embodied in *must*, another reason for its infrequency may be that it is more personal than *have to*, in that the latter is used to convey obligation from 'outside' (Swan, 1995: 352) or 'objective obligation' (Simpson, 1997: 137), whereas *must* is used to convey the opinion of the speaker (ibid.). In an institutional environment, *have to* would usually be seen as more appropriate.

References

Bargiela-Chiappini, F. and Harris, S. (1997) *Managing Language: The Discourse of Corporate Meetings*, Amsterdam: John Benjamins.

Biber, D., Conrad, S. and Reppen, R. (1998) *Corpus Linguistics: Investigating Language Structure and Use*, Cambridge: Cambridge University Press.

Biber, D., Johansson, S., Leech, G., Conrad, S. and Finnegan, E. (1999) *Longman Grammar of Spoken and Written English*, London: Longman.

Boden, D. (1994) *The Business of Talk: Organizations in Action*, Cambridge: Polity Press.

Bülow, A. (2009) 'Negotiation studies', in Bargiela-Chiappini, F. (ed.) *The Handbook of Business Discourse*, Edinburgh: Edinburgh University Press, 142–54.

Carter, R. (2004) *Language and Creativity: The Art of Common Talk*, London: Routledge.

Carter, R. and McCarthy, M. (2006) *Cambridge Grammar of English*, Cambridge: Cambridge University Press.

Channell, J. (1994) *Vague Language*, Oxford: Oxford University Press.

Charles, M. (1996) 'Business negotiations: Interdependence between discourse and the business relationship', *English for Specific Purposes*, 15, 19–36.

Charles, M. and Charles, D. (1999) 'Sales negotiations: Bargaining through tactical summaries', in Hewings, M. and Nickerson, C. (eds.) *Business English: Research into Practice*, London: Longman.

Cutting, J. (ed.) (2007) *Vague Language Explored*, Basingstoke: Palgrave.

Drew, P. and Heritage, J. (1992) 'Analysing talk at work: An introduction', In Drew, P. and Heritage, J. (eds.) *Talk at Work*, Cambridge: Cambridge University Press, 3–65.

Evison, J., McCarthy, M. and O'Keeffe, A. (2007) 'Looking out for love and all the rest of it: Vague category markers as shared social space', in Cutting, J. (ed.) *Vague Language Explored*, Basingstoke: Palgrave.

Fairclough, N. (1989) *Language and Power*, London: Longman.

Fairclough, N. (2000) *New Labour, New Language?*, London: Routledge.

Farr, F., Murphy, B. and O'Keeffe, A. (2001) 'The Limerick Corpus of Irish English: Design, description and application', *Teanga*, 21, 5–29.

Gee. J.P., Hull, G. and Lankshear, C. (1996) *The New Work Order*, London: Allen and Unwin.

Goffman, E. (1981) *Forms of Talk*, Philadelphia: University of Pennsylvania Press.

Halliday, M. (1985) *Spoken and Written Language*, Victoria: Deakin University.

Halliday, M. (1994) *An Introduction to Functional Grammar*, London: Edward Arnold.

Handford, M. (2007) *The Genre of the Business Meeting: A Corpus-based Study*, PhD thesis, University of Nottingham (Unpublished).

Handford, M. and Koester, A. (2010) '"It's not rocket science": Metaphors and idioms in conflictual business meetings', *Text and Talk*, 30, 27–51.

Hoey, M. (2005) *Lexical Priming*, Abingdon: Routledge.

Holmes, J. (2000) 'Doing collegiality and keeping control at work: Small talk in government departments', in Coupland, J. (ed.) *Small Talk*, Harlow: Pearson Education, 32–61.

Holmes, J. (2006) 'Workplace narratives, professional identity and relational practice', in de Fina, A., Schiffrin, D. and Bamberg, M. (eds.) *Discourse and Identity*, Cambridge: Cambridge University Press, 166–87.

Holmes, J. (2007) 'Making humour work: Creativity on the job', *Applied Linguistics*, 28, 4, 518–37.

Holmes, J. and Stubbe, M. (2003) *Power and Politeness in the Workplace*, London: Longman.

Hunston, S. (2002) *Corpora in Applied Linguistics*, Cambridge: Cambridge University Press.

Hutchby, I. and Wooffitt, R. (2008) *Conversation Analysis* (Second edition), Cambridge: Polity Press.

Hyland, K. (1998) 'Persuasion and context: The pragmatics of academic metadiscourse', *Journal of Pragmatics*, 30, 437–55.

Iedema, R. (1997) 'The language of administration: Organizing human activity in formal institutions', in Christie, F. and Martin, J. (eds.) *Genre and Institutions*, London: Continuum, 73–100.

Koester, A. (2004) 'Relational sequences in workplace genres', *Journal of Pragmatics*, 36, 1405–28.

Koester, A. (2006) *Investigating Workplace Discourse*, Abingdon: Routledge.

Koester, A. (2010) *Workplace Discourse*, London: Continuum.

Lampi, M. (1986) *Linguistic Components of Strategy in Business Negotiations*, Helsinki: Helsinki School of Economics.

Maynard, D. (1984) *Inside Plea Bargaining: The Language of Negotiation*, New York: Plenun.

McCarthy, M. (1998) *Spoken Language and Applied Linguistics*, Cambridge: Cambridge University Press.

McCarthy, M. (2000) 'Captive audiences: Small talk and close contact service encounters', in Coupland, J. (ed.) *Small Talk*, Harlow: Pearson Education, 84–109.

McCarthy, M. and Carter, R. (1997) 'Grammar, tails and affect: Constructing expressive choices in discourse', *Text*, 17, 3, 405–29.

McCarthy, M. and Handford, M. (2004) '"Invisible to us": A preliminary corpus-based study of spoken business English', in Connor, U. and Upton, T. (eds.) *Discourse in the Professions: Perspectives from Corpus Linguistics*, Amsterdam: John Benjamins, 167–201.

McKenna, R. (1993) *Relationship Marketing*, Cambridge, MA: Perseus Books.

Nelson, M. (2000) *A Corpus-based Study of Business English and Business English Teaching Materials*, PhD thesis, University of Manchester (Unpublished).

Neu, J. and Graham, J. (1995) 'An analysis of language use in negotiations: The role of context and content', in Ehlich, K. and Wagner, J. (eds.) *The Discourse of Business Negotiation*, Berlin: Mouton de Gruyter, 243–72.

O'Keeffe, A. (2003) '"Like the wise virgins and all that jazz" – using a corpus to examine vague language and shared knowledge', in Connor, U. and Upton, T. (eds.) *Applied Corpus Linguistics: A Multidimensional Perspective*, Amsterdam: Rodopi, 1–20.

O'Keeffe, A., McCarthy, M. and Carter, R. (2007) *From Corpus to Classroom: Language Use and Language Teaching*, Cambridge: Cambridge University Press.

Paulin, M., Ferguson, R. and Payaud, M. (2000) 'Effectiveness of relational and transactional cultures in commercial banking: Putting client-value into the competing values model', *International Journal of Bank Marketing*, 18, 7, 328–37.

Paulin, M., Perrien, J. and Ferguson, R. (1997) 'Relational norms and the effectiveness of commercial banking relationships', *International Journal of Service Industry Management*, 8, 5, 435–52.

Poncini, G. (2002) 'Investigating discourse at business meetings with multicultural participation', *International Review of Applied Linguistics*, 40, 345–73.

Poncini, G. (2004) *Discursive Strategies in Multicultural Business Meetings*, Peter Lang, Linguistic Insights Series.

Simpson, P. (1997) *Language Through Literature*, London: Routledge.

Spencer-Oatey, H. (2000) *Culturally Speaking: Managing Rapport through Talk across Cultures*, London: Continuum.

Sunaoshi, Y. (2005) 'Historical context and intercultural communication: Interactions between Japanese and American factory workers in the American South', *Language in Society*, 34, 185–217.

Swan, M. (1995) *Practical English Usage*, Oxford: Oxford University Press.

Tannen, D. (1993) 'Rethinking power and solidarity in gender and dominance', in Tannen, D. (ed.) *Gender and Conversational Interaction*, Oxford: Oxford University Press, 165–88.

Trompenaars, F. and Hampden-Turner, C. (1998) *Riding the Waves of Culture: Understanding Diversity in Global Business*, New York: McGraw-Hill.

Weiyun He, A. (1993) 'Exploring modality in institutional interactions: Cases from academic counselling encounters', *Text*, **13**, 4, 503–28.

Wenger, E. (1998) *Communities of Practice: Learning, Meaning and Identity*, Cambridge: Cambridge University Press.

Zupnik, Y. (1994) 'A pragmatic analysis of the use of person deixis in political discourse', *Journal of Pragmatics*, **21**, 339–83.

7 Interpersonal creativity: *Problem, issue, if,* and metaphors and idioms

Creativity is not always a word that springs to mind when thinking about work or business. Indeed, even developing the strategy of an organization, traditionally viewed as a highly creative endeavour (Mintzberg, 1994; Hamel, 2007) has recently been interpreted as a practice that managers become socialized into and perform within the constraints of the organizational context (Rigby, 2003; Johnson et al., 2007; Samra-Fredericks, 2009). However, according to de Bono, creativity is central to success in business:

Creativity is used to solve problems, resolve conflicts, simplify procedures, cut costs, improve motivation, design new products and services, and fashion strategies. Any situations that require thinking demand creativity. Without it, we are condemned to repeating the standard routines. (de Bono, 2006: 355)

Of course, a considerable amount of the working day is made up of standard routines, several of which are explored in this study, allowing for an essential degree of efficiency that constantly creating everything anew would prevent. Nevertheless, de Bono highlights a crucial tension in business: how can business people deal with challenging, immediate situations, often categorizable as potential or actual problems, in real time in an effective way? While this is a huge, nebulous issue that demands a truly interdisciplinary approach, CANBEC data does allow for insights on creativity at the level of discourse through an analysis of the items *problem, issue, if,* and metaphors and idioms. These items have been chosen because they are among the most statistically and stylistically or culturally significant interpersonal items in CANBEC: *problem, issue* and *if* are among the most important keywords in the corpus, and metaphors and idioms (hereafter referred to as MIDs – see Handford and Koester, 2010) are extremely common in meetings, accounting for one in every 50 items, as we will see below. Furthermore, the items, through what is termed here 'interpersonal creativity', can construct the overall process of creative problem-solving through indexing specific discursive practices related to each stage of that process that were pinpointed in Chapter 5. To clarify this, it is necessary to briefly outline what is meant here by interpersonal creativity, and its relationship with language and problem-solving.

Interpersonal creativity concerns the following three interrelated aspects of creativity: creative problem-exploration (tied to the discursive practice of focusing on decisions, through the key-words *problem* and *issue*), creative thinking (tied to hypothesizing/speculating, through the use of *if*) and linguistic creativity (tied to the practice of evaluating, in the form of MIDs). Moreover, creative group problem-solving provides an overarching framework for these three aspects of creativity and the interpersonal practices of focusing on decisions, hypothesizing/speculating and evaluating. The term 'interpersonal creativity' is therefore used here to refer to the language that invokes the interpersonal discursive practices, the practices themselves, the specific stages of the creative problem-solving process that the practices construct, and the overall process itself. One of the clearest expositions of creative problem solving is provided by Henry (2001).

According to Henry (ibid.: 7), much of the literature on creativity in business is concerned with creative problem-solving and decision-making. She states: 'Clearly to solve problems effectively you need flexibility to use both imaginative and evaluative thought'. She argues that creative problem-solving models tend to have three parts:

- a problem-exploration stage
- an idea-generation stage
- a final action-planning stage

Each stage also has two phases: a first, expansive phase where imaginations are put to work, and a second phase, in which options from the first phase are chosen.

If we accept that business meetings are often concerned with discussing, preventing, and sometimes offering solutions to and solving real and hypothetical problems (that is, they are either fully or partly 'problem-oriented'), then there should be clear, recurrent traces of these practices in the discourse. As mentioned above, the language items to be analysed in this chapter are the keywords *problem*, *issue*, *if*, and MIDs. *Problem* and *issue* shed light on and index the creative process or action of pinpointing and exploring problems, even though they are not necessarily used in a linguistically creative sense, as is often the case, for instance, with MIDs.

The keyword *if* – arguably one of the biggest statistical surprises, in that it is so much more frequent in spoken business English compared to everyday conversation (see Chapter 4 for a list of keywords) – is highly multifunctional. For instance, it frequently appears in politeness-marking clusters, such as *if you look at* (see Chapter 5 for a discussion of clusters containing *if*). Notwithstanding this, in CANBEC *if* is often used to discuss hypothetical and probable situations, and unreal worlds, largely in the time frames of the present and future, and contributes to an understanding of the second stage of creative problem-solving: idea generation (see Willing, 1992, for a discussion of hypothesizing at this stage of problem-solving). Furthermore, *if*, perhaps more than any other lexical item, communicates creative thought.

Evaluation is a constant in many areas of institutional discourse. It is intrinsic to all stages of problem-solving (Hoey, 1983; Henry, 2001), and particularly in the final stage of developing the best course of action, so it is perhaps unsurprising that MIDs – which are inherently evaluative (Strässler, 1982; Moon, 1992, 1998; McCarthy, 1998; Carter, 2004; Handford and Koester, 2010) and which in themselves can often be interpreted as creative language use (Gibbs and Gerrig, 1989; Carter, 2004) – play a central role in many meetings. Furthermore, given the ever-present issue of relationships and face needs in business (Spencer-Oatey, 2000; McCarthy and Handford, 2004; Koester, 2010), MIDs (along with other critical items) elucidate how interlocutors in business manage collaboration and conflict when addressing or sidelining problems. Of course, this is not to suggest that these particular items are only found in creatively framed, problem-focused contexts: they can fulfil many functions and help to constitute a wide range of practices. Nevertheless, as Koester (2006: 101) shows, MIDs can play an important and statistically probable role in each stage of the problem-solving process. For instance, she mentions that the first stage features metaphors relating to pain (an example from CANBEC is *It's a pain having stuff here once it's done*), and the second stage includes items such as *figure out* and *sit down and* (*think/talk about*), which again are replicated in CANBEC. The third stage is explored in detail below.

Through exploring the critical items of *problem, issue, if* and MIDs from the corpus (as in step 2 of the methodology outlined in Chapter 2, page 39: 'pinpoint potentially important lexico-grammatical items and linguistic features'), we can begin to see how creativity, collaboration and conflict are discursively and interpersonally achieved in transactional and relational discourse. Furthermore, Chapter 2 (pages 46–7) showed how the concept of interdiscursivity can account for creativity in terms of the combination and embedding of genres, discourses and social practices (for example, Candlin and Maley, 1997). Lee (2008), discussing the potential benefits of corpora for discourse analysis, argues that collocations and clusters on the one side and intertextuality and interdiscursivity on the other refer to 'the same phenomenon: that language is never created fresh and from scratch, but borrows, repeats, quotes, implies and alludes to prior texts and prior ideas' (ibid.: 91). It is insights such as this which support the argument that repeated lexico-grammatical items can index existing practices in a recognizable and contextually constrained way, but which can nevertheless be applied to new problems and action points in meetings.

7.1 *Problem* and *issue*

As noted above, business is concerned with problems and decisions, both real and hypothetical. Conflict can arise from perceived problems, and decisions may be made in response to actual or potential problems. The purpose of this section is to analyse how problems are raised, bypassed or postponed through the items *problem* and *issue* and their collocates, thus beginning the explication of interpersonal creativity, and in particular the first stage of the creative problem-solving process, problem exploration (Henry, 2001). This will also show how speakers evaluate the situation and thus reflect their stance on the issue in question. For instance, S1's stance towards the issue of her pay is clear in the following exchange:

(7.1)

> *Internal meeting*
> Relationship of speakers: manager–subordinate
> Purpose: reviewing; planning
> Topic: HRM (performance review)

S1: But starting salaries for business advisors in Business Link Northants is twenty one thousand a year and I I'm I'm paid an awful lot less than that.
S2: Mm.
S1: Erm and it's not rea= I've already talked about it more than I even wanted to. It's not a huge **issue** but it it may become one one day.

Before moving on to the full investigation of *problem* and *issue* and how they invoke key aspects and practices of business meetings, it is worth briefly discussing what is meant by problem-solving. There are at least two contrasting positions regarding the processes of problem-solving and decision-making in business meetings. The first posits that, while decisions are eventually made in meetings, their occurrence is far less frequent, obvious or causal than is generally assumed. Issues are frequently discussed, but pin-pointing an explicit, recognizable decision made in relation to a specific issue is often difficult. The second position is more in accordance with the everyday view of decision-making, in that decisions are frequently made in meetings and follow a clear causal chain of problem–discussion–decision (compare Hoey's sequence of problem–response–evaluation, 1983). The former position is powerfully argued by Boden (1994), and work by Watson (2002) on (the lack of) causality in decision-making in organisations supports her stance, as does research by Mirivel and Tracy (2005). The latter position is upheld by Holmes and Stubbe (2003) and arguably underpins Koester's definition of genre (2006).

Boden argues that, in large, formal meetings, the purpose is often information-oriented, but in smaller meetings, 'the focus is 'at least in spirit' on decision-making. This is not to say that many decisions are actually *made* in most meetings' (1994: 84). She states:

Actual decisions in organisations are virtually invisible, yet they are the 'quanta' out of which pivotal choices are made, undesirable strategies avoided, and critical paths taken . . . decisions, as identifiable items, become clear only after their constitution. (Boden, 1994: 183)

Holmes and Stubbe (2003) argue that the type of workplace will affect the type of decision-making: in hierarchical establishments, a contentious decision will merely require the ratification of the chair, but in more egalitarian companies, such decisions will be approached collaboratively and with much negotiation. Decision-making is often 'the primary function of the meeting' (ibid.: 75).

Whilst the purpose of this section is not to evaluate these two contrasting positions, it is important to note that decision-making may not be as clear and obvious as might be expected. As such, if we accept that the word *problem* is often tied to decision-making (Hoey, 1983; McCarthy and Handford, 2004; O'Keeffe et al., 2007), and that *issue* is closely related to *problem* both semantically and in terms of collocation (as will be shown later on in this chapter), then these two major keywords may help to shed light on this process. In extract 7.2, the relationship between problems and decisions is clearly articulated by S3.

(7.2)

> *External meeting*
> Relationship of speakers: contractually bound
> Purpose: reviewing; planning
> Topic: logistics; production

> S1: Oliver Steffi is there anything else you want to sort of add to the agenda?
> S3: Yeah. (1 second) I would like to use the option to talk about the file which we created in regard to the last [inaudible].
> [drink being poured]
> S3: So in general this would show you (1 second) erm the problems which we have to to know the information which is behind all the different+
> S5: (clears throat)
> S3: +er decisions.

We could summarize this reasoning further as: raise problem – collect information – make decision. This clearly resembles Henry's three stages (2001), with the collecting of information being achieved through and therefore roughly equivalent to generating ideas.

Goals can also be directly related to the problem-solving process – both in terms of achieving higher-level goals (such as making a profit) and more local goals (such as improving the efficiency of a specific aspect of the company's operation). In answer to the question of where discursive practices fit into this process, Brown and Duguid's perspective that practice is 'the internal life of process' (2000: 95) is apposite, with each of the stages of the process a potential practice or bundle of practices.

This section now moves on to a discussion of two keywords from the corpus: *problem* and *issue*. These synonyms occur very high on the keyword list presented on page 106 of Chapter 4 (rank 31 and 34 respectively), and as such play a far more frequent role than they do in everyday speech. Not only do the two items share meaning at the semantic level, and can appear in the same stages of the unfolding discourse, they also exhibit parallel patterns in semantic/collocational/colligational terms. Table 7.1 shows the top ten collocations for each item. The contents of the brackets indicate the position of the collocate left (L) or right (R) of the node – for example, (L1) is the word immediately to the left of the keyword, and (R4) is the word four spaces to the right of the keyword.

Table 7.1   Collocates of **issue** *and* **problem**

#	Issue	Problem
1	the (L1)	the (L1)
2	that (L4)	that (L4)
3	and (R1)	with (R1)
4	not (L2)	it's (L3)
5	yeah (R2)	yeah (R2)
6	it's (L3)	you (R4)
7	that's (L2)	have (L2)
8	but (L5)	that's (L2)
9	with (R1)	not (L2)
10	you (R4)	and (L4)

The two lists of collocates are strikingly similar, not just in that nine of the ten words are shared (only *have* with *problem*, and *but* with *issue* are not shared), but also the positions of the collocates. Both nouns form the following patterns:

Collocational and colligational patterns for **issue/problem**

	L3	L2	L1	node	R1	R2
S1			the	issue/problem	with	
		that's	the	issue/problem		
	(it's)	not	the	issue/problem		
S2						Yeah
S1	anaphoric deictic pronoun	+(negative adverb *not*)	+definite article	+node		
S2						+affirmative informal response token

The following concordances show how these patterns feature in co-text.

Concordance lines for **problem** *and* **issue**

Because that's the **problem** with the standing edition is that erm we weren't anticipating spending all that time actually working on a keyboard.

[S1:] Right. The point is of now after we've met [inaudible] that's the **issue**. [S6?:] Okay. Yeah. But+

No but that that's not the **issue** is it. He doesn't want to have that thing collapse on the front of a train and derail it

---

These findings lend weight to the argument that these two words are potentially synonymous, because at the colligational and collocational levels they are virtually identical, apart from the verb *have* which competes for position L2 among the collocates of *problem*. If one were to accept the view that meaning is contained within the words themselves, then it would be reasonable to expect that these words, their collocations and colligations would occur in a similar fashion across different business contexts.

However, when these two words are compared in terms of specific contexts, it becomes clear that there are significant differences in their use, supporting the argument that meaning is embedded in the context rather than in the words themselves (as we have already seen with the deontic clusters *you have to* in Chapter 2 and *you need to* in Chapter 5). In terms of the relationship of speakers, while the occurrence of the two items is similar in external meetings, it is very different in the internal meeting categories: whereas *problem* occurs more in peer communication, *issue* occurs more in manager–subordinate communication. Moreover, in terms of company, there are some striking differences. *Problem* occurs most frequently in a range of (British) manufacturing companies, but far less frequently in international pharmaceutical companies, whereas for *issue* the opposite holds. Equally significant are the topic results. While *problem* occurs most frequently in procedure and technical meetings, *issue* does not occur at all in these meetings. While both *problem* and *issue* occur in sales and marketing meetings, *issue* is approximately five times less likely in such meetings. Both items occur with fairly equal frequency in logistics meetings. Factors such as the size of the organization and speaker birthplace do not seem to affect the figures.

It should therefore be clear that these two apparent synonyms behave very similarly at the lexico-grammatical level and very differently at the contextual level. Occurrences vary considerably depending on topic, relationship of speakers and company type, and yet in terms of collocation and colligation they are largely equivalent. The following extract (7.3) from a meeting between managers of a museum shows how these two nouns can occur together, but with slightly different functions:

(7.3)

> *Internal meeting*
> Relationship of speakers: peer
> Purpose: reviewing
> Topic: marketing; production

S3: I mean there are two **issues**. The first is c= can you access that infor-mation off Leon's computer.
(2.5 seconds)
S1: Erm (4 seconds) yeah. Theoretically. Yeah. It depends where it is.
S3: Cos the other thi=. [laughs] Well I I thi= think that's another **issue**. And the other the and and another **issue** which comes on= onto that is that erm I'm still waiting he s= that cos (1.5 seconds) apparently one of the **problems** with getting some of the information off the computer is the fact that erm that particular (1 second) the s= the software is not as powerful as the stuff we've got on the the new computer that he's got. (3 seconds) There was an **issue** about getting the stuff off+
S4: No. He's got the same+
S3: +in the format.

This extract shows that, whilst the two nouns are closely related, they are not necessarily interchangeable. Although both here have a discourse prosody of difficulty, *problem* is more similar to an obstacle or something specific that should be solved, whereas *issue* may be perceived as being more nebulous, perhaps broader, and requiring consideration and discussion. *Problem* may also be more categori-cal, which would help to explain why it is more frequent in peer than manager–subordinate communication: there seems to be less attention paid to face concerns in peer meetings (Holmes and Stubbe, 2003), so we can find *issue* being used euphemistically by managers rather than the less equivocal and therefore more face-threatening *problem*.

When comparing internal and external meetings, the behaviour of *problem* and *issue* suggests that considerable differences may exist in the decision-making process. For example, in external communication, decisions may not be made in the meeting itself: instead, external meetings often provide a platform for explaining or informing partici-pants about decisions already made, or rejecting or agreeing to deci-sions already made, or signalling agreement or discontent with decisions made, or discussing or hinting at the possible implications of decisions made.

In internal meetings a different situation exists. The purpose of manager–subordinate meetings often contrasts with peer meetings. Manager–subordinate meetings frequently involve the conveying of information from manager to subordinate, whereas peer meetings are often called to discuss problems and make decisions. Strategy meetings would be the clearest example of this, which by definition are decision-focused (Johnson et al., 2007). In the strategy meeting below (extracts 7.4 and 7.5), members of the upper management are foregrounding practical problems concerning design issues with a new factory that require solutions (or actions) via appropriate deci-sions. S1 is the managing director, S2 is the technical director and S3 is the finance director.

(7.4)

> *Internal meeting*
> Relationship of speakers: peer
> Purpose: planning
> Topic: strategy

> S2: And these= and remember this is where there's been a **problem** so you've got an imbalance of your chemicals.
> S1: Okay so right. So there may be some=
> S2: So these are the ones that we need to get out of the building quickly.

Interestingly, this meeting features more occurrences of the word *decision* (eight occurrences) than the combined total of *issue* and *problem* (seven). This is the only meeting in the whole corpus to exhibit such behaviour, and *decision* is far more common in strat-egy meetings than any other type of meeting. The use of *decision* in this meeting is more in line with Holmes and Stubbe's (2003) more explicit portrayal of decision-making outlined earlier in this chapter.

(7.5)

> S1: Right. So in fact there's e= th= the there's actions outstanding for this week still which we can finalize when when Derek's here.
> (1 second)

S3: Yeah.
S1: I've got a feeling he'll bottle out (1 second) of **decision making**. ... But I I'll= I wanna make that **decision**. Harry said we could make that **decision** providing we've got er a refund clause.

It is also worth noting that, while *issue* and *problem* are keywords in the full CANBEC corpus, and in both the external meeting and internal meeting sub-corpora (outlined in the Appendix), indicating that they are used more frequently in both internal and external meetings than in everyday social and intimate conversations, the word *decision* is not. In a ten-million-word corpus of written business English (the Wolverhampton Business Corpus), the situation is somewhat different, with *problem* occurring far less than *issue*, and the frequency of *decision* falling between the two.

The items *problem* and *issue* are highly significant in many types of business meetings, especially internal meetings, and are potentially primed (Hoey, 2005) to both occur at different stages of and to bring into focus certain decision-related practices and processes. These include flagging something as needing discussion (*this is a problem*), or showing a decision is not needed (*so not a problem there*), or hinting that something may become an issue in the future. We also saw how much the context affects the frequency and use of these items, even when the collocations are largely the same. Such findings clearly demonstrate that concordance lines of whole corpora can only contribute so much to the understanding of particular items, and that Sinclair's idiom principle (1991, and see Chapter 4 of this volume) does indeed require a contextual foundation in order to more fully account for the way items behave in discourse.

7.2 *If*

In Chapter 5, hypothesizing/speculating was categorized as a recurrent interactional practice in business meetings, with the keyword *if* often forming part of clusters used to index this practice – for example, *if you* and *so if*. This section will look at the role *if* can play in what Cook describes as 'the relationship between the manipulation of linguistic forms and the generation of hypothetical realities' (2001: 36)[1], which concerns creative thinking in our framework of interpersonal creativity, and can elucidate Henry's (2001) second stage of creative problem-solving (idea generation) at the text level.

This section first looks at the collocations, colligations and some of the most frequent clusters involving *if*, before going on to discuss how it is used in internal and external meetings. The most frequent collocations of *if* are shown below in their most typical positions in relation to the node word.

Collocational patterns for if

L2	L1	node	R1
Yeah	and/but	if	you/we/they/it's
	that	if	you

The most frequent top ten verb lemmas that are found in the R2/R3 positions after *if* (that is, the second or third word after the node) are *can, have, get, got, want, say, look, could, are* and *gonna*. Typical collocations are shown below.

Collocational and colligational patterns for if (R2 and R3)

L2	L1	node	R1	R2	R3
Yeah	and	if	you/we	can/could	have/get/
		if	you/we	have/get/want/got	want /say the
(affirmative informal response token)	+conjunction	+node	+pronoun	+verb	

Yeah can be used here as a backchannel which precedes the take-up of the turn by another participant with *if*. *If* is therefore in turn-initial position. Alternatively, the speaker may use *yeah* rhetorically within a turn. These collocations are grammatically interesting, as eight out of the ten verbs are in the present tense, further reinforcing the notion that much business talk[2] involves present and particularly future situations (which the high frequency of simple past forms in the negative-keyword list in Chapter 4 would also indirectly suggest). By hypothesizing about contemporaneous problems, or possible future problems, or desirable situations, business people hope to understand, prevent or encourage them through the creation of irrealis modes. According to McCarthy and Handford (2004), and O'Keeffe et al. (2007) it is characteristics such as these that mark spoken business discourse as a distinct institutional order.

*Table 7.2   Four-word clusters with **if***

Cluster	Internal meetings total	Density	External meetings total	Density
I don't know if	81	0.12	11	0.046
if we can get	49	0.073	17	0.072
if you look at	45	0.07	9	0.038
you know if you	29	0.043	10	0.042
I think if we	28	0.041	10	0.042
if you want to	26	0.039	10	0.042
I mean if you	24	0.035	7	0.03
see if we can	24	0.035	8	0.034
if we look at	21	0.031	9	0.037

Table 7.2 shows the top four-word clusters involving *if*, providing a snapshot of those in the corpus. The second and third columns in this table show the results from internal meetings, with the total number of occurrences and the density figures (calculated by multiplying the number of occurrences by 1,000 and then dividing that number by the total in the relevant sub-corpus). The fourth and fifth columns show the equivalent results for external meetings.

Biber and Conrad's (1999) proposal that ten occurrences per million words is significant means that all of these clusters are very significant: the least frequent cluster in external meetings – *I mean if you* – occurs 30 times per million words, and the most frequent in internal meetings – *I don't know if* – occurs 120 times. As the figures show, many of these clusters occur fairly equally in external meetings and internal meetings. Exceptions are *I don't know if* and *if you look at*, which are more than twice as frequent in internal meetings. Interestingly, *if we look at* is more frequent in external meetings, which is explicable in terms of the display of collaboration and convergence invoked by inclusive *we* (see Chapter 6 for a discussion of *we*). These three clusters, along with the fragment *see if we can* are often not strictly conditionals, but instead are employed to issue face-protecting 'politeness directives' (Carter and McCarthy, 2006: 757) – for example, pointing participants to some aspect of the agenda or presentation. Next, the highly significant two-word cluster *if you* will be analysed to show a small degree of its multifunctionality in internal and external meetings.

CLUSTER: *if you*

Key practice: hypothesizing

Occurrence in external meetings: 375
✎ *frequency per million words: 1,762*
Occurrence in internal meetings: 934
✎ *frequency per million words: 1,422*

If you is the eleventh most frequent two-word cluster, occurring 1,309 times, and is more frequent in external than internal meetings. It is not practically possible to outline all the different contexts in which it is used and the different uses it has, so here we will see how it forms the head of a 'frame' (O'Keeffe et al., 2007) which occurs in many meetings. This frame collocates with verbs relating to speech and tends to be used in negotiation phases of meetings. The colligation can be summarized and exemplified as follows:

*Colligational patterns for **if you***

If	you	say	"Well we'll do that"
If	you	were to say	"Right"
(If)	+(personal pronoun)	+reporting verb	+discourse marker + reported clause

Extract 7.6 from a sales meeting shows the sales person (S1) outlining a possible, desirable future situation, with the client (S2) hypothetically buying more stock (*up to sixteen*) and the sales person therefore being able to offer a more competitive price (*we're prepared to do something*).

(7.6)

External meeting
Relationship of speakers: non-contractually bound
Purpose: buying/selling/promoting a product
Topic: sales

S1: Erm but you know we're prepared to do something like **if you say** **"Well** look I'm pretty sure that we're gonna be up to sixteen by by Christmas time or+
S2: Yeah.
S1: +by er April".

This cluster is used to speculate, or to create a notion of irrealis. And, as is often the case with this semi-fixed expression in external meetings, it is employed here to show why a mutual relationship would be beneficial through an imagined scenario in which the two companies are collaborating more closely.

The same cluster is also found in internal meetings, and yet it tends to have a very different discourse prosody. There is a strong contrast when *if you* is used in internal meetings (generally negative possibility) compared to external meetings (positive possibility). In internal meetings, speculation and irrealis are often employed to predict and therefore prevent possible or actual problems mushrooming, whereas, in external meetings, the same language can be used to visualize a better future situation between the two companies. In other words, in internal meetings the cluster is used to (negatively) evaluate situations and thus direct the participants towards certain actions. The extract below from an internal meeting in an IT company further highlights this, with the manager (S1) explaining to his subordinate the possible problems involved with the proposed procedure.

(7.7)

> *Internal meeting*
> Relationship of speakers: manager–subordinate
> Purpose: reviewing; planning
> Topic: technical

S1: But I still don't wanna go to John and say "John. Here's a purchase requisition for eighteen thousand pounds". In a month when we know we will not do well in sales+

S2: Yeah.

S1: +er and also what it means is that he will then raise "Well hang on. You told me we were gonna get [inaudible] on a per user basis so start charging users". Which is a massive project. I don't think he is aware of how much is involved. And also the amount of aggro it will cause with customers **if you say "Right** we're taking this away from you now".

This extract contrasts strongly with extract 7.6 from the external meeting in terms of discourse prosody, and the colligation serves a preventative function (warning against or emphasizing the potential negative effects of an action), as opposed to the encouraging role noted in many external meetings. It is also worth noting how the discursive practice of directing a subordinate is achieved through again imagining possible conversations.

It is also evident that, like *I don't know if*, several clusters involving *if* (such as most of those in table 7.2) do not neatly fit into traditional grammatical descriptions of conditional statements. Indeed, within the corpus the types of past and, to a lesser extent, present, unreal conditionals found in language textbooks are relatively rare (such as *if I had done it, I wouldn't have . . .* or *if I was there, I would . . .*), and the corpus highlights several *if* clusters that have nothing to do with conditionality. Findings like this add considerable support to the argument that language-driven studies of discourse can yield results which more top-down approaches cannot (Sinclair, 1991).

This section has explored how *if* is used in external and internal meetings to generate ideas, hypothesize, speculate and indirectly encourage or direct interlocutors towards or away from a particular situation, action or decision. As is the case with so many of the items in the book, only a brief discussion is possible, and further research is required to find out more about this fascinating word and its col-locations. Context has been shown once again to have a consider-able bearing on the use of the item, particularly in terms of discourse prosody and the practices the item reflexively constitutes.

7.3 Metaphors and idioms

This section will look at interpersonal creativity in terms of linguis-tic creativity, and how it invokes evaluation in problem-focused and action-planning discourse. Linguistic creativity can involve forms such as idioms, metaphors, repetition, relexicalization, metonymy, meronymy, hyperbole and litotes (Low, 1988; Tannen, 1989; Gibbs, 1994; McCarthy, 1998; Carter, 2004; O'Keeffe et al., 2007), although research on such creative language use in workplace discourse is still relatively nascent (but see Koester, 2000, 2006; McCarthy and Handford, 2004; Handford and Koester, 2010). The focus here is on all linguistic, as opposed to conceptual (Lakoff and Johnson, 1980), meta-phors, as well as idioms, across the nine business meetings in the sub-corpus (see the Appendix for a breakdown of this sub-corpus), showing how they have been pinpointed, how they have been categorized and what roles they play in the discourse. The approach used here has been developed from work by Moon (1998), Cameron (2003), Carter (2004) and Koester (2006) and applied to conflictual meetings from the CANBEC and ABOT corpora by Handford and Koester (2010). As only a cursory discussion of the identification and categorization proc-esses is possible here, the reader is directed towards the Handford and Koester article, which explores these areas in much more depth.

Cameron (2003) states that there are three basic approaches to the study of naturally occurring (as opposed to invented) linguistic metaphors and idioms. The first method involves looking for items that are 'indisputably figurative' (ibid.: 58) across various texts. Important work by Deignan (1999, 2005) has been carried out on the British National Corpus (BNC) using this method. The second method involves pinpointing items that have a particular function in the discourse – for example, work by Drew and Holt (1998, 2005), which looks at how idiomatic language can be used to summarize, close or shift the topic. The third approach, applied here, involves the analyst deciding on each potentially metaphorical and idiomatic item as it occurs within a complete text. While such an approach is a far more time-consuming and inferential process than the first two approaches, it does allow for 'far greater insights into the pragmatic, semantic and lexico-grammatical realization of idiomatic language as it occurs in real-time discourse' (Handford and Koester, 2010: 29). It also enables the discussion of the use of metaphors and idioms across whole texts, unlike the first two approaches (Cameron, 2003).

In terms of how an item (a word or phrase) can be identified as being 'potentially metaphoric', Cameron (ibid.) proposes the following two steps:

1 It appears incongruous with its context of use, as there is another (more 'literal' or basic) way of interpreting the item which is inconsistent with its present discourse context.
2 The incongruity can be resolved – that is, it is neither a mistake nor nonsense.

Moon's (1998) definition has been applied to pinpoint idioms. According to her, idioms are items that cannot be broken down into their constituent parts because a semantic, pragmatic or grammatical anomaly would result. The metaphors and idioms (MIDs) are categorized in table 7.3 (page 202) with examples[3].

Extract 7.8, from the beginning of an external, non-contractually bound meeting, shows how some of the examples given in table 7.3 feature in problem-solving discourse. Each item's possible categorization is put in square brackets. This process was conducted for the 88,492 words in the sub-corpus. The extract also shows how MIDs are often indirect and thus allow speakers to deal with potentially face-threatening topics (such as deciding what will be discussed, the type of foreseen relationship and the financial obligations that the future relationship would incur) in a collaborative, non-conflictual way.

Table 7.3   Categories of MIDs, based on Moon (1998) and Koester (2006)

Metaphors	Extended opaque frozen metaphors ('classic' idioms): *spending money like water*
	Extended spatial/motion metaphors: *plunge into the technical aspects*
	Other metaphors and metaphorical collocations: *they'd been bitten by a couple of other ISPs; looking to raise awareness*
Formulae	Cultural allusions – proverbs, maxims, catchphrases: *donkeys' years*
	Idiomatic prefabricated phrases or clauses: *in our favour; issues (you) still have outstanding; bearing in mind*
Anomalous collocations	*day in day out; other than the fact that*
Idiomatic phrasal verbs	*fill you in on; put together a meeting*

(7.8)

External meeting
Relationship of speakers: non-contractually bound
Purpose: giving and receiving information/advice
Topic: sales; technical

S2: Thank you very much. Erm okay before we sort of **plunge into** [*spatial metaphor*] the technical aspects of this is is there any commercial **issues that you still have outstanding** [*idiomatic prefabricated phrase / anomalous collocation*] at the moment?

S1: Well no **other than the fact that** [*anomalous collocation*] erm (2 seconds) when we spoke last+

S2: Mhm.

S1: +I t= I I gave you a brief outline of what **we are looking to** [*metaphor*] **put together** [*idiomatic phrasal verb*].

S5: Yeah.

S1: And **had a look at** [*idiomatic prefabricated phrase*] the resell agreement et cetera.

S2: Mhm.

S1: Erm **bearing in mind** [*metaphor / idiomatic prefabricated phrase*] that we're not a reseller.

Table 7.4   Breakdown of MIDs for all meetings

Category	Amount/density per 1,000 words
Metaphor (total)	898 / 10.1
Extended opaque frozen metaphor	117 / 1.3
Extended spatial/motion metaphor	297 / 3.4
Other metaphors and metaphorical collocations	484 / 5.47
Formulae (total)	253 / 2.85
Cultural allusions	82 / 0.9
Idiomatic prefabricated phrases/clauses	171 / 1.93
Anomalous collocations	232 / 2.62
Idiomatic phrasal verbs	333 / 3.76

Overall density of MIDs: 19.4

Table 7.4 shows that a MID occurs almost every 50 words in the sub-corpus, which is almost three times higher than in Koester's workplace corpus (2006). This suggests that MIDs may be more frequent in business meetings than in other types of institutional discourse, as Koester's corpus embodies a wide range of workplace genres. As business meetings are arguably the most transactional form of business discourse (Boden, 1994), this finding appears to run counter to Carter (2004: 79), who argues that the more transactional a speech event, the less likely we are to find instances of linguistic creativity. The density of items reported here is also much higher than that recorded by Strässler (1982), who analysed idioms in spoken interactions of various types. Therefore, while more systematic research across genres and registers is needed to corroborate these tentative claims (ideally by inter-rater analysis – see Cameron, 2003; Handford and Koester, 2010), the statistics presented here suggest the importance of MIDs in the interactional construction of business meetings.

As table 7.4 shows, the most frequent type of MIDs is metaphor, which totals more than the other three categories combined and accounts for slightly over one per cent of the data. Other metaphors (sometimes involving single words) and metaphorical collocations account for the largest number of examples from this category. Cultural allusions – for instance, proverbs and maxims – are least frequent overall. When they do occur, they are uttered overwhelmingly by the most senior person present, as are frozen metaphors.

Cultural allusions and metaphors also tend to be extremely evaluative, a finding duplicated in Koester's study (2006). Lyotard, commenting on popular sayings, proverbs and maxims, states, 'they are like little splinters of potential narratives, or moulds of old ones, which have continued to circulate on certain levels of the contemporary social edifice' (1979: 22). Here, the level is that of the powerful speaker judging and/or advising on the issues at hand or the endeavours of others in internal and external meetings. Spatial and motion metaphors, in addition, are often employed to outline or review, and evaluate, processes or plans. The remaining categories are found to fulfil a variety of roles, which will be discussed further. The ratio of each type of idiom is very similar throughout each individual meeting.

When internal meetings and external meetings are compared, the most striking finding is the relative frequency of MIDs, with densities per 1,000 words of 22.6 and 15.4 respectively (see figure 7.1 for a more detailed breakdown). The overall ratio of different types of idiom remains fairly constant, however, with metaphors totalling more than the other three categories combined in both internal meetings and external meetings (the relative ratio for metaphors, formulae, anomalous collocations and idiomatic phrasal verbs in external meetings and in internal meetings is approximately 16:4:4:6).

In determining what factors may affect the use of MIDs, the topic of the meeting does not seem to have much bearing. Whereas one internal sales meeting in the sub-corpus has a density of 18.3, the external sales meeting has a density of 13.7. An even greater difference is found between internal and external production meetings (with the density in two internal meetings approximately double the 10.8 found in an external meeting). While both internal and external procedure meetings have high densities (26.3 internal and 23.1 external), they also contain a high level of disagreement, particularly the external meetings. The relationship between disagreement and the use of MIDs will be further explored below. Company size does not appear to influence the density either, with the highest (26.3) and the lowest (10.8) figures both coming from companies with over 10,000 employees. Nor does the type of company seem to be relevant.

The relationship of speakers, in contrast, does appear relevant: as noted above, idioms are much more frequent in internal meetings than external meetings, and figure 7.1 shows that MIDs are very frequent in manager–subordinate meetings and even more so in peer meetings. External contractually bound meetings feature the lowest density overall, although one highly conflictual, non-contractually

Figure 7.1   Density of MIDs according to relationship

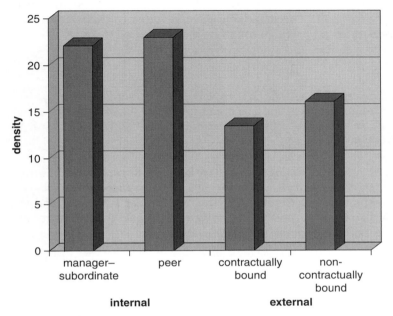

bound meeting has a very high density. We will now examine some extracts from internal and then external meetings.

As shown in extract 7.8, the beginning of external meetings (stage 1 in Chapter 3), in which the participants confirm the agenda, can feature a high proportion of MIDs, and there are similarities at the beginning of internal meetings as well. The first 844 words of the internal manager–subordinate sales meeting in extract 7.9 involve a monologue by the managing director, in which he reviews and evaluates the problematically poor sales over the past few months and the recent, better results, particularly by one sales team, *WHL*. This review phase has a density of MIDs of 35.5. This is extremely high, and almost double the density across the whole meeting. Over a third of this language comprises extended opaque frozen metaphors, and as such is strongly evaluative: *cut back to the bone*; *diabolical month*; *crawl back out of the woodwork*. This monologue reflects and reinforces (negotiates) the power role of the managing director (it would be inappropriate for one of the sales staff to address the managing director in such baldly evaluative language), but also creates a sense of convergence. MIDs can be used to increase degrees of intimacy and soften the force of negative evaluations (Carter, 2004), and extract 7.9 demonstrates this. The choice of pronouns further enhances this convergent tone, and also mitigates the potential face-threat to the staff. The managing director talks of the shared pain, and encourages all participants to *keep our fingers crossed*.

(7.9)

> *Internal meeting*
> Relationship of speakers: manager–subordinate
> Purpose: reviewing
> Topic: sales

> S1:   if things keep **coming back** and we **keep our fingers crossed** ... erm ... so that's worked well. WHL h= have had ... an **absolutely cracking** ... September and October. Particularly October (1 second) and the November looks pretty good as well. So the **pain** that we've got will be more than compensated for by WHL.

Later in this monthly sales review meeting, each member of the sales team reports on his or her progress over the past month and any relevant decisions and action plans that have been made. Each of the five members of the sales team finishes the update with a metaphor or idiom, which is consistently followed by a positive idiomatic evaluation by the managing director. In extract 7.10, the sales person announces the decision that the team has to *sit tight* (that is, do nothing for the moment), but that (slow) progress is being made (*moving forward*). The managing director then evaluates this situation and decision positively.

(7.10)

> S4:   So we've gotta sort of **sit tight** with that. But no it's it's= it is **moving forward** but it is ... still little bit slow.
> S1:   **Magic**. (1 second) **Looking good**. Thanks Phil. Eddie what you got?

The use of such MIDs by staff members allows the other participants to realize that the speaker has come to the end of the turn, and the evaluative, power-invested MID helps create a sense of cooperative autonomy: the sales person is displaying control over his or her area of work and is therefore of worth to the group. By positively evaluating each update through MIDs, the managing director addresses the face needs of his staff – which should further motivate them – and he signals his necessary agreement that this sales person's turn is complete. He also fulfils his position of power: it is the prerogative of the manager and the manager alone to evaluate the performance of the subordinate staff in this context, and to signal that the discussion should move on to the next speaker.

MIDs can also be found during small talk – for instance, before the formal beginning of the meeting. In the following peer meeting, S1 is the technical director and S2 is the finance director; they are both waiting for the sales director to arrive. There has been a certain amount of inter-departmental tension in the company at the directors' level, which appears again later in the meeting. This small-talk phase, however, is much more light-hearted.

(7.11)

Internal meeting
Relationship of speakers: peer
Purpose: planning
Topic: procedure

S1: But er= oh. Cos there's **inter-manager bickering going on** at the moment.

S2: [laughs]

S1: [inaudible]

S2: Erm yeah I met quite a few customers this morning. Erm anyway **cut a long story short** Doyle Grant who are an accountants in= said would we be prepared to do a talk.

[5 turns removed from extract]

S2: Then about three press **came up to** me. Really **stroppy big sort of lady came up to me and said** "Why don't we ever get any copy from you?" you know in a sort of South African accent. And I said "**Darling** who are you?" [laughs] And I was talking to the Doyle Grant lady+

Here the story creates a sense of convergence, which may be highly purposive in light of the bickering referred to half-jokingly at the beginning of the extract. The MIDs help to introduce the frame (*cut a long story short*) and embellish the story (*stroppy big sort of lady*). It is also a vehicle for humour (*Darling*), which is 'a useful means for creating solidarity' (Holmes and Stubbe, 2003: 134; see also Holmes, 2007, for a discussion of creativity, humour and the achievement of relational and transactional goals in the workplace).

Extract 7.12 is taken from later in this meeting. It shows the finance director (S2) and sales director (S3) telling the technical director (S1) that the attitude of the technical staff needs to change. Once again, this highly evaluative and face-threatening proposal is hedged using idiomatic language.

(7.12)

> S2: I think it's also really important+
> S3: Yeah. That's not a bad idea.
> S2: +something we need to **work forward to** is is= which is a bit controversial but is also the attitude as well is that it is very **now**. If this is going to happen and it's project management driven to be honest with you Doz their+
> S1: Mm.
> S2: +**attitude's got to be customer**. You know **"Good morning this is your salary talking"**+
> S1: Mm.
> S2: +is very much gonna be the way **it'll go forward**.

This decision concerning the required change in the technical staff's attitude was made in a previous meeting, with the support of the company managing director, and was then communicated to the technical staff by the technical director on the same day in subsequent meetings. The extract is also interesting because it features the very common conceptual metaphor of (forward) movement as progress (Handford and Koester, 2010): *something we need to work forward to; the way it'll go forward.*

While the parity of the status of the speakers in the peer meeting above is straightforward, the same is not true in all peer meetings, and can lead to interesting negotiation of identities and issues. In extract 7.13 from an internal peer meeting, the British chair (S1) is not the most senior person present in terms of status, and the most senior person (S4, referred to as *Lee*), from Vietnam, does not appear to want to agree with the course of action proposed by the chair (in a follow-up interview, the chair commented that this was usual behaviour on the part of S4). There is much disagreement, and it is often expressed through MIDs. It seems that both speakers seek to assert power through the use of this language. This meeting has the highest overall density of MIDs across all nine meetings (26.3), and supports Koester's (2006) finding that it is problem-focused and decision-making discussions that feature the highest density of idiomatic language. In the extract below, S1 and S4 have been discussing the time schedule for the proposed changeover. S4 is proposing changing the chair's plan, but the chair is not keen on his idea.

(7.13)

> *Internal meeting*
> Relationship of speakers: peer
> Purpose: planning; task-/problem-oriented
> Topic: technical; procedure

S1: I think it's **quite late in the day** Lee to erm= (1.5 seconds) for us to **set up** a+

S4: Okay.

S1: +server to test. I mean it's just can we is it is it possible=

S4: No I mean I probably have a machine that er+

S1: Yeah.

S4: +only have er two connection and just repatch one of them to (1 second) [inaudible]

S1: I think **you're blazing a trail**. So we might have to just try it. And=

S4: Well **we're blazing a trail** but we do that anyway. I mean this is+

S1 attempts to dissuade S4 and show that his suggested course of action is a problem by using the extended opaque frozen metaphors *late in the day* and *blazing a trail*. As noted by Koester (2006), such metaphors, along with cultural allusions, tend to be the most evaluative form of idiom, so these metaphors emphasize the chair's lack of enthusiasm for the proposals. S4 also employs what Kotthoff terms an 'opposition format' (1993: 202) – that is, when a 'rhetorically important word of the previous utterance is picked up and builds the centre of the countermove' (ibid.) – by adopting the *blazing a trail* metaphor to support his position. Such conflictual turn-structure will be discussed further in Chapter 8. His choice of pronoun is also significant, lending the collaborative weight of *we* to his position: in this meeting that involves six speakers and 11 participants, he is the only one to make this proposal to change the schedule; moreover, despite his senior position, he is the only employee present from his section.

Although it is a peer meeting (given the role of the chair and the decision-making purpose of the meeting), the relative statuses of the participants are still relevant and alluded to. This is evident in the following phatic interlude (extract 7.14) towards the end of the meeting when the chair (S1, referred to here as *John*) has managed to persuade S4 to agree with the proposed course of action.

(7.14)

S4: So John you gonna **take us out** when this [inaudible]?
(2 seconds)
S1: Er yeah I'm sure the network team will be **taking you all out** when we're all **on** their new network.
S4: No I want you. You.
[laughter]
S4: You. [inaudible]
S1: It's it's still not my project. [inhales] It never was.
S4: Oh it's not your project? Oh I thought it was your project.
S1: No **I've just got the biggest mouth**.
SM: [laughs]
S1: Erm.
S4: **He's backing off now** so that's good. It's okay.
S1: You have to disassociate yourself [inaudible].
SM: [laughs]

It would be arguably inconceivable for a subordinate of S1 to utter the metaphorical metastatement *He's backing off now so that's good*, which asserts the relative power of the speaker even more through the choice of the pronoun *He* (thus addressing the 'audience' and not S1, and denying S1 the right to respond without considerable threat to S1's own face), as well as the potentially face-threatening *I want you. You.* Even the request to be taken out might be seen as inappropriate. This demonstrates that even in a phatic exchange, with a socializing topic that it is not related to the agenda, the status of the speakers is still relevant and is evident in their choice of language. S4 subtly, or not so subtly, reminds S1 and the other participants of his seniority. S1 could be seen as employing a negative politeness strategy by self-deprecatingly saying *I've just got the biggest mouth*, which may be politic given that he has not allowed his senior to direct the course of action (in a follow-up interview, S1 described their relative status as follows: 'Lee (S4) was an all-powerful director, and I was a grunt'). The choice of pronoun in *He's backing off now* can also be seen to be a power token, in that S4 is addressing the other participants and commenting on S1's stance. The alternative *You're backing off now* appears, comparatively, less divergent, less evaluative and less dominant.

In extract 7.8 from the external non-contractually bound sales meeting (and also in extract 3.10 from the contractually bound pharmaceutical meeting analysed in Chapter 3 – refer to pages 84–5 for the extract), we saw how MIDs are often employed to soften evaluations and potentially face-threatening communication. For instance, in extract 3.10, a lot of time is spent discussing potential and actual problems and solutions in projects. This involves many spatial/ motion metaphors, such as *we're saying bring forward increase quantity* (lines 23–4). Where problems exist, they are often downplayed through metaphor (combined with other interpersonal items such as vague language and the indeterminate *we*): *If we haven't got things in place* (line 31). Such spatial/motion metaphors also indicate the positive progress being made, as well as the worth and efficacy of the relationship, as in these examples from a different stage of the meeting: *we've got a way ahead, we are on the same level* and *I can see where you're coming from.*

Compared to the internal meeting analysed in extracts 7.13 and 7.14, the chair's status in the long pharmaceutical meeting is not challenged or negotiated to the same extent through idiom, although S1 (the chair) does use more idioms than the other speakers. This lack of negotiation partly explains the low density of MIDs apparent in this meeting (a density of 10.8). The meeting also involves three L2-English speakers, which could be an additional factor in the ability and/or willingness of participants to use metaphorical language (see Prodromou, 2008). Nevertheless, in the corpus there is plenty of evidence of L2 speakers of English regularly using metaphorical language appropriately – for instance, S4 from Vietnam in extracts 7.13 and 7.14, or S3 from Germany in 7.2. This is an area that requires further systematic research, and will be touched on again in Chapter 9.

In general, external meetings in CANBEC, like internal meetings, do not feature explicit conflict. While the requisite negotiation of obligation and relationships in both internal and external business meetings means that the potential for conflict is ubiquitous, the preference in meetings in CANBEC favours the collaborative, non-face-threatening language options. Nevertheless, conflict does on occasion spiral clearly upwards, and one external meeting, from which extract 7.15 is taken, consistently features the two participants attempting to assert superiority and aggressively threaten each other's personal and professional (Charles, 1996) sense of face. This is consistently achieved during the meeting through MIDs: *it's not rocket science, the rent's stupid, you must be welcomed up and down the country.* The density of idioms as stated earlier is very high (23.1, compared to 15.4 for all external meetings), even compared to internal meetings, and is accounted for by the consistent movement towards divergence throughout the meeting. Divergent turn-taking and repetition will be discussed in Chapter 8 (see also Handford and Koester, 2010), but extract 7.15 shows how the speakers aggressively disagree with each other over perceived problems through face-threatening MIDs. S1 in this extract is the operations controller of a pub chain and S2 is the estates manager from the brewer.

(7.15)

External meeting
Relationship of speakers: contractually bound
Purpose: buying/selling/promoting a product; task-/problem-oriented
Topic: procedure; logistics

S2: Erm and these are the er= these are the letters. (1.5 seconds) Er there's two of each. (1.5 seconds) Basically it s= doesn't really anything that I haven't already told you. (1.5 seconds) Apart from **stinging** you for the legal fees.

(1.5 seconds)

S1: **Beg your pardon?**

(3 seconds)

S2: It's only a hundred and fifty quid a pub.

S1: **You are having a laugh.**

S2: You can afford it.

S1: **You are having a laugh.** (1 second) How can that possibly be ... right?

(1.5 seconds)

S2: Well the things cost money.

S1: Yeah but why are we paying for it?

(2.5 seconds)

S2: Well you've got more money than we have.

S1: [inaudible] **No come on.** Seriously. How how can that possibly be [inaudible]?

S2: Well if you have an **extreme** er **problem** with it then I can er=

S1: I have got an **extreme problem** with it yeah. 'Specially for hundred and fifty quid. That's **absolute madness.**

According to Carter, '[c]reativity in common speech often seems to be connected with the construction of a relationship and of interpersonal convergence' (2004: 9). Gibbs and Gerrig (1989) also propose that metaphor is used to foster intimacy between interlocutors: as understanding metaphor relies more heavily on shared mutual knowledge or conversational common ground than understanding literal knowledge, the function of metaphor is to highlight this common ground. Although CANBEC also features a high degree of collaborative metaphors, the three meetings in the sub-corpus with high levels of disagreement or conflict have the highest density of idioms. The meeting from which extract 7.15 is taken, for instance, contains almost twice as many idioms as the other two external meetings in the sub-corpus, and these idioms are often face-threatening (see Handford and Koester, 2010). Moreover, as extract 7.15 shows, informal language can be used for threatening an interlocutor's face and not just for convergence (Handford and Koester, 2010).

This section has shown that MIDs play a key role in meetings in the achievement of goals and their enabling practices. MIDs can help achieve transactional goals (Koester, 2006), including the action-planning, or evaluation, stage of the creative problem-solving process, as well as more interpersonal (but not necessarily convergent) goals and practices, such as signalling stance, negotiating (im)politeness / face issues, and negotiating discursive roles and identities. These interpersonal goals and practices are evident in both transactional, on-topic discourse, and in convergent and potentially divergent small talk. Furthermore, the discursive practices of summarizing a stretch of discourse or closing a topic often feature MIDs. Similar results have been reported by Koester (2006, 2010).

The concept of a workplace as a community of practice (Wenger, 1998) outlined in Chapter 2, and the related notions of shared expertise and terminology associated with particular communities, are of value in explaining the use of such language in business meetings. This is because metaphors and idioms are examples of the shared repertoire of linguistic tools we find in such communities. It goes some of the way to explaining why metaphors are more common in internal meetings than external meetings, because, in all likelihood, a community within a particular company, or the company as a whole, would have developed more shared linguistic tools (in the form of language and the shared discursive practices that give them meaning) than would two separate companies which are working together.

7.4 Summary

This chapter has explored the use of the statistically significant items *problem, issue, if*, and metaphors and idioms in terms of interpersonal creativity. It has shown that these items can all play a central part in the creative processes of problem-solving and dealing with decisions, with *problem/issue, if* and MIDs each relating to one aspect of the overall process of creative problem-solving as outlined by Henry (2001).

Problem and *issue* clearly have the most obvious literal link to the exploration of problems, and by association decision-focused processes and practices. These two keywords were shown to be particularly significant in internal meetings, which allowed certain inferences to be made about problem-solving in such meetings. Interestingly, differences were found between the two words at the contextual level, even when they share the same collocations and colligations. Such findings suggest that a discourse-sensitive conception of semantic or discourse prosody, as opposed to an approach that prioritizes the semantic content of the words themselves, is appropriate.

One theme of this chapter concerns evaluation. All of the items discussed here can be employed evaluatively, most obviously metaphors and idioms and *problem* and *issue*, but also *if*, when used in certain clusters. For instance, the cluster *if you say "Well ..."* can communicate an encouraging or discouraging discourse prosody. This chapter has also shown how these items can be used outside of problem-solving: *if* can be used as a politeness marker, and idioms and metaphors enable interlocutors to converge during small talk. Furthermore, *if* has been shown to index several discursive practices, such as 'speculating' and 'hypothesizing'.

In terms of metaphors and idioms, there were several interesting findings that warrant further research. While there is evidence to support the position that idioms are markers of convergence, the opposite is also seen to hold in meetings featuring conflict and disagreement. A comparison of external meetings and internal meetings revealed significant statistical differences, with MIDs being far more common in the latter. The overall proportional breakdown of types of MIDs was seen, however, to be highly consistent across all meetings. MIDs also featured most highly in internal meetings involving participants from different departments, which can partly be explained by the lack of ingrained power positions and subsequent attempts to assert control over the direction of the discourse and the decision-making process. In terms of creative problem-solving, MIDs were shown to index evaluative discursive practices, enabling speakers to propose, negotiate and agree on action plans.

Finally, if we look at the quantitative, interpersonal findings, combining results from the whole corpus and the sub-corpus, we can begin to build a rough, composite picture of the business meeting in terms of the probabilistic frequencies of certain interpersonal items. Firstly, we can say that, in every 200 words, we can expect on average four metaphors or idioms, four instances of *we*, about two and a half of the six two-word hedges (*I think, you know, I mean, sort of, kind of, a bit*), two instances of *just*, two of *well*, slightly less than one frequent modal deontic verb (*need to, have to, should* or *gotta*), slightly more than one *if*, two instances of *er*, and three and a half of *yeah*. In Chapter 8, the occurrence of such interpersonal items in and across speaker turns will be explored.

Notes

1. Although Cook was discussing specifically non-work-related discourse, this relationship is nevertheless central to much workplace discourse.
2. This is not to suggest that the same tendency does not occur in everyday speech: many of the most frequent collocates of *if* in the R2 position in the CANCODE corpus of everyday discourse are also in the present simple tense or are present modals – for example, *want, can, do, have, go* and *win*.
3. The boundaries of this categorization are fuzzy (Koester, 2006), and there is considerable overlap: 25 per cent of Moon's items can be placed in two of the five categories, and one per cent in three (Moon, 1998). Moon also discusses the inevitability of disagreement over categorization, due to idiolect and idiosyncrasy (ibid.: 23). While I have attempted to be consistent in deciding on and categorizing the lexical items, it seems likely that there is much scope for disagreement. Ideally, inter-rater analysis would be applied to the data, but given that the two 15-minute meetings analysed by Handford and Koester (2010) took over 50 hours to inter-rater categorize, it has so far proven impossible to find a qualified and available researcher who is willing to invest the requisite amount of time to inter-rater analyse all the data in the sub-corpus.

References

Biber, D. and Conrad, S. (1999) 'Lexical bundles in conversation and academic prose', in Hasselgard, H. and Oksefjell, S. (eds.) *Out of Corpora: Studies in Honor of Stig Johansson*, Amsterdam: Rodopi, 181–90.

Boden, D. (1994) *The Business of Talk: Organizations in Action*, Cambridge: Polity Press.

Brown, J. and Duguid, P. (2000) *The Social Life of Information*, Boston: Harvard Business School Press.

Cameron, L. (2003) *Metaphor in Educational Discourse*, London and New York: Continuum.

Candlin, C. and Maley, A. (1997) 'Intertextuality and interdiscursivity in the discourse of alternative discourse resolution', in Gunnarsson, B., Linell, P. and Nordberg, B. (eds.) *The Construction of Professional Discourse*, London: Longman.

Carter, R. (2004) *Language and Creativity: The Art of Common Talk*, London: Routledge.

Carter, R. and McCarthy, M. (2006) *Cambridge Grammar of English*, Cambridge: Cambridge University Press.

Charles, M. (1996) 'Business negotiations: Interdependence between discourse and the business relationship', *English for Specific Purposes*, 15, 19–36.

Cook, G. (2001) *Language Play, Language Learning*, Oxford: Oxford University Press.

de Bono, E. (2006) 'Creating corporate creativity', in *Business: The Ultimate Resource*, London: A and C Black, 355–6.

Deignan, A. (1999) 'Corpus-based research into metaphor', in Cameron, L. and Low, G. (eds.) *Researching and Applying Metaphor*, Cambridge: Cambridge University Press, 177–202.

Deignan, A. (2005) *Metaphor and Corpus Linguistics*, Amsterdam: John Benjamins.

Drew, P. and Holt, E. (1998) 'Figures of speech: Figurative expressions and the management of topic transition in conversation', *Language in Society*, **27**, 495–522.

Drew, P. and Holt, E. (2005) 'Figurative pivots: The use of figurative expressions in pivotal topic transitions', *Research on Language and Social Interaction*, **31**, 1, 35–61.

Gibbs, R. W. (1994) *The Poetics of Mind: Figurative Thought, Language and Understanding*, Cambridge: Cambridge University Press.

Gibbs, R. W. and Gerrig, J. R. (1989) 'How context makes metaphor comprehension seem "special"', *Metaphor and Symbolic Activity*, **4**, 145–58.

Hamel, G. (2007) *The Future of Management*, Boston: Harvard University Press.

Handford, M. and Koester, A. (2010) '"It's not rocket science": Metaphors and idioms in conflictual business meetings', *Text and Talk*, **30**, 27–51.

Henry, J. (ed.) (2001) *Creative Management*, London: Sage.

Hoey, M. (1983) *On the Surface of Discourse*, London: Allen and Unwin.

Hoey, M. (2005) *Lexical Priming*, Abingdon: Routledge.

Holmes, J. (2007) 'Making humour work: Creativity on the job', *Applied Linguistics*, **28**, 4, 518–37.

Holmes, J. and Stubbe, M. (2003) *Power and Politeness in the Workplace*, London: Longman.

Johnson, G., Langley, A., Melin, L. and Whittington, R. (2007) *Strategy as Practice*, Cambridge: Cambridge University Press.

Koester, A. (2000) 'The role of idioms in negotiating workplace encounters', in Trappes-Lomax, H. (ed.) *Change and Continuity in Applied Linguistics*, Clevedon: Multilingual Matters, 169–83.

Koester, A. (2006) *Investigating Workplace Discourse*, Abingdon: Routledge.

Koester, A. (2010) *Workplace Discourse*, London: Continuum.

Kotthoff, H. (1993) 'Disagreement and concession in disputes: On the context sensitivity of preference structures', *Language in Society*, **22**, 193–216.

Lakoff, G. and Johnson, M. (1980) *Metaphors We Live By*, Chicago: Chicago University Press.

Lee, D. (2008) 'Corpora and discourse analysis: New ways of doing old things', in Bhatia, V., Flowerdew, J. and Jones, R. (eds.) *Advances in Discourse Studies*, Abingdon: Routledge, 86–99.

Low, G. (1988) 'On teaching metaphor', *Applied Linguistics*, **9**, 2, 125–47.

Lyotard, J-F. (1979) *The Postmodern Condition: A Report on Knowledge*, Minneapolis: University of Minnesota Press.

McCarthy, M. (1998) *Spoken Language and Applied Linguistics*, Cambridge: Cambridge University Press.

McCarthy, M. and Handford, M. (2004) '"Invisible to us": a preliminary corpus-based study of spoken business English', in Connor, U. and Upton, T.

(eds.) *Discourse in the Professions: Perspectives from Corpus Linguistics*, Amsterdam: John Benjamins, 167–201.

Mintzberg, H. (1994) *The Rise and Fall of Strategic Planning*, London: Prentice Hall International.

Mirivel, J. and Tracy, K. (2005) 'Premeeting talk: An organizationally crucial form of talk', *Research on Language and Social Interaction*, 38, 1, 1–34.

Moon, R. (1992) 'Textual aspects of fixed expressions in learners' dictionaries', in Arnaud, P. and Béjoint, H. (eds.) *Vocabulary and Applied Linguistics*, London: Macmillan, 13–27.

Moon, R. (1998) *Fixed Expressions and Idioms in English: A Corpus-based Approach*, Oxford: Oxford University Press.

O'Keeffe, A., McCarthy, M. and Carter, R. (2007) *From Corpus to Classroom: Language Use and Language Teaching*, Cambridge: Cambridge University Press.

Prodromou, L. (2008) *English as a Lingua Franca: A Corpus-based Analysis*, London: Continuum.

Rigby, D. (2003) 'Management tools survey 2003: Usage up as companies strive to make headway in tough times', *Strategy and Leadership*, 31, 5, 4–11.

Samra-Fredericks, D. (2009) 'Ethnomethodology', in Bargiela-Chiappini, F. (ed.) *The Handbook of Business Discourse*, Edinburgh: Edinburgh University Press, 92–104.

Sinclair, J. (1991) *Corpus, Concordance, Collocation*, Oxford: Oxford University Press.

Spencer-Oatey, H. (2000) *Culturally Speaking: Managing Rapport through Talk across Cultures*, London: Continuum.

Strässler, J. (1982) *Idioms in English: A Pragmatic Analysis*, Tübingen: Gunter Narr Verlag.

Tannen, D. (1989) *Talking Voices: Repetition, Dialogue and Imagery in Conversational Discourse*, Cambridge: Cambridge University Press.

Watson, T. (2002) *Organising and Managing Work*, London: Prentice Hall.

Wenger, E. (1998) *Communities of Practice: Learning, Meaning and Identity*, Cambridge: Cambridge University Press.

Willing, K. (1992) 'Problem-solving discourse in professional work', *Prospect*, 7, 2, 57–65.

8 Turn-taking: Power and constraint

Turn-taking is concerned with exploring the (largely orderly) transition from one speaker to the next in naturally occurring speech (Levinson, 1983: 297) – that is, how turns are taken, managed and combined to form sequences by interlocutors in spoken interactions. Studies of turn-taking address the issue of how 'the utterances in question conform or depart from the expectations that are attached to the 'slots' in which they occur' (ibid.: 12). Two types of expectations, or constraints, are pertinent here: one is that the expectations of the utterance in question are established by the immediately preceding turn (to form 'adjacency pairs', such as a question being followed by an answer); the second relates to the evident, conventionalized assumptions attached to the wider social context in which the turn occurs, and the social identities of those who perform the social actions (ibid.). The notion of preference (Pomerantz, 1984) is critical to an understanding of turn-taking and the degree to which utterances conform to or depart from the expected constraints of the discourse. A preferred response is one which is structurally expected (such as a greeting following a greeting), and is therefore direct and to the point, whereas a dispreferred response is marked in terms of its more complex structure – for instance, by hedges, pauses and accounts. Rejecting an offer would usually be a dispreferred response (but see Kotthoff, 1993, Handford and Koester, 2010, and below). We can therefore say that analysing turn-taking shows how the discourse is shaped and constrained by the participants' orientations to the context. According to Drew and Heritage (1992: 16), examining how the context affects the unfolding language in and across turns and how language is used to achieve social actions furthers our understanding of institutional discourse, of which business meetings are an example. It has been argued throughout this book that the differing power relationships between speakers is one of the most relevant contextual categories in accounting for particular constraints in business-meeting discourse. This chapter will proceed by taking illustrative examples from each of the relationship categories of meeting, and will ask the relevant questions concerning power and constraint in order to give an account of the turn-taking in each example.

Before moving on to the analysis of the data, it is worth discussing the relationship between turn-taking, power and constraint a little further. In institutional discourse, speaker turns are constrained to varying degrees, depending on factors such as the roles and goals of the participants (Atkinson and Drew, 1979; Drew and Heritage, 1992; Schegloff, 1992; Bargiela-Chiappini and Harris, 1996, 1997; Heritage, 1997, 2005; Holmes and Stubbe, 2003). The institutional culture itself, coupled with the type of work the institution is involved in, can also heavily influence the turn-type. When discussing different institutions and their respective 'opportunities for action', or constraints in turn organization, Heritage (1997) contrasts those where departures from the turn organization can be explicitly sanctioned – for example, a courtroom cross-examination or a police interview – and those where the turn organization is a product of the task in which the participants are involved, or 'some other feature of the interaction' (ibid.: 165). In this second type of institution, turns are less rigid and less predictable. Business meetings would tend to be found in this category.

One such 'feature of the interaction' is the relative power of the participants. Hutchby and Wooffitt define power as 'the structurally provided ability to constrain the actions of others' (1998: 170), and such a definition suggests that the greater the organizationally sanctioned power difference between the speakers, the greater the opportunity for constraint. They are careful to clarify, nevertheless, that a conversation-analysis approach to such contextual features does not entail a causal link between the relationship of the speakers and the possible actions of those involved:

... the participants could conceivably make things different; although obviously departures from the normative conventions, though possible, would be treated by other participants as accountable and open to challenge ... (therefore) the exercise of powerful discursive resources can always be resisted by a recipient. (Hutchby and Wooffitt, 1998: 170)

This quotation raises several points which are relevant to business meetings and the wider institutional context they reflexively recreate, including the notion of 'normative conventions', or, in other words, the expected discursive, professional and social practices. These include certain preferred turn-taking styles – that is, structural norms at the turn-design, sequence and genre level that allow interlocutors to make conventionalized inferences concerning the type of activity they are involved in. Such styles are important, because 'the design features of preferred and dispreferred responses can be used as a resource for the maintenance of social solidarity in talk-in-interaction' (Hutchby and

Wooffitt, 2008: 48). The longer quotation from Hutchby and Wooffitt (1998) above is also a reminder that those with less power can contest the constraints imposed on them, although this admittedly carries an element of risk. This is a source of potential conflict that analyses of 'the new work order' (Gee et al., 1996; Sarangi and Roberts, 1999) are centrally concerned with, given that some workplaces (particularly multinational corporations) openly talk about the need to 'socialize' people into becoming members of communities of practice, and hence develop 'certain kinds of people' (Gee et al., 1996: 21). For further discussion of critical approaches to business discourse, see Deetz and McClellan (2009).

Furthermore, the opportunity for constraint does not mean that those in discursively powerful positions actively choose or need to overtly constrain the less powerful interlocutors. As we have repeatedly seen, meeting discourse often unfolds in a 'quasi-conversational' (Heritage and Greatbatch, 1991: 98) way. Even in manager–subordinate meetings, where the roles tend to be most distinct, the interaction may share many features with everyday communication, such as hedging, vagueness, overlaps and humour. As discussed in section 8.1, within the same manager–subordinate meeting there may be differing degrees of topic management and self-appointed turn-taking, depending on the specific topic under discussion and the changing goals and also roles of the speakers (Holmes and Stubbe, 2003). Even in meetings where constraint is not immediately apparent, it is important to remember that the participants are still members of particular communities of practice, and what may look like relaxed communication may in fact be the members very much conforming to and replicating the expectations and practices of the unfolding, dynamic context (for instance, the analysis of the small talk from extract 6.1, beginning on page 152).

The issue of power and turn-taking is also explored by Heritage (1997), who outlines six categories, briefly discussed in Chapter 4, for analysing the institutionality of interaction:

1 Turn-taking organization
2 Overall structural organization of the interaction
3 Sequence organization
4 Turn design
5 Lexical choice
6 Forms of asymmetry (such as differences in power between speakers)

Overall structural organization was discussed in Chapter 3, whereas lexical choice was the focus of Chapters 4 (which also touched on turn design), 5, 6 and 7. Forms of asymmetry, mainly in terms of the relationship of the speakers, have been discussed throughout the book. Heritage states that, while categories 2–5 interlink rather like a 'Russian doll' (1997: 179), the first and the last categories (turn-taking organization and forms of asymmetry) are wild cards: while a distinct turn-taking system has a strong influence on various levels of the organization of interaction, asymmetry actually pervades all the other levels of the interaction's organization. Expertise (and lack of it) may also be a source of asymmetry, and Bargiela-Chiappini and Harris (1996) show how expertise as well as status allow for greater control over the turn-taking style within an institution's meetings.

This chapter will explore the relationship between these two 'wild cards' of institutional discourse – asymmetry and turn organization – and their manifestation in internal and external meetings. Throughout this chapter, I will also be applying frameworks developed by Holmes and Stubbe (2003) and colleagues on the LWP corpus (*Language in the Workplace*, mentioned previously in Chapters 1–3). They state that meetings, at both the overall structural and individual phase levels, involve a tripartite structure: the opening or introductory section, the central development section, and the closing section (ibid. – see Chapter 3 of this volume for a discussion of the number of stages in business meetings). At both these macro and micro levels, they argue, the first and last sections are the prerogative of those in power (extract 8.1 provides an example of this). The central section of each stage of a meeting (for instance, stage 2 in the meeting structure presented in Chapter 3), and each phase that makes up a stage, tend to be less overtly controlled by powerful speakers (ibid.).

At a very general level, Holmes and Stubbe (2003: 70) also argue that the following are interrelated:

- function of meeting
- relationship of speakers
- predominant structural pattern

'Function of meeting' is largely equivalent to 'meeting purpose' as outlined in Chapter 1. 'Predominant structural pattern' refers to both the general level of organization and linear and spiral patterns of turns, with linear patterns following a more traditional, on-topic, incremental structure – as in the manager–subordinate meetings outlined in Chapter 3 – and which tend to be 'driven by the manager's agenda' (ibid.). Spiral patterns of turns have speakers returning to an unfinished topic after several turns, and shifting topic very frequently.

Holmes and Stubbe point out that, while peer-type meetings often involve spiral patterning, most meetings in their data contain a mixture of both spiral and linear patterns. In addition, the specific topic – that is, the subject under discussion – also affects the pattern.

In addition to the purpose of the meeting, the relationship of the speakers, and the predominant structural pattern as outlined by Holmes and Stubbe, this chapter will demonstrate how a fourth factor, the role of the chair, is also related to turn-taking. The dynamic role which the chair can play in the same meeting will be discussed below, as well as the effect this has on the turn organization in both internal and external meetings.

8.1 Turn-taking in internal meetings

This section will analyse how the relationship of the speakers involved in different types of internal meetings and the purpose of the meeting in question (for example, reporting) influence the turn-taking organization. As already noted, other contextual factors, such as the topic being addressed, can also influence the turn-taking behaviour, and these will be foregrounded when appropriate. Given that the issue of asymmetry is so central to understanding all aspects of institutional discourse, and turn-taking in particular (Heritage, 1997), the following two sub-sections discussing internal meetings are separated into manager–subordinate communication and that involving peers.

Holmes and Stubbe argue that meetings involving participants who are 'equal in status' – that is, peer – tend to be more cyclical in structure, with speakers tending to 'engage in more extended exploratory talk' (2003: 70), whereas those between managers and subordinates are more linear with more requests for action and clear directives. In terms of meeting purpose, they state that information-gathering or reporting (here called 'reviewing') meetings will also tend to follow a linear structure, determined by the manager's agenda.

Most meetings in the sub-corpus (see the Appendix for a breakdown of this) involve more than two speakers, which allows for a comparative study of the number of turns taken by each speaker. In dyads, the proportion will obviously be 50:50 or thereabouts (although the length of turns will not in all likelihood be 50:50). In a study of British meetings, Bargiela-Chiappini and Harris (1996) state that the most senior speakers speak for the most amount of time, so it seems plausible that they will also take the most number of turns. Indeed, in formal meetings, the role played by the chair is, by definition, explicit, as is often the case in manager–subordinate meetings (Holmes and

Stubbe, 2003). In such meetings, we could expect the discourse, there-fore, to be controlled by and through the chair, with him or her taking up a high proportion of the turns. In peer meetings, by contrast, we could expect the chair to take a lower proportion of turns.

Turn-taking in manager–subordinate meetings

In the sales meeting at a foam manufacturer explored in extracts 8.1 and 8.2, there are four speakers present apart from the managing director: two sales executives and two sales administrators, who are reporting on recent sales. According to Holmes and Stubbe's (2003) rationale, this meeting is likely to be linear in turn organization, because the relationship of the speakers is manager–subordinate, the managing director is chairing what is a weekly sales review meeting as the sales director is absent, and the purpose is primarily reviewing. In addition, we can expect the proportion of turns taken by the chair to be higher than in peer meetings, as the chair plays a more controlling role. There is an extra constraint in this meeting which would also reduce the likelihood of an open, exploratory event, that being time. The managing director (S1) refers to this explicitly at the beginning of the meeting in extract 8.1.

(8.1)

> *Internal meeting*
> Relationship of speakers: manager–subordinate
> Purpose: reviewing; planning
> Topic: sales

S1: We've gotta rattle through quickly today. Wanna get finished by ... eleven if we can. E= e= in plus or y= plus or minus five or ten minutes so we'll just ... really rattle through the key points.

The managing director then continues by explicitly allocating the next speaker (line numbers are added to this section of the extract for reference):

S1: So Julie since you are immediately there can you just ... c= go through yours?
S2: Yeah. We didn't actually get a set of 'em so [inaudible] this time.
S1: Haven't you?
5 S3: No.
S1: Can you not remember what you wrote? [laughs]

S2: I know sorry [laughs] I've got mine but not everybody else's.
S1: Right. Oh right. Okay.
S2: So.
10 S1: Well we we can share around okay. (1 second) I mean just pick out any key points.
S2: Erm (1 second) just imagine order some mats for use with that inflatable play area. It's self-explanatory on there.
S1: Right.
15 S2: Henley's have ordered a new tool which GNRT it are actually paying for so they've finally committed to this. It's+
S1: Excellent.

The sales executive, Julie (S2), has not made enough copies of her sales report for this meeting, and the chair is directing her to explain her results anyway. There is some misunderstanding early on when the chair appears to think she has completely forgotten to bring the report. This accounts for his laughter, which can be seen to soften the potential face-threat embodied in the direct question *Can you not remember what you wrote?* [*laughs*] (line 6) which seems more accusatory than the affirmative alternative: *Can you remember what you wrote*, or than the more informal contracted negative form: *Can't you remember what you wrote* (Carter and McCarthy, 2006: 537). Following the repair, he goes on to give the directive again to deliver a report with an imperative form, but in a very hedged manner, using *I mean, just* and *any*: *I mean just pick out any key points* (lines 10–11). This combination of imperative forms with hedges in manager–subordinate directive discourse has also been described by Koester (2006: 45).

This short extract is typical of the reviewing stages of this meeting, in that the chair takes up a large proportion of the turns. In fact, overall he takes up 38 per cent of all the turns in the meeting, which, considering that there are five speakers present, is a relatively high proportion. Once S2 is reporting on recent sales, the chair regularly provides backchannels, which are often positive (for example, *excellent*), thereby attending to the sales executive's positive face needs and encouraging her to continue talking.

Even though most of this meeting is taken up with reviewing recent sales results, there are also some problem-solving/planning phases. When the topic changes, the style of turn-taking also changes, with the chair (S1) playing a less active role, a pattern reflected in other meetings. In extract 8.2, the participants are discussing a problem with a foam exercise mat they produce and market.

(8.2)

Internal meeting
Relationship of speakers: manager–subordinate
Purpose: reviewing; planning
Topic: sales

S1: The orange peel. (1 second) Th= we still don't know why that happens do we.

S4: No.

S2: I think it's where the p= it tends to be the ones I've seen say I was
5   sitting on an ab ... cradle when [inaudible] did it and Eddie. Where you're actually sitting and you're just doing it. I don't know if it's cos (1 second) where the pressure's been applied in that ... particular bit. It seems= so I don't know whether the erm ... adhesive comes away from the foam. D'ya know. I don't know.

10 S4?:[inaudible]

S2: If you like punch s= d'ya know like imagine you per= you punch something for long enough. That's ... it's where the impact is+

S3: Cos the [inaudible] does=

S2: +even just by sitting on it by impact I mean just where your (1 second)
15   backside is.

S5: How's the foam underneath? Is it like= does it crumble or is it?

S2: It's just like bubbly.

S4?:I don't know if it's+

S5: U= un= underneath the er the vinyl?

20 S4?:+under the vinyl. I don't think anyone's cut one up to look at it.

S5: Hmm.

S2: That's what we maybe should do.

Compared with extract 8.1, the difference in turn-taking in extract 8.2 is immediately noticeable: each of the participants takes multiple turns, apart from the chair, who only takes one turn. He introduces the problem-solving frame with the tag *do we* (line 2) and then allows his staff to come to a decision about the problem. The extract highlights an important aspect of the relationship between turn-taking and speaker goals. Holmes and Stubbe argue that apparent digressions can facilitate 'the achievement of other goals, such as a greater involvement from the group in the decision-making process' (2003: 69). The non-involvement of the chair in this non-agenda-related discussion can be interpreted in this way, as his overt presence in the discussion would probably mean that the other participants would be less empowered to arrive at a decision by themselves. By not involving himself, he provides an opportunity for the sales staff to freely talk about the problem without an overt gatekeeping or leading presence.

The lexico-grammatical choices in extract 8.2 also indicate that the topic is concerned with problem-solving, and that the staff are searching for consensus. As shown in Chapter 7, hypothesizing language is frequent in problem-solving, and again it is evident how convergence and consensus are reached in meetings through the use of modals, hedges and the multifunctional *if*. For example, the second part of S2's first turn contains the hedged, speculative, face-protecting clusters *I don't know if* and *I don't know whether*, the modal *it seems*, and the explicit statement of uncertainty at the end which invites her colleagues to comment further *D'ya know. I don't know* (lines 6–9).

Turn-taking in peer meetings

The peer meeting which we will look at in extract 8.3 is from the same foam manufacturer as extracts 8.1 and 8.2, and S1 is the same managing director, who is also chairing this meeting. All other members are also upper management. We could expect the proportion and length of the turns by the chair to be lower than those in the manager–subordinate meeting (from which extracts 8.1 and 8.2 are taken), given that this is a peer meeting. As it is also a planning meeting, we could expect the approach to the topic to be relatively more exploratory (Holmes and Stubbe, 2003), which would also suggest a more cyclical, less rigid turn organization. In extract 8.3, the first turn of which was replicated in the discussion of decision-making language in Chapter 7 (extract 7.5), the managing director is explaining why the group should make a decision about sending money as a deposit, despite the probable unwillingness of the absent *Harry* (the company accountant) to do so.

(8.3)

> *Internal meeting*
> Relationship of speakers: peer
> Purpose: planning
> Topic: strategy

S1:   I've got a feeling he'll bottle out (1 second) of decision making. ... But I I'll= I wanna make that decision. Harry said we could make that decision providing we've got er a refund clause.
[11 turns removed from extract]

S2: All depends how him= important that start date is. W= whenever it is+

S1: Yeah.

S2: never sure which month it is but

S3: W= ar= are we= we're all we were talking first of all is to start production aren't we.

(2 seconds)

S2: All we're saying is we're saying twenty four weeks right?

S1: Yeah.

S2: He's committed to twenty four weeks+

S1: Yep.

S2: +as soon as he gets the ... cheque.

S1: Yeah.

S3: [inaudible]. But if we don't get the cheque to him by Christmas then he might revisit that.

S1: Yeah. Well it makes you [inaudible]. Yeah.

S2: And now

[9 turns removed from extract]

S4: Erm so [inaudible] ... gotta ... take the risk.

S1: Yeah. ... I think we've got to.

S4: Especially cos they've got that clause saying that

S2: Yeah.

S4: +wherever possible they would+

S1: Th= they'll refund=

S4: +[inaudible] what they could.

(2 seconds)

S1: But it's hell of a gamble. Hundred and eleven thousand or hundred thirteen thousand pounds or whatever to put down as a deposit but we've gotta do it.

(3 seconds)

S2: Yep.

As with the decision-making sequence in the manager–subordinate meeting in extract 8.2, there are multiple turns and there does not seem to be a fixed order of speakers. The participants gradually come to a consensual decision through tying together a series of related issues. In describing such a process, Boden states:

People build layers of discussion, debate and eventual decision on a given topic or activity, diffusing possible disagreement while molding decision through multiple occasions of interaction. Their conversational collusion is a matter of weaving, turn by turn, one agenda into another. (Boden, 1994: 164)

In extract 8.3, the following issues are woven into the final decision: Harry's procrastination, the refund clause, the importance of

the production start date, the initial time period, the possible repercussions of not paying by Christmas, the issue of the refund clause
again, the size of the deposit and therefore the size of the risk, and,
finally, the necessity of deciding on that risk.

While the proportion of turns taken by the chair in this peer meeting
is lower than in the manager–subordinate meeting referred to in
extracts 8.1 and 8.2, the total number of words is higher: he accounts
for 45 per cent of all words uttered in the peer meeting, compared to 38
per cent in the manager–subordinate meeting (even taking the number
of speakers into account – four compared to five – proportionally he
still speaks more in the peer meeting). If power is a relative concept
(Holmes and Stubbe, 2003: 3) and is dynamically related to the positions of the other participants, as Hutchby and Wooffitt's (1998)
definition given on page 219 suggests, then the managing director
would have less power in a peer meeting than in a manager–subordinate meeting, but in fact he talks more in the peer meeting. In
another meeting taken from CANBEC (see extract 8.4), the chair –
who is not actually the most senior person present – takes an even
higher proportion of turns once the total number of speakers has
been taken into account. These findings problematize Bargiela-
Chiappini and Harris's (1996) assertion that the more powerful the
speaker, the more he or she speaks.

It is also interesting that, in all the multiparty talk in the CANBEC
sub-corpus, just two speakers account for over 50 per cent of the
turns: in the multinational bank meeting analysed in extract 8.4,
for example, S4, who is more senior than the chair, and the chair
(S1) account for 61 per cent of all turns taken, even though there are
seven speakers present. These meetings often involve direct discussion
between the two participants, as extract 8.4 – the end of a problem-
solving phase of a technical meeting – demonstrates:

(8.4)

Internal meeting
Relationship of speakers: peer
Purpose: reviewing; planning
Topic: technical

S4: No problem.
S1: So okay. So assuming that is sorted out+
S4: Okay.
S1: +one way or another on Thursday.

S4: [inaudible] I think we don't have any more problems. I think [inaudible]+

S1: So+

S4: +[inaudible].

S1: +so let's let's assume it's approaching Thursday+

S4: Mm.

S1: +six o'clock.

S4: Mm.

S1: The process the sequence of events is about six o'clock=

S4: I give a call to whoever it is. Command centre you call it.

SM: [laughs]

Section 8.1 has discussed turn-taking in internal manager–subordinate and peer meetings, with particular attention paid to linear and cyclical patterns, the role of the chair, and other power-related issues. In section 8.2, certain aspects of turn-taking in external meetings will be explored.

8.2 Turn-taking in external meetings

The focus in this section, as in the previous section, will be on the rationale of the meeting and the status of the speakers and their relationship, and how these factors influence turn-taking. According to Heritage (1997: 163), the institutional goal orientations and status of the participants have a direct bearing on the turn-taking organization, and it is at the level of speaker goals that internal and external meetings can clearly diverge. For instance, while internal meetings may be concerned with a manager reviewing the weekly progress of his or her subordinate with a long-term view of promoting the subordinate, external meetings are often concerned with developing sound inter-organizational relationships and the best price for products or services. The importance of power asymmetries was also discussed at the beginning of this chapter, and again this can be a fecund source of comparison between internal and external meetings. Within a company, the status and role of the speaker are usually a given, whereas, in external communication, such issues may require more negotiation, might be initially unknown to at least some of the participants, or might not be particularly relevant. Related to this is the issue of face (Goffman, 1967). Charles (1996: 24) talks of 'corporate face' in sales negotiations – that is, a notion of face that captures the 'tactical and professional nature of the status and roles' of participants as representatives of their company, and it is argued here that this concept is relevant to other inter-organizational communication.

Therefore, in external communication, there are issues of personal face and corporate face that need consideration. However, as with the corporate *we* discussed in Chapter 6 (and Chapter 4), corporate face is unlikely to be relevant in internal communication.

The issues raised in the preceding paragraph can also be used to differentiate between types of external meetings – for instance, goals can differ greatly depending on whether the relationship is contractually bound or non-contractually bound. The depth of the relationship between the speakers present can also be a factor, as in some meetings the participants may never have met before, whereas in others they may have worked together for a number of years. The attention given to (corporate and personal) face, and the scope for conflict can also differ considerably depending on the external relationship. These and other issues and the effect they can have on turn-taking will be discussed below.

Turn-taking in non-contractually bound meetings

The role played by the chair in business meetings has been shown to have direct relevance to the turn organization (Boden, 1994; Bargiela-Chiappini and Harris, 1996, 1997; Holmes and Stubbe, 2003). In multiparty discourse, where there is more potential variety in interaction than in dyads, the chair can enforce the agenda. Alternatively, the chair can encourage 'off-topic' discussion by either engaging with or withdrawing from the interaction, or by doing both, as shown in the linear and cyclical turn patterns in extracts 8.1 and 8.2.

The relationship between the transactional goals of the institution, the meeting itself and the importance of the chair is outlined by Bargiela-Chiappini and Harris: 'In all business meetings, the achievement of specific organizational goals depends on accomplishing the main task through the discussion of the agenda by the Chair and the Group' (1997: 208). They argue that within meetings there are three possible directions for exchanges. They are:

- chair to participants
- participant(s) to chair
- participant(s) to participant(s)

While this is the case for internal meetings, the picture may be more complex for external meetings. As the data discussed in Bargiela-Chiappini and Harris (ibid.) were all taken from internal meetings, references to the chair and the participants are from an internal perspective, which I argue can be substantially different from external meetings in that these (particularly non-contractually bound meetings) do not always have a chair.

In the following sales meeting between a manufacturing company and a promotional magazine (extract 8.5), none of the participants seems to be consistently fulfilling the role of chair. In the internal meetings examined in CANBEC, typically the chair takes the most turns, whereas in this meeting, the managing director – at whose company the meeting is being held and who we might thus assume is the chair – takes the least number of turns (22 per cent, compared to 32 per cent for his sales-manager colleague and 43 per cent for the guest sales person). While this does not prove that the managing director is not the chair, when we also consider that the sales person has requested this meeting, and that he sets out the agenda at the opening stage of the meeting, it seems that the sales person might fit the description of chair according to Bargiela-Chiappini and Harris (1997) and Holmes and Stubbe's (2003) description of the role of chair. Extract 8.5 shows the sales person (S1) outlining the topic of the meeting, which is to discuss the possibility of altering the relationship between the companies from one where the buyer buys magazine space on an ad hoc basis, to one where the relationship is contractually bound through the purchasing of an annual package.

(8.5)

> *External meeting*
> Relationship of speakers: non-contractually bound
> Purpose: buying/selling/promoting a product
> Topic: sales

S1: What I said George I don't know how much sort of Kevin's spoke to you and so forth. I mean what what we're trying to do we're doing it more and more. I mean obviously sort of Kevin like I suppose he gets fed up of me phoning them up and so forth. But what what we're trying to do with most companies is sort [inhales] like a package out. (1.5 seconds) So for example you know exactly what you're spending with Coal PLC erm as a company (1 second) and therefore you know I'm not having to contact you. You you've got all your copy deadlines et cetera et cetera. (2.5 seconds) Starting from Coal PLC you you probably (2 seconds) have seen our editorial programme for next year.
[knock on door]
SM: Hello.

Bearing in mind the considerable unequal status of a seller in a new relationship like this one and the fact that a buyer 'is expected to exert a degree of control over a seller and the situation' (Charles, 1996: 23), to describe a visiting sales person as chair is not a valid proposition. The degree of negative politeness strategies (Brown and Levinson, 1987), such as hesitation, indirectness, hedging, vagueness and self-deprecation in this extract, is also pertinent. The sales person very cautiously justifies his visit, thereby implicitly acknowledging the imposition caused by the meeting. Such linguistic behaviour is typical of speakers who are in subordinate power positions (Holmes and Stubbe, 2003), as well as sellers at an early stage of an external buyer–seller relationship (Charles, 1996). This absence of a clear chair is a feature of non-contractually bound meetings in the corpus.

An aspect of this meeting which is also apparent in other non-contractually bound meetings concerns the length of the turns taken by one speaker. The linear and cyclical turn patterns discussed by Holmes and Stubbe (2003) are also evident in external meetings, but in non-contractually bound meetings in particular, there are often very long turns made by one speaker in the meeting. While these can take the form of a formal or informal presentation, more commonly they involve extended monologues. In the meeting from which extract 8.5 is taken, for example, the seller regularly talks at length without interruption from the buyer, despite the greater power of the buyer[1].

In extract 8.6, taken from an initial, exploratory meeting between two IT companies, there is a similar pattern of long turns from one speaker. An IT broker (whose function is compared to that of a 'matchmaker' between general companies and IT companies who can provide technical support to the general companies) is visiting an internet service provider in order to find out about this company's technical and service capabilities, with a view to starting a contractually bound relationship. In extract 8.6, the technical director of the internet service provider (S3) can be seen to be doing most of the talking, which is consistent with the asymmetrical turn-taking rights his role as expert allows (Bargiela-Chiappini and Harris, 1996). Nevertheless, he speaks far more than any of the other five participants present, despite already having given a lengthy presentation. At the end of the extract, he even answers a question that is directed away from him and specifically at his colleague, *Luke*, stating that the topic is his *kettle of fish* – that is, his area of expertise.

(8.6)

External meeting
Relationship of speakers: non-contractually bound
Purpose: buying/selling/promoting a product
Topic: sales; technical

S3: So we would never claim to be something we're not.

S4: Okay. Fine. Do you er run any er SP services [inaudible]?

S3: No.

S4: You don't.

5   S3: We did think about it. Er (2 seconds) partly because we've got Batlax down the road. Their head office is about a mile and a half away from us.

S4: Mm.

S3: And we had this raging debate about whether or not we should do

10   it. Erm and we just= we just never did. I think by the time we we're= we're generally fairly cautious erm you know so it's it's not a case of see an opportunity jump at it and and make market. We would rather kind of sit back a little bit and say "Well yeah. What are the risks of doing this?" And= so we sat back long enough to realize that

15   the EDP market wasn't gonna= model wasn't gonna work and then everything went tits up anyway. So luckily we didn't+

SM: [laughs]

S3: +you know= we didn't get burnt by that. Er we have customers who offer EDP services so I s= I suppose you could say in a way we have

20   some responsibility for the delivery. But largely you know we we're= we're navvies basically. Our job+

SM: [laughs]

S3: +is to deliver packets from one place to another place. Where where we believe we're capable we will move up the value chain. So erm

25   you know we are n= we are= (2 seconds) unlike other ISPs we don't stop at a leased router er on our customer's site. You know we're interested in how they're gonna deliver the internet infrastructure into their own organizations. We're a networking company we can do that. We don't sort of think "Oh blimey we don't want to touch

30   their own network when they've got remote offices. Blimey what will we do?" That's bread and butter to us.

S4: Yeah.

S3: Yeah?

S1: Okay. Erm Luke last time we met+

35   S5: Mm.

S1: +you mentioned you're considering ADSL broadband DSL services.

S5: Mhm.

S1: Is that s= is that= has that moved along at all?

S3: Yeah.

40   S5: Yeah.

S3: Oh I I can answer that+

S5: Mm.

S3:   +cos that's+
SM: Yeah.
45   S3:   +my my kettle of fish.

The high degree of strategy-level evaluation, reflected in the density of idiomatic language – *raging debate* (line 9), *see an opportunity jump at it* (line 12), *sit back a little bit and say* (line 13), *sat back* (line 14), *went tits up* (line 16), *didn't get burnt* (line 18), *we're navvies* (line 21), *move up the value chain* (line 24), *that's bread and butter to us* (line 31) – is also interesting, given that S3's expertise is in the technical sphere. Ethnographic research within this company brought to light, however, how much power and influence on key strategic decisions this technical director exerted. The combination of self-directed positive corporate face-work (by explaining the good judgment of the company) and a degree of informal self-deprecation (*we're navvies basically*) can be interpreted as convergence, as, through this, S3 arguably addresses the professional and interactional expectations of the visiting company. The professional expectation (that the internet service provider is a worthy partner for the visiting company) is met through S3 showing that his company is expert in its field and understands the market, and the interactional expectation (that S3's company is easy to develop a relationship with) is addressed through the self-deprecatory humour.

A further feature of non-contractually bound meetings concerns the negotiation of the agenda[2] and the roles of the participants. For instance, in extract 8.7 from early on in this same meeting, the chief technical officer of the IT broker explains his responsibilities to the sales director of the internet service provider.

(8.7)

External meeting
Relationship of speakers: non-contractually bound
Purpose: buying/selling/promoting a product
Topic: sales; technical

S5:   Great. Great. I mean sorry. Just just so I know who you are?
S4:   I'm CTO at Max Mouse Systems.
S5:   Right.
S4:   And also advise clients erm on sort of technical side of their enquiries.
S5:   Right.

S4: So if someone calls up and asks for a particular solution I'll sort of draw down and say "Well why why are you actually going for that?" and+

S5: Okay.

S4: +erm "[company name]'s the place to be for that sort of system" or whatever.

S5: Yeah.

S4: So erm sort of just involved in that= in that respect.

S5: Right. Okay. So you call= you speak to most most people+

S4: Erm s= s=

S5: +making enquiries?

S4: If if it sort of falls into into that category. I don't really tend to do sort of web design type stuff.

S5: Yeah.

S4: Or= but more [knock on door] erm sort of Max Mouse Systems's core business [door opens] namely hosting or erm leased lines. That s=

S5: Yeah.

S4: That sort of stuff.

S5: Okay. Okay. So you have a bit of a= bit of a run through with the customer+

S4: Yeah exactly.

S5: +on what they're looking for. And=

S4: Exactly.

Such negotiation of roles (and agendas) is a common feature of non-contractually bound meetings, where, unlike internal meetings and many contractually bound meetings, the participants may be meeting for the first time, the host company may not be aware of the visiting company's business, and the exact purpose of the meeting may not be clear to either side. Furthermore, the status of the individuals present may be less relevant than in other meetings, and therefore this issue of power is less explicit. Notwithstanding this, power in terms of expertise and professional ability may be more relevant, and may be a critical factor when deciding whether to proceed with a relationship. Hence the ability to communicate these credentials in a recognizable and convincing way, through accepted practices, will be a key skill for those involved in such meetings.

Extract 8.7 is also interesting in terms of convergence – for instance, the summary offered by S5 at the end of the exchange, which is positively endorsed by S4. Examples of such cooperative discourse are the norm in the non-contractually bound meetings in CANBEC. This is unsurprising given the emphasis placed on developing a relationship and the tentative nature of the relationship itself. In contractually bound meetings, which will be discussed in the next section, we see far more evidence of conflict as well as evidence of convergence.

Turn-taking in contractually bound meetings

As mentioned above, there are several differences between non-contractually bound and contractually bound external meetings, and one of these concerns the chair. Where the relationship is contractually bound and where there are regular meetings, the senior person from the host company may act very much like a chair in an internal meeting. This is evident in the following extract (8.8) from the meeting between a large pharmaceutical company and their supplier, which was also analysed in Chapters 3 and 6 (extracts 3.10 on pages 84–5 and 6.1 on pages 152–3). In this six-participant meeting, the chair takes 46 per cent of the turns, which is a higher proportion (2.77 times that of the average) than any of the internal meetings in the sample. Extract 8.8 shows how the chair (S1) is attempting to address the issue of the guest company's internal communication.

(8.8)

> *External meeting*
> Relationship of speakers: contractually bound
> Purpose: reviewing; planning
> Topic: logistics; production

	S3: So this will be a double work for us to to say okay we have to cancel one order and er (1 second) increase the the next order. Because they are on a different different erm (1.5 seconds) time line.
	S1: You mean at the moment you've got probably three packing orders.
5	S3: Yeah.
	S1: You it's probably all from the same bulk. Yeah?
	S3: [inaudible]
	S1: It's all from the same bulk yeah?
	S3: But they have different=
10	S1: They're different packing order numbers yeah so they're in the packaging plan as three different orders at three different time points.
	S3: Yeah.
	S1: The question is do can you go into that first one and increase it to
15	two thousand and then cancel the next two. That's a question. Don't want an answer.
	S3: Yeah. Yeah.

S1:   In terms of what that means yes it means extra work up front in
        terms of doing that.
20   S3:   Yeah.

Certain lexico-grammatical and discursive items signify S1 as
someone exerting his power – for example, the interruption followed by the perfunctory agreement *They're different packing order
numbers yeah* (line 10) and the face-threatening metastatements
(Lakoff, 1973) *The question is* (line 14), *That's a question* (line 15),
Don't want an answer (lines 15–16) and *In terms of what that means
yes it means* (line 18). He also opens and closes the meeting, sets and
distributes the agenda and manages the turn-taking and topic, stick-
ing mainly to a linear pattern. He is therefore largely equivalent to a
chair in an internal manager–subordinate meeting.

Not all contractually bound meetings exhibit these overtly powerful and potentially divergent aspects, and it should be remembered that there are many types of contractually bound relationship
between different types of companies. Moreover, disagreements can
become overt in internal meetings (Koester, 2006; Handford and
Koester, 2010), as shown in Chapter 7. Nevertheless, we find greater
degrees of overt conflict in some of the contractually bound meetings
than in any other type of internal or external meeting in the corpus.
How conflict can be manifested through metaphorical and idiomatic
use was discussed in Chapter 7, and here we will explore conflict at
the turn level, with particular reference to the meeting between the
operations controller of a pub chain (S1 in extract 8.9) and the estates
manager from the brewer (S2), examined previously in extract 7.15.

In this meeting, the power relationship between the speakers is quite
complex, because S1 is at the executive level within his company,
whereas S2 is a lower-level manager. However, S1's company is contractually obliged to accept most of the conditions outlined by S2.
Furthermore, S2's company is considerably larger than that of S1.
According to Hutchby and Wooffitt's (1998) definition of power
as a participant's ability to constrain (given here on page 219), it
would therefore seem that S2 has more power. Interruptions themselves are potentially face-threatening, and arguably more so in external meetings, because of the combination of personal and corporate
face, and the relative fragility of the relationship. S1's interruption
in extract 8.9 is therefore a departure 'from (the) normative conventions' (Hutchby and Wooffitt, 1998: 170) of external (and indeed
many internal) meetings. The fact that the interruption is explicitly
challenged by S2 (*You didn't let me finish the sentence*) is also noteworthy: it is an example of the speaker exercising his power, as the

long silence (3.5 seconds) which follows the challenge also appears to be. Extract 8.9 shows how a speaker can break the normative conventions, and how such perceived inappropriacy can be reprimanded and sanctioned (Levinson, 1983: 320) by a powerful speaker. A less powerful speaker would probably have refrained from commenting on the interruption.

(8.9)

External meeting
Relationship of speakers: contractually bound
Purpose: buying/selling/promoting a product; task-/problem-oriented
Topic: procedure; logistics

S2: Well if you have an extreme er problem with it then I can er=
S1: I have got an extreme problem with it yeah. 'Specially for hundred and fifty quid. That's absolute madness.
S2: You didn't let me finish the sentence. (3.5 seconds) If you have any [laughs] if you've got an extreme problem with it (1 second) then we can pay it.

Heritage talks of the 'bias intrinsic to many aspects of the organisation of talk which is generally favourable to the maintenance of the bonds of solidarity between actors and which promotes the avoidance of conflict' (1984: 265). Even when disagreement does occur, according to Greatbatch, we tend to find sequences through which the disagreements 'are routinely exited through a process in which the speakers deescalate their disputes by moderating their positions' (1991: 277). At other times, the conflictual topic will be ignored or postponed, because '[d]eferring disagreement or debate is not a casual or random matter; it is central . . . to the smooth and practical everyday enactment of the organisation' (Boden, 1994: 155). One of the key factors in understanding why conflict is unwelcome is face, as disagreement will often involve threats to positive and negative face (Brown and Levison, 1987; Spencer-Oatey, 2000).

The importance of attending to face needs in external meetings has been discussed several times in this book. However, face is not attended to consistently throughout such meetings, as extract 8.8 from the external, contractually bound meeting (which discussed the guest company's inefficiency) demonstrates. Indeed, in the contractually bound meeting between the operations controller of the pub chain (S1) and the estates manager from the brewer (S2), face seems to be purposefully aggravated (Muntigl and Turnbull, 1998), as extract 8.10 shows. The brewer has a contract which means they can decide which beers are sold by three pubs which they own, as well as how much rent is charged, even though the pubs are managed by the pub chain.

(8.10)

    S1: And the rent's (1 second) stupid. So.

    S2: Not as stupid as I was trying to make it.

    S1: It's ridiculous already. The the the amount you were trying to make it was absolutely erm (1 second) beyond any business sense whatso-

5   ever.

    S2: [inhales]

    S1: And if it was=

    S2: That [inaudible].

    S1: Any kind of independent operator would've probably thrown the

10   keys back at you.

    S2: Ah yeah.

    S1: So.

    S2: But we wouldn'ta caught them because you're not allowed to do that.

15   (2.5 seconds)

    S1: [laughs] So what else can we get out of you other than this?

    S2: Absolutely nothing. The erm the retail link scheme ends at the end of this year erm and these are our proposals to kick in at the end of September this year for the rest of your lease. (2 seconds)

20   That's what I've gotta be clear on telling you. (1.5 seconds) There is a however however. The however is that on each of your pubs [S2 continues the turn]

The use of repetition combined with idiomatic and metaphorical language is one way the roles are negotiated (Handford and Koester, 2010), at times with the communication resembling verbal jousting – particularly, but not solely, on the part of S2. McCarthy and Carter (2004: 66) state that the main purpose of repetition is often 'to co-construct interpersonal convergence and to creatively adapt to the other speaker(s)', and McCarthy (1998: 143) shows how idioms and metaphors, through their indirect semantics, can help speakers work towards convergence. The repetition of the metaphorical *stupid* and the relexicalization to *ridiculous* in lines 1 and 3 of extract 8.10 are clearly not markers of convergence here. Instead, what seems to be happening is an example of an 'opposition format' (Kotthoff, 1993), touched on in Chapter 7, where 'there is no preference for agreement any more', and where a speaker uses a term of the other speaker in his or her own argument 'in such a way that the claim loses the power to influence'. Another instance of an opposition format is the impressively agile metaphorical exchange in lines 9–14.

There are various other features in extract 8.10 that signal the level of divergence: the emphatic stance markers (Koester, 2006) *absolutely . . . beyond any . . . whatsoever* (lines 4–5), with *absolutely* being repeated later in the extract (line 17); the idiom *kick in* (line 18), which has an aggressive undertone; the repetition of *however* (line 21); and the metapragmatic act (Thomas, 1984: 227) *That's what I've gotta be clear on telling you* (line 20), which is 'incontrovertibly rude' (Lakoff, 1973: 304). The final adjacency pair also seems particularly telling:

> S1: [laughs] So what else can we get out of you other than this?
> S2: Absolutely nothing.

As discussed at the beginning of this chapter, refusals or disagreements in the second part of adjacency pairs tend to be dispreferred, and, as such, the turn shape tends to be more complex than a preferred, or expected, response. The adjacency pair in extract 8.11 from an internal manager–subordinate meeting highlights typical elements of a dispreferred second (one-second pause, token agreement, hesitation, self-editing in terms of pronoun choice – Levinson, 1983).

(8.11)

> *Internal meeting*
> Relationship of speakers: manager–subordinate
> Purpose: reviewing
> Topic: technical

> S1: Okay. Who= has anyone reviewed that?
>   (1 second)
> S2: Yes you we're I'm just putting it together now.

The tenses are also indicative: the manager (S1) uses the present perfect, which reflects his opinion that the task should have already been completed, and the subordinate uses the present progressive, signalling that it is being done, but is not yet completed. The underlying principle is that the preferred response to a question concerning completion of work is a positive one. When the response is negative, or in this case dispreferred, we can expect it to be hedged, longer and more complex. What we find in the final adjacency pair in extract 8.10, unusually, is a completely unhedged refusal. Indeed, the refusal is accentuated by the emphatic marker *absolutely*. According to Kotthoff (1993: 201), disagreement can become the preferred context and be 'stressed and oriented to', which seems to be the case here. Such turn structure is extremely atypical in business meetings, and both reflects and creates the high degree of conflict. Again, face needs are far from being addressed, and we can see how the negotiation of power issues (such as assertion) in external, contractually bound meetings can be aggressively enacted through linguistic divergence, and partly through unusual turn structures. In fact, much of the linguistic surface evidence of conflict in this meeting, such as turn structure, seems to reflect and be caused by the bald expression of constraint and the aggressive reaction against it. In the exchange in extract 8.12, which occurs towards the end of the meeting, a deterioration into personal abuse is evident, with S2 responding to S1's highly sarcastic parting remark with a highly critical insult:

(8.12)

> S1: John. (1 second) I don't envy you. You must be welcomed up and down the country.
> S2: Well yeah. Most people are= most people are kinder than you are but there you go.

8.3 Summary

This chapter has explored turn-taking in business meetings, with particular focus on issues of asymmetry and turn organization. As claimed by Holmes and Stubbe (2003), in internal meetings the relationship of speakers and the meeting purpose were shown to be key factors in determining the turn organization (supporting findings by Holmes and Stubbe, 2003), as was the role played by the chair. Depending on the chair's level of involvement, it was demonstrated that the turn organization can vary greatly within the same meeting, and this involvement or non-involvement of the chair was interpreted from a speaker-goals perspective.

By considering the relative status of the speaker, some interesting findings concerning the number of turns taken by the chair became apparent. The internal meeting with the highest proportion of turns taken by the chair was a peer meeting, and even in a peer meeting where the chair took proportionally fewer turns than in the manager–subordinate meeting, the actual amount he spoke was not found to greatly vary. This problematizes the notion that the amount someone speaks is directly related to their power.

In external meetings, the role played by the chair was seen to be highly variable: in a regular contractually bound multiparty meeting, the person in charge of the meeting was argued to be equivalent to a chair. In the non-contractually bound meetings, by contrast, it was not possible to clearly identify the chair, and it was therefore proposed that, within external meetings, the notion of chair is problematic. Again, we found that powerful speakers do not always talk the most. Further research is required, however, in these areas.

In terms of conflict and collaboration, in both of the contractually bound external meetings discussed here, rather than paying consistent attention to the face needs of the interlocutor, we found considerable threats to face as well as seemingly deliberate divergence. The findings support the position of Holmes and Stubbe, who argue that conflict 'may occasionally arise through miscommunication, but power issues, relationships and people's potentially competing face needs are much more likely to give rise to problematic talk' (2003: 162). In a meeting where conflict had become contextualized, it was found that turn length and complexity were also affected, with disagreement becoming the 'preferred' response. In the non-contractually bound meetings in CANBEC, however, the corporate and personal face needs of the participants were often addressed. This suggests that participants may be expected to pay more attention to face in non-contractually bound meetings, whereas in contractually bound meetings, where there is already a relationship with contractually defined obligations, this is not necessarily the case.

Notes

1. Indeed, such passive behaviour on the part of the buyer, thus understating interest in the seller's products, could be interpreted as a negotiating practice.
2. See extract 7.8 in Chapter 7 (page 202) for the initial negotiation of the agenda in this meeting.

References

Atkinson, J. and Drew, P. (1979) *Order in Court*, London: Macmillan.
Bargiela-Chiappini, F. and Harris, S. (1996) 'Interruptive strategies in British and Italian management meetings', *Text*, **16**, 3, 269–97.
Bargiela-Chiappini, F. and Harris, S. (1997) *Managing Language: The Discourse of Corporate Meetings*, Amsterdam: John Benjamins.
Boden, D. (1994) *The Business of Talk: Organizations in Action*, Cambridge: Polity Press.
Brown, P. and Levinson, S. (1987) *Politeness: Some Universals in Language Usage*, Cambridge: Cambridge University Press.

Carter, R. and McCarthy, M. (2006) *Cambridge Grammar of English*, Cambridge: Cambridge University Press.

Charles, M. (1996) 'Business negotiations: Interdependence between discourse and the business relationship', *English for Specific Purposes*, **15**, 19–36.

Deetz, S. and McClellan, J. (2009) 'Critical studies', in Bargiela-Chiappini, F. (ed.) *The Handbook of Business Discourse*, Edinburgh: Edinburgh University Press, 119–31.

Drew, P. and Heritage, J. (1992) 'Analysing talk at work: An introduction', In Drew, P. and Heritage, J. (eds.) *Talk at Work*, Cambridge: Cambridge University Press, 3–65.

Gee. J.P., Hull, G. and Lankshear, C. (1996) *The New Work Order*, London: Allen and Unwin.

Goffman, E. (1967) *Interaction Ritual: Essays on Face-to-face Behaviour*, New York: Anchor Doubleday.

Greatbatch, D. (1991) 'On the management of disagreement between news interviewees', in Drew, P. and Heritage, J. (eds.) *Talk at Work*, Cambridge: Cambridge University Press, 268–301.

Handford, M. and Koester, A. (2010) '"It's not rocket science": Metaphors and idioms in conflictual business meetings', *Text and Talk*, **30**, 27–51.

Heritage, J. (1984) *Garfinkel and Ethnomethodology*, Cambridge: Polity Press.

Heritage, J. (1997) 'Conversation analysis and institutional talk', in Silverman, D. (ed.) *Qualitative Research: Theory, Method and Practice*, London: Sage, 161–82.

Heritage, J. (2005) 'Cognition in discourse', in te Molder, H. and Potter, J. (eds.) *Conversation and Cognition*, Cambridge: Cambridge University Press, 184–202.

Heritage, J. and Greatbatch, D. (1991) 'On the institutional character of institutional talk: The case of news interviews', in Boden, D. and Zimmerman, D. (eds.) *Talk and Social Structure*, Cambridge: Polity Press.

Holmes, J. and Stubbe, M. (2003) *Power and Politeness in the Workplace*, London: Longman.

Hutchby, I. and Wooffitt, R. (1998) *Conversation Analysis*, Cambridge: Polity Press.

Hutchby, I. and Wooffitt, R. (2008) *Conversation Analysis* (Second edition), Cambridge: Polity Press.

Koester, A. (2006) *Investigating Workplace Discourse*, Abingdon: Routledge.

Kotthoff, H. (1993) 'Disagreement and concession in disputes: On the context sensitivity of preference structures', *Language in Society*, **22**, 193–216.

Lakoff, R. (1973) 'The logic of politeness; or minding your p's and q's', *Papers from the 9th Regional Meeting of the Chicago Linguistic Society*, Chicago: Chicago Linguistic Society, 292–305.

Levinson, S. (1983) *Pragmatics*, Cambridge: Cambridge University Press.

McCarthy, M. (1998) *Spoken Language and Applied Linguistics*, Cambridge: Cambridge University Press.

McCarthy, M. and Carter, R. (2004) 'There's millions of them: Hyperbole in everyday conversation', *Journal of Pragmatics*, **36**, 2, 149–84.

Muntigl, P. and Turnbull, W. (1998) 'Conversational structure and facework in arguing', *Journal of Pragmatics*, **29**, 225–56.

Pomerantz, A. (1984) 'Agreeing and disagreeing with assessments: Some features of preferred/dispreferred turn shapes', in Atkinson, J. and Heritage, J. (eds.) *Structures of Social Action*, Cambridge: Cambridge University Press, 57–102.

Sarangi, S. and Roberts, C. (eds.) (1999) *Talk, Work and Institutional Order*, Berlin: Mouton de Gruyter.

Schegloff, E. (1992) 'On talk and its institutional occasions', in Drew, P. and Heritage, J. (eds.) *Talk at Work*, Cambridge: Cambridge University Press, 101–34.

Spencer-Oatey, H. (2000) *Culturally Speaking: Managing Rapport through Talk across Cultures*, London: Continuum.

Thomas, J. (1984) 'Cross-cultural discourse as 'unequal encounter': Towards pragmatic analysis', *Applied Linguistics*, **5**, 3, 226–35.

9   *Teaching and learning implications*

Although the contribution of corpus studies to developments in various fields of applied linguistics over the past two decades has been profound, applying findings from corpus research in the development of teaching and learning materials is neither straightforward (Lee and Swales, 2006), nor universally embraced (Widdowson, 2000; Cook, 1998). These issues, combined with the tendency of many to steer clear of research that seems incongruous with accepted pedagogical content and practices, help explain why corpus texts and corpus findings have not been widely exploited in much language teaching material over the same 20-year period. While this situation is gradually changing (O'Keeffe et al, 2007), such advances in business language teaching materials, particularly in relation to spoken discourse, are still slow (Koester, 2010).

According to Koester (2010), research into business discourse can inform business teaching and learning and therefore business teaching materials in addressing the following five areas:

1 The different goal orientations of business discourse as compared to everyday communication
2 The appropriate and frequent vocabulary used in business, particularly in terms of clusters, and how such language is different from everyday English
3 The ways workplace genres are constructed
4 The importance of problem-solving at work and the range of skills needed to achieve it
5 The importance of relational as well as transactional aspects of communication

These are indeed all crucial areas for teaching and learning, and there is obvious overlap between them and the content and findings explored here. A further key issue concerns the discursive and professional practices that can constitute or index these five areas, and how learners can be made aware of and given the opportunity to acquire them. By focusing on these areas in the classroom and training room, through awareness-raising activities, discussions and practice, the learner should be better equipped for succeeding at work. This chapter will therefore firstly discuss what is meant here by 'learner', what has appeared in language teaching books, and then finally there will be a discussion of exploiting corpora such as CANBEC in terms of language, skills and activity types for materials development purposes.

9.1 Who is the learner?

Traditionally, a learner of business English has been considered to be a 'non-native speaker', seemingly with the implicit assumption that he or she is inherently lacking in the requisite knowledge, skills and language compared to the 'native speaker' model. In Chapter 5, the issue of the 'native speaker' ('NS') / 'non-native speaker' ('NNS') distinction was briefly discussed, along with its relevance in terms of business contexts where English is used. We saw that, in terms of frequent clusters, the international meetings[1] in CANBEC are quite similar to the meetings where all the participants are British. Furthermore, while certain clusters may indeed be the preserve of British speakers (such as *this that and the other*) and others may be used only by Western Europeans (*at the end of the day*), this appears to be the exception rather than the rule. Many of the most important keywords and clusters, such as *if* or *we need to* are used regularly across nationalities in the corpus. Similar findings on the use of vague language have been reported by Cheng (2007), who showed that it is used equally by L1 and L2 users of English in the Hong Kong Corpus of Spoken English. It is findings such as these that can, it is argued here, help improve educational business materials. How this can be achieved will be demonstrated below.

The use of metaphors and idioms by L1 and L2 speakers of English in CANBEC is also noteworthy. According to Prodromou (2008), while idiomatic language enables L1 users to communicate more easily, the same language is deeply problematic for L2 users, whatever their level of proficiency. However, as mentioned in Chapter 7, there are several instances of L2 speakers of English in CANBEC both responding successfully to and producing idiomatic language in the same evaluative, discursive manner as their L1-English colleagues, both in Britain and in countries where English is not the predominant first language. This is particularly noticeable with L2 users in management positions in multinational companies.

There is also an increasing awareness that L1 speakers of English are often not the most effective international business communicators (Marriott, 1995; Du-Babcock, 1999; Seidlhofer, 2004). This has been confirmed by L2-English trainees with whom I have conducted consultancy work. They have commented that it tends to be more difficult to communicate successfully with US and UK speakers than with continental Europeans or Asians (they state this is often because of rigidly idiomatic, verbose and insufficiently enunciated language). This seems to suggest that the view of the 'NS' as a standard or model for communication, with the 'NNS' as deficient (for example as seems to be assumed in the Common European Framework and many mainstream language textbooks[2]), should be replaced with a dynamic skills-set which enables the learner to navigate successfully through communicative international and intercultural situations, at least with regard to business communication. One section of a potential skills-set is outlined below.

A discussion of these issues is important because, undoubtedly, a perceived lack of linguistic capital (Bourdieu, 1991), particularly in terms of English proficiency, can lead to individuals being denied opportunities in the seemingly globalized workplace (see Piller, 2009), and employees can be denied advancement opportunities, apparently because of differing tacit communicative practices and expectations (Roberts and Campbell, 2005). It is also clear that discrimination, unequal opportunity or hegemony continue to exist in business (see Parker and Grimes, 2009; Mullany, 2009), and examples of convergent discourse between British managers demeaning various 'others' can be found in CANBEC. Furthermore, the 79 per cent male / 21 per cent female gender breakdown in CANBEC could be interpreted as reflecting gender/power biases in society, bearing in mind that CANBEC is largely a corpus of management talk.

In discussing traditional English language teaching methodologies, which have arguably influenced business English materials, Graddol states, 'there is an inbuilt ideological positioning of the student as outsider and failure – however proficient they become' (Graddol, 2006: 86). De-prioritizing 'NS' norms, raising awareness among L2 and L1 users alike of the implications of certain discursive practices and assumptions, and accepting that we are all learners are possible ways, among many others, to address such issues. As Ochs states when discussing the novice/expert distinction, 'the socialization of a humane world depends on a continual human willingness to assume the status of novice as parents, as teachers, and as culture-travelers' (1996: 432). To that list we might add 'business people'.

Perhaps in response to the changing perceptions over 'NS' norms, communication-skills training of L1-English business people who have to use English internationally is a growing market. Within the UK, for instance, this has become a government-level national issue, as reflected in the launching of the National Occupational Standards for Intercultural Working in 2008 (http://www.ukstandards.org.uk).

While more systematic research is required in these areas, and given that there are undoubtedly linguistic differences between L1 and L2 speakers (not least in the way the language has been acquired – Hoey, 2005), there is the realization that the 'NS'/'NNS' distinction may not be the most relevant or productive issue for those involved in learning how to do business, and that we need a broader notion of 'learner' than merely 'non-native speakers of English'. This holds for those in tertiary education and those involved in in-house company training. Moreover, authentic workplace corpora can be seen, rather than as a model of prescriptive 'NS' usage, as a collection of expert performances (Bazerman, 1994) for learners, teachers and materials developers to explore. A parallel approach has been suggested by Lee and Swales (2006) for learners of academic writing.

Of particular relevance here is the notion of what it means to be an 'expert' in the profession or genre in question, and how learners, whether they be L1 or L2 speakers of English (Firth, 2009), move through the various stages of apprenticeship to approach the goal of becoming expert within their community of practice. As Hoey states:

[T]he distinction between a native speaker and non-native speaker starts to evaporate when we recognize that we are all learners in some areas of our language and beginners in others ... no L1 speaker is primed to deal with every situation they might encounter. (Hoey, 2005: 184)

As proposed in Chapter 4, 'priming' here concerns both language and discursive practices that constitute spoken business discourse. Of course, the backgrounds of learners, their needs and therefore their learning materials may be different, but the goal is essentially the same. Discussing authentic international written business transactions, Barbara and Scott (1999) argue that appropriacy and mutual intelligibility are the crucial factors involved in producing and interpreting a text – not whether the texts are produced by L1 or L2 users – and it is surely these two factors that should be given priority by learners of business English who have entered or will enter the workplace. By 'business English', I mean not only the special nomenclature that reflects content knowledge, but also the interpersonal discourse that has been the central concern of this book.

Therefore, in answer to the question of who is the learner of business English, we could say it is somebody who wants to be an expert user of the various business genres, such as meetings and presentations, in English, used within a particular profession and community, including L1 and L2 users. As discussed already, the institutional relationship and status of the speakers, along with the goals of the encounter, appear to have the foremost effect on the communication, with both L1 and L2 clients and managers having more power and discursive opportunities than subcontractors or subordinates (although it should be remembered that power is not always top-down and can be negotiated or contested). It is a practical understanding of and ability to successfully negotiate issues such as these that enable the learner to move towards being an expert business person. Focusing on 'NS' and 'NNS' differences will not.

This is not to say that an understanding of intercultural communication is not of value: awareness of and experience in intercultural issues and contexts are profoundly important for the learner and teacher of business English (or any other mode of communication), and can bring long-lasting professional, personal and relational benefits. However, teaching and training materials may approach intercultural communication in terms of unquestioned national or even continental stereotypes, such as 'If you want to do business in South America for instance, you have to be aware that Latin people are warm and friendly' (Cotton et al., 2006: 159), or that a particular nationality is 'traditionally suspicious of "foreign devils"' (Lewis, 1999: 42), or that members of another are 'among the worst listeners in the world' (ibid.: 34). Materials that deal uncritically with such issues risk causing 'pragmatic failure' on the part of learners, which 'carries the risk of being attributed to flaws of personality or ethnocultural origins and may carry grave social implications' (Blum-Kulka, 1997: 57). Educational materials might better benefit learners through the critical exploration of authentic professional and institutional intercultural contexts, roles and dilemmas, which may have a far greater impact on the unfolding discourse and the assumptions of the participants than simplistic ethnocentric national stereotypes[3]. For instance, in my role as a consultant to companies that use English internationally, I have often heard the comment that it is easy for fellow engineers or industry-specific researchers to understand each other, even though their first languages may be different; however, communication between, for example, sales people and researchers who share the same first language and who work in the same industry (or even in the same company) can be far more taxing and problematic. One sales person for a Japanese vehicle manufacturer recently announced to me during a training session, 'the engineers [in our company], I just do not understand them. I don't know why they do things. I don't like them', provoking much concurring laughter and nodding among his sales colleagues (no engineers were present). Moreover, there is also a strong case for a greater focus on how successful multicultural communication in authentic business contexts is discursively achieved – for example, through exposition of the findings of Poncini (2004) – rather than approaching cultural differences in the traditional, Hofstedian way, as 'a nuisance at best and often a disaster' (http://www.geert-hofstede.com). Work by Spencer-Oatey on rapport management (2000) and, more recently, on the *Global People* project (http://www.globalpeople.org.uk), is particularly relevant and useful for those who work and communicate internationally.

9.2 Teaching materials: What do they teach?

The preceding section has argued that business English teaching materials need to develop the language and skills of L1 and L2 English speakers who are apprentices in business contexts. This section will discuss what is taught in business materials. The relationship between skills and practices will also be touched on in section 9.3.

Language teaching materials have the potential to offer a short-cut to learners to acquire helpful items and features of language that are 'in harmony with those of their listeners' (Hoey, 2005: 186). Therefore, studying materials based on authentic data should be an effective way of shortcutting language learning and also the apprenticeship stage, to become an accepted member of the business community in question.

Nevertheless, according to Hoey (ibid.), the opposite is often the case, with textbooks often teaching grammar points with no consideration of the characteristic lexis, leading to 'unnatural output'. While 'natural language' is a thorny concept which may, for some, suggest 'native speaker' normative use, it is taken here to mean language that is used within the particular communities of practice in question: if business people use language that is not in harmony with that of their colleagues or clients, they are open to risk and possible censure, irrespective of their first language. For all members of a community of practice, moving through the stages of apprenticeship to becoming an expert requires, among other things, learning the appropriate ways of communicating (Gee et al., 1996; Wenger, 1998). Certain ideational and interpersonal business collocations, their discourse prosodies (Stubbs, 2001) and the discursive practices of the genres used by that community form a central part of any expert's communicative range, which can then be applied or strategically exploited. For the individual hoping to succeed in the new or future workplace, or new work context (such as in a new department or with a new set of clients), whether he or she be an L1 user, bilingual or L2 user, learning the language of that context is a *sine qua non*.

Hoey's (2005) criticism of textbook language mentioned in the previous paragraph could also be applied to many business English textbooks[4]. Instead of textbooks teaching attested collocations, or items with demonstrable discourse prosodies as suggested by Nelson (2006), several studies over the past 20 years (Williams, 1988; Nelson, 2000; Koester, 2006) demonstrate the 'mismatch that continues to exist between teaching materials and real language' (Bargiela-Chiappini et al., 2007: 9). Nelson's distinction between language *about* business and language to *do* business (discussed in Chapter 5) is again useful: increasingly, mainstream business textbooks can claim a degree of authenticity through the use of written texts and experts talking about business – for example, MacKenzie (2002) features interviews with real business professionals talking about aspects of business. However, from my own analysis (Handford, 2009) of over 20 of many of the best-selling business textbooks, from intermediate to advanced level, I found no examples of lessons based on business people actually doing spoken business; that is, there were no lessons based around real meetings, telephone calls, presentations and so on. Such genres were taught, but seemingly based on contrived or simulated scripts.

This brings to mind Nelson's statement: 'Next time somebody tries to sell you a BE [business English] book, you are entitled to ask them, "How do you know it is business English?"' (*The Guardian Weekly*, 20/3/03, quoted in Bargiela-Chiappini et al., 2007: 91). This is an important question, because one of the features of business English is that it has constrained collocations (Nelson, 2000), meaning that certain language may be highly unlikely in real business contexts. This issue has been explored in several chapters throughout this book, usually with reference to face (Goffman, 1967); for instance, the use of certain modal forms of obligation such as *must*, while formally possible, are highly unusual and potentially hazardous in business meetings. Similarly, expressions such as *I disagree with you* are not uncommon in textbooks and language classrooms (McCarthy, 1998), but in CANBEC the phrase does not appear once in over 900,000 words of meetings. (Nor were there any instances in the five-million CANCODE corpus of everyday speech – McCarthy, 1998). There are plenty of disagreements in CANBEC, but these tend to be prefaced by expressions like *yeah but*, which occurs over 200 times, or *Well* + hedging expressions. *I disagree with you*, like *you must*, is potentially highly face-threatening in many situations. By presenting language such as *you must* or *I disagree with you* as unmarked, effective and appropriate examples of communication for international business situations, learners are in danger of acquiring linguistic behaviour that may be highly detrimental to their professional career. Notwithstanding this, face is a highly culture-specific notion (Spencer-Oatey, 2000), and what may be rude in one culture can, of course, be acceptable in another. Therefore, a key step in the intercultural classroom or training room is to raise awareness that communicative practices can affect the relationship, by discussing examples such as *I disagree with you* and the issue of appropriacy (Handford, 2002).

A further problem with many English language business textbooks concerns interpersonal discourse. According to Koester, '[t]he interpersonal dimension of language has largely been neglected in the teaching of General and Business English ... The pervasiveness of relational elements of talk within all kinds of task-oriented interaction needs to be recognized and built into the language teaching syllabus' (2006: 162). Koester also argues that, even when relational communication is taught in business courses, it is only in the form of small talk and socializing, which stand outside the business side of communication. Furthermore, there is a strong tendency in teaching materials to prioritize unequivocal communication in all situations, yet research shows that vagueness is a common, constructive feature of cooperative, ideational communication in business and other institutional discourses (Koester, 2006; Cutting, 2007). In surveys I have conducted with companies that work internationally, it is consistently interpersonal and interactional skills that are of greatest concern to their L2-English-speaking staff – or, in the words of Holmes and Stubbe, issues of power and politeness (the subtitle for their 2003 book). These include things like small talk and chatting in coffee breaks, but also issues such as clarifying meanings, blocking interruptions, politely containing a garrulous interlocutor and directing the other company to follow the desired procedure. It is argued here that such skills and the language that achieves them should be taught with reference to actual, equivalent encounters from real businesses, rather than being based on the impressions of a textbook author. The situation with training materials can also be similarly troubling, with Sarangi and Roberts describing the depictions of communication in 'how to' manuals as 'absurdly simple' (1999: 2). A final, related issue that is often ignored in business materials is the intertextual nature of naturally occurring discourse: how encounters are built on and draw from previous encounters, how participants discuss and relate preceding and future communication to the ongoing encounter, and how spoken business English often references written texts, such as emails, reports and agendas. Making learners aware of this intertextuality is an important pedagogical aim. The following section will explore how a corpus such as CANBEC can be exploited for pedagogical purposes.

9.3 How can a corpus such as CANBEC be exploited?

At the time of writing, the most significant contribution from corpora to language learning has been in terms of lexico-grammar, with dictionaries in particular having been revolutionized over the past 20 years (O'Keeffe et al., 2007). The importance and usefulness of clusters in context continue to receive much attention in applied linguistics research (Nattinger and deCarrico, 1992; McCarthy, 1998; Wray, 2002; O'Keeffe et al., 2007; Adolphs, 2008), but this research has not always crossed over to teaching materials, particularly in business English. Given the genre-creating, identity-signalling, fluency-enabling multifunctionality of many clusters, their potential value to learners cannot be overemphasized. In addition, the importance of statistically significant keywords and how they are used in context would benefit those intending to succeed in their chosen professions, as argued at the end of Chapter 5. Many lexico-grammatical findings in CANBEC question the traditional separation of vocabulary and grammar (such as the pragmatic clusters involving the keyword *if* serving politeness or baldly unconditional functions, or the tendency of *I* in particular to form clusters, such as *I think*) and, at a theoretical level, add to the growing need for a radical rethink of the traditional paradigmatic and syntagmatic distinction (see Stubbs, 2007). How these theoretical developments can or should feed into learning remains to be seen (see Carter, 1998 and Cook, 1998).

Apart from lexico-grammar, specialized spoken corpora such as CANBEC can also shed light on turn-taking practices which would be useful for learners, and will be discussed below. Transcripts of recordings can also be used for listening exercises, both without alteration for higher-level learners, and in simplified form for those who may struggle because of lower comprehension ability. Even though the latter would not qualify as strictly 'authentic' texts, they are still preferable to purely contrived dialogues (see Chapter 7 of Koester, 2010, for example exercises).

This book has been centrally concerned with discursive practices, which raises the paradox of how these can be explicitly taught, as practices are by definition tacit. Nonaka (1994), dealing at the level of organizations, talks about the externalization and then internalization of a company's implicit knowledge and practices, with successful Japanese companies converting useful tacit knowledge into explicit knowledge (externalization) which can then be shared across the company and internalized. Similarly, once useful tacit discursive practices have been identified, as in this study, they can then be categorized as skills for the learner to notice, acquire and practice (internalization). The intention is that this will speed up the learning/apprenticeship process[5].

Notwithstanding this, corpora also allow for a critical approach in the apprenticeship process. This can be critical in terms of the items and features that are chosen for study, and critical in the way the learners are encouraged to view the language. For instance, should the very frequent five-word cluster *this that and the other* be taught to L2 learners of business English, bearing in mind that it seems to be used solely by British male managers with their peers? One argument is that it could be taught receptively, but only with this important contextual information, and probably at an advanced level, to those likely to deal with British managers. There are countless other items that are more widespread, more useful and less culturally bound, such as *we need to*.

A further aspect of a critical approach to language learning in business contexts is that teaching materials may be one of the few 'spaces', publisher permitting, that allow for criticality in contemporary society of the modern workplace and its practices by those desiring membership of such workplaces. As Gee et al. state:

As the distinction between 'learning' and 'doing' collapses in the contemporary work world, thanks to the knowledge and information explosion and to new technologies, we need to ask where the space for reflection and critique apart from immersion in the core values and communities of practice of the business will exist. (Gee et al., 1996: 67–8)

The classroom or training room can become such a space. Furthermore, a specialized corpus like CANBEC, which has been analysed thoroughly, can allow the materials developer to ask questions about authentic language, content and practices in context from various perspectives that simulated or created examples cannot, as it is a record of what actually happens in and between businesses. While such questions may not be welcomed by the members of the Discourses themselves (Gee et al, 1996: 13), it is the responsibility of educators to raise awareness of issues, values and practices, as well as the implications of choices we all make, and materials developers have an arguably greater opportunity and thus responsibility than most to encourage consideration and reflection as part of learning. As Kress stated a quarter of a century ago with reference to the overt discussion of the ideological orientation of written genres, we need to provide learners 'with the essential skills necessary to manipulate, control, and organize language for their *own* purposes' (Kress, 1982: 13, italics in the original). The same holds for learners of spoken business genres.

We now turn to the practical question of what could be taught in business English classes and in-house training about how to communicate at work. Following a review of the key findings of this study, one possible option, that has much in common with that of Koester (2010) which was described at the beginning of this chapter, is outlined here. As we saw in Chapter 1, the language in CANBEC meetings can be grouped into four general purposes or functions, which for teaching purposes could also be categorized as higher-level skills:

- procedure-focusing
- information-focusing
- decision-focusing
- negotiating-focusing

Learners of business English should be encouraged to develop competencies in performing all four key skills, which are applicable in face-to-face meetings and other work genres (such as telephone calls, interviews and training sessions).

On a more detailed level, a review of the discursive practices in Chapter 3 and the key functions of clusters in Chapter 5 indicates several essential skills learners should develop, each of which can be subsumed under one or more of the above higher-level skills. Among these are: clarifying what you have said, clarifying what your interlocutor has said, clarifying your general position, and asking for clarification. Similarly, learners need to be able to summarize effectively. Decision-making and problem-solving can be unpacked into several skills, such as raising an issue, discussing the issue, discussing solutions, reaching consensus, and postponing or evading decisions. Other skills include planning and making arrangements, exchanging information, evaluating, dealing with conflict and hypothesizing. Moreover, the interpersonal aspects of communication discussed throughout the book show that building, maintaining and occasionally ending a business relationship, attention to face and positive and negative politeness strategies (such as showing appreciation and hedging impositions, respectively) all deserve consistent attention in the classroom.

As mentioned above, awareness of turn-taking styles is another area that can benefit learners and accelerate the process of apprenticeship, for instance the issue of preference (Pomerantz, 1984) during agreements and disagreements: the preferred turn structure for agreements in convergent communication is for short, unhedged positive responses, whereas in conflictual, divergent communication, disagreements tend to be unhedged and abrupt, as we saw in Chapter 8. Disagreement during cooperative business communication, which CANBEC suggests is far more usual than outright conflict, tends to feature silences, hedges and accounts. Learners need to be made aware of this. As noted above, however, textbooks often teach disagreeing through expressions such as *I disagree with you*, with no attention given to turn structure. In addition, the importance of status within the meetings and how it allows or restricts opportunities to take the floor or open or close topics should also be taught. Once again, such awareness-raising can be dealt with critically, with learners being encouraged to consider the appropriacy of such norms to their own specific context.

In answer to the question of what language should be taught in business English classes, there is obviously a great need for the learning of business terminology. This involves language primarily *about* business – for example, *merger*, *forecast* and *brand placement*. As we have seen, however, when business people are actually doing business, then various clusters and keywords are far more frequent and versatile. The following paragraph outlines several of the key lexical and grammatical categories apparent in CANBEC.

Hedging and indirect language make up a considerable amount of CANBEC, in the form of clusters such as *I don't know*, *I think*, *I mean* and *I guess*. They occur in all types of meetings and tend to have a clear face-protecting role. As such, they are useful during disagreements, when making suggestions and when offering any kind of criticism. Vague language is also very common in business meetings and allows the speaker to show shared understanding – for instance, *and things like that* and *and everything else*. Vague language can also be used in 'win–win' and 'win–lose' negotiations. Modality is another area that deserves considerable attention in the classroom – for example, modal verbs and expressions of obligation and possibility. In terms of the former, the statistical behaviour of deontic modal verbs outlined in Chapter 6, showing that *need to* and *have to* are extremely frequent, whereas *must* is rarely used, is of obvious interest to learners. The same can be said of the multifunctional keyword *if*, which is found in many lexical clusters such as *I don't know if* and *if we can*, as well as politeness expressions such as *if you look at*, which also forms more traditionally recognizable conditional clauses. As mentioned above, pronouns and backchannels deserve attention in the classroom and training room, as do discourse markers such as *so* and *the next point is*. *So* is particularly interesting from a turn perspective, because 27 per cent of its occurrences are at the beginning of a speaker's turn, compared to, for example, less than ten per cent for another statistical keyword, (*the*) *problem*, and less than five per cent for *if*. This also suggests learners may benefit from more information on which items tend to be found in the turn-initial or 'head' (Carter and McCarthy, 1995) position of the turn, and which may be more typical at the end of turns, such as question tags. Such findings can be related to the heads, bodies and tails model briefly discussed in Chapters 4 and 5 (see pages 111–12). Another category that needs more attention is that of metaphors and idioms. Metaphors and idioms are often taught as somewhat flowery replacements for more literal expressions, and yet they have quite distinct discursive roles, not least that of evaluating, and are often used by powerful speakers. As with many other language items, a purely semantic approach to teaching business English or any other language will put the learner at a pragmatic disadvantage when it comes to dealing with real business people in real situations and to using language that is 'in harmony' with the community of practice. Such a disadvantage could potentially have serious consequences for the employee concerned, such as losing an argument, a client or a job.

The language discussed in the preceding paragraph comprises essentially interpersonal items and categories and, as mentioned above, these are largely ignored in business language materials (Koester, 2006). They enable the speaker to communicate the message clearly, achieve the communicative goals of the discussion, and deal with the relationship appropriately. Of course, with each item and skill, there are issues of power and social distance that need to be considered – for instance, is the discussion between a manager and subordinate or between peers? Whether the communication is internal or external also needs consideration, most evidently when dealing with inclusive and exclusive *we*, but also in terms of appropriate listenership and backchannels. As discussed in Chapter 6, the non-committal *hmm* may create a negative impression with a potential client, whereas *sure* may have a better chance of allowing the listener to achieve his or her transactional goal.

Figure 9.1 shows a sample exercise taken from a business course published by Cambridge University Press, which applies findings from CANBEC and other corpora (at the time of writing, this course is under development). The extract explores the use of metaphors in conflictual communication, and is intended for an upper-intermediate/advanced language level.

In figure 9.1, the 'text' referred to is a transcript from the conflictual meeting discussed in Chapter 7 (extract 7.15) and Chapter 8

Figure 9.1   Sample material taken from Handford et al. (forthcoming)

Language: metaphors and conflict

A metaphor involves using one idea to talk about and usually evaluate another (*I'm completely lost*). A metaphor can be used to make the message seem more cooperative and perhaps indirect (*Everything's moving in the right direction*), or more conflictual (*these four vehicles are a pain in the neck from my point of view*). Metaphors are surprisingly common in business.

1 Here is a selection of phrases from the meeting that include metaphors. With a partner, find them in the text, and then decide where they fit on the following scale:

Conflictual	Neutral/not sure	Friendly

your letter found its way to me
dive in
grab a chair
I'm in the dark
I'll give you the story
it's not rocket science
the rent's stupid
not as stupid as I was trying to make it
you must be welcomed up and down the country
it's beyond any business sense
would have thrown the keys back at you
we wouldn't have caught them
you're clear where we're coming from

2 Now, look at the text again where the conflictual metaphors occur, and discuss with a partner what you could say to make the communication less conflictual. For instance, instead of saying *the rent's stupid*, you could say *we think the rent is an issue/we would like to look at negotiating the rent*. Then role play each section of the text in a more friendly way.

3 Would you be comfortable using this type of language at work? Do you want to use conflictual language in business? What are the dangers of conflict in business, and what are the possible benefits?

4 Think of two or three groups that you are a member of (your nation, company, university, sports team, friends, family etc.). Is conflict accepted or even encouraged in these different groups? Why, or why not? Which is the least conflictual group, and which is the most? Discuss with a partner.

(extracts 8.9, 8.10 and 8.12). After listening to the dialogue, the learners analyse the language, decide on the discourse prosody of each item in context, find suitable alternatives that make the communication less conflictual, and then critically evaluate the use of such language from their personal perspective and the wider world of work. Furthermore, they can begin to realize that metaphors may also be primed (Hoey, 2005) for conflictual as well as convergent contexts (Handford and Koester, 2010) and, depending on the learners, a critical discussion is possible which addresses issues such as using metaphorical language in international situations, or the use of idioms and the impact on learner identity. Subsequent application activities can also allow the learners the opportunity to use such language and deal with conflictual situations in a controlled environment. Furthermore, it should be noted that these items are not being taught in the traditional sense of 'Here's a list of ("native speaker") metaphors; memorize and use them': the purpose of the exercise is to raise awareness that metaphors can be used in conflictual as well as convergent contexts, and it is ultimately the learner's decision about how to use this information. This use of metaphors as depicted here may be more typical of L1 business English (although further research is required to explore this – see Chapter 7 of Koester, 2010), and yet to deny L2 learners access to this rhetorically powerful use of language seems highly questionable. Moreover, merely from a receptive perspective, such awareness is bound to be beneficial to the business person. The final two questions in figure 9.1 attempt to look at the issue of conflict and language from a cultural perspective, but one that is not wholly focused on nationality. Linguistic insights and exercises such as these would also be beneficial to the less-experienced L1 business user as well as L2 users and future users of business English.

9.4 Summary

As discussed in Chapter 1, CANBEC is simultaneously a big corpus (relative to other fully transcribed corpora of spoken business English, and as a corpus of business meetings) and a small corpus (relative to the amount of business communication going on in the world, and relative to many general corpora). In terms of what CANBEC demonstrates, only rudimentary interpretations of selected prosodic features such as intonation are possible, although the recordings could in theory be re-transcribed. What CANBEC does allow us to see is the recurrent, critical language that is such an integral part of business meetings in a range of contexts, and to infer the practices that construct the genre, the identities of the speakers and their communities. The fully transcribed corpus has illuminated several significant discursive features of business meetings, including keywords (*if*), clusters (*if you say "Well . . ."*), the impact of context on different discourse prosodies and meanings of such features, and the frequency of certain discursive practices in certain types of meetings.

Corpora such as CANBEC provide a snapshot of language used in a selection of business contexts. Nevertheless, more corpora of authentic business communication from around the world and from as many industries and organizations as possible will help develop a clearer picture of what business people really do in meetings, presentations, over lunch, at the photocopier, on the phone and so on. CANBEC is primarily, though not completely, a corpus of British L1 (male) users of business English in meetings. Separate corpora would allow us to further evaluate how generalizable these findings are, not only in terms of the occurrence of particular language and practices, but also in terms of their relative frequency. For instance, do different groups of expert users of business English summarize and clarify less or more often than other speakers in equivalent situations and, if so, how does this affect communication? In addition, the development of multimodal business corpora of authentic interactions that allow for the analysis of non-verbal features of communication would be of considerable benefit to those involved in business teaching, training and learning.

Firth (2009) calls for the urgent development of more L2 corpora outside of educational settings, to allow us to see how learners, even when they are not learning in the traditional sense, fulfil work roles and responsibilities. His research shows that L2 speakers use 'nonstandard' forms tactically to converge with their interlocutors – that is, they repeat language that traditionally would be seen as an error in order to develop the relationship and highlight cooperation rather than divergence, and prioritize the transactional task at hand above the language. This insight raises important considerations, such as whether this is the appropriate way to behave given institutional and personal goals (such as the transactional and relational goals in the context), and whether this information should be dealt with in the L2 business language classroom. My response to both these questions would be a resounding 'Yes!'

Notes

1. As outlined in Chapter 1, international meetings included meetings with participants from different countries, recorded both in the UK and elsewhere, mostly in multinational corporations.

2. See also Chapter 8 of Coyle et al. (2010) for a discussion of related issues involving CLIL (content and language integrated learning).
3. On a related point, according to Gee et al. (1996: 41), a feature of the global workplace is that: 'Elites who control information and culture share more in cultural and aesthetic values with their peers across the developed world than they do with their less advantaged fellow citizens.'
4. Two exceptions to this, cited by Bargiela-Chiappini et al. (2007) – although neither is, strictly speaking, a textbook for the ELT business market – are Koester (2004) and Hogarth and Burnett (1995).
5. Vygotskian socio-cultural theory (Vygotsky, 1978) can also shed light on such processes, particularly the concepts of 'scaffolding' and the 'zone of proximal development': see Lantolf (2000) and Walsh (2006). See also O'Keeffe et al. (2007: 228–45) for a discussion of teaching implications of corpora and socio-cultural theory.

References

Adolphs, S. (2008) *Corpus and Context: Investigating Pragmatic Functions in Spoken Discourse*, Amsterdam: John Benjamins.

Barbara, L. and Scott, M. (1999) 'Invitations for bids', in Bargiela-Chiappini, F. and Nickerson, C. (eds.) *Writing Business: Genres, Media and Discourses*, Harlow: Longman, 227–54.

Bargiela-Chiappini, F., Nickerson, C. and Planken, B. (2007) *Business Discourse*, Basingstoke: Palgrave.

Bazerman, C. (1994) 'Systems of genres and the enhancement of social intentions', in Freedman, A. and Medway, P. (eds.) *Genre and New Rhetoric*, London: Taylor and Francis, 79–101.

Blum-Kulka, S. (1997) 'Discourse pragmatics', in van Dijk, T. (ed.) *Discourse as Social Interaction*, London: Sage Publications, 38–63.

Bourdieu, P. (1991) *Language and Symbolic Power*, Cambridge: Polity Press.

Carter, R. (1998) 'Orders of reality: CANCODE, communication, and culture', *English Language Teaching Journal*, **52**, 1, 43–55.

Carter, R. and McCarthy, M. (1995) 'Grammar and the spoken language', *Applied Linguistics*, **16**, 2, 141–58.

Cheng, W. (2007) 'The use of vague language across spoken genres in an intercultural corpus', in Cutting, J. (ed.) *Vague Language Explored*, Basingstoke: Palgrave, 161–81.

Cotton, D., Falvey, D. and Kent, S. (2006) *Market Leader: Upper Intermediate Coursebook*, Harlow: Longman.

Cook, G. (1998) 'The uses of reality: A reply to Ron Carter', *English Language Teaching Journal*, **52**, 1, 57–63.

Coyle, D., Hood, P. and Marsh, D. (2010) *CLIL: Content and Language Integrated Learning*, Cambridge: Cambridge University Press.

Cutting, J. (ed.) (2007) *Vague Language Explored*, Basingstoke: Palgrave.

Du-Babcock, B. (1999) 'Topic management and turn taking in professional communication', *Management Communication Quarterly*, **12**, 4, 544–74.

Firth, A. (2009) 'Doing not being a foreign language learner: English as a *lingua franca* in the workplace and (some) implications for SLA', *International Review of Applied Linguistics in Language Teaching*, **47**, 1, 127–56.

Gee. J.P., Hull, G. and Lankshear, C. (1996) *The New Work Order*, London: Allen and Unwin.

Goffman, E. (1967) *Interaction Ritual: Essays on Face-to-face Behaviour*, New York: Anchor Doubleday.

Graddol, D. (2006) *English Next*, British Council. Available at: http://www.britishcouncil.org/jp/learning-research-english-next.pdf [Accessed 4th December 2009].

Handford, M. (2002) 'Developing sociocultural awareness in the ESL classroom', *Nottingham Linguistic Circular*, **17**, 1–16.

Handford, M. (2009) Analysis of authentic spoken texts in business textbooks (Unpublished document).

Handford, M. and Koester, A. (2010) '"It's not rocket science": Metaphors and idioms in conflictual business meetings', *Text and Talk*, **30**, 27–51.

Handford, M., Lisboa, M., Koester, A. and Pitt, A. (forthcoming) *Business Advantage. Upper Intermediate Student's Book*, Cambridge: Cambridge University Press.

Hoey, M. (2005) *Lexical Priming*, Abingdon: Routledge.

Hogarth, W. and Burnett, L. (1995) *Talking it through: Teacher's guide and classroom materials*, Macquarie University, Sydney: National Centre for English Language Teaching and Research.

Holmes, J. and Stubbe, M. (2003) *Power and Politeness in the Workplace*, London: Longman.

Koester, A. (2004) *The Language of Work*, London: Routledge.

Koester, A. (2006) *Investigating Workplace Discourse*, Abingdon: Routledge.

Koester, A. (2010) *Workplace Discourse*, London: Continuum.

Kress, G. (1982) *Learning to Write*, London: Routledge.

Lantolf, J. (2000) 'Introducing sociocultural theory', in Lantolf, J. (ed.) *Sociocultural Theory and Second Language Learning*, Oxford: Oxford University Press, 1–26.

Lee, D. and Swales, J. (2006) 'A corpus-based EAP course for NNS doctoral students: Moving from available specialized corpora to self-compiled corpora', *English for Specific Purposes*, **25**, 56–75.

Lewis, R. (1999) *Cross Cultural Communication: A Visual Approach*, Warnford: Transcreen Publications.

MacKenzie, I. (2002) *English for Business Studies*, Cambridge: Cambridge University Press.

Marriott, H. (1995) 'The management of discourse in international seller-buyer negotiation', in Ehlich, K. and Wagner, J. (eds.) *The Discourse of Business Negotiation*, Berlin: Mouton de Gruyter, 103–26.

McCarthy, M. (1998) *Spoken Language and Applied Linguistics*, Cambridge: Cambridge University Press.

Mullany. L. (2009) 'Gender studies', in Bargiela-Chiappini, F. (ed.) *The Handbook of Business Discourse*, Edinburgh: Edinburgh University Press, 213–25.

Nattinger, J. and DeCarrico, J. (1992) *Lexical Phrases and Language Teaching*, Oxford: Oxford University Press.

Nelson, M. (2000) *A Corpus-based Study of Business English and Business English Teaching Materials*, PhD thesis, University of Manchester (Unpublished).

Nelson, M. (2006) 'Semantic associations in business English: A corpus-based analysis', *English for Specific Purposes*, 25, 217–34.

Nonaka, I. (1994) 'A dynamic theory of organizational knowledge creation', *Organizational Science*, 5, 1, 14–37.

O'Keeffe, A., McCarthy, M. and Carter, R. (2007) *From Corpus to Classroom: Language Use and Language Teaching*, Cambridge: Cambridge University Press.

Ochs, E. (1996) 'Linguistic resources for socializing humanity', in Gumperz, J. (ed.) *Rethinking Linguistic Relativity*, Cambridge: Cambridge University Press, 407–37.

Parker, P. and Grimes, D. (2009) '"Race" and management communication', in Bargiela-Chiappini, F. (ed.) *The Handbook of Business Discourse*, Edinburgh: Edinburgh University Press, 292–304.

Piller, I. (2009) 'Intercultural communication', in Bargiela-Chiappini, F. (ed.) *The Handbook of Business Discourse*, Edinburgh: Edinburgh University Press, 317–29.

Pomerantz, A. (1984) 'Agreeing and disagreeing with assessments: Some features of preferred/dispreferred turn shapes', in Atkinson, J. and Heritage, J. (eds.) *Structures of Social Action*, Cambridge: Cambridge University Press, 57–102.

Poncini, G. (2004) *Discursive Strategies in Multicultural Business Meetings*, Peter Lang, Linguistic Insights Series.

Prodromou, L. (2008) *English as a Lingua Franca: A Corpus-based Analysis*, London: Continuum.

Roberts, C. and Campbell, S. (2005) 'Fitting stories into boxes: Rhetorical and contextual constraints on candidates' performances in British job interviews', *Journal of Applied Linguistics*, 2, 1, 45–73.

Sarangi, S. and Roberts, C. (1999) 'The dynamics of interactional and institutional orders in work-related settings', in Sarangi, S. and Roberts, C. (eds.) *Talk, Work and Institutional Order*, Berlin: Mouton de Gruyter, 2–57.

Seidlhofer, B. (2004) 'Research perspectives on teaching English as a lingua franca', *Annual Review of Applied Linguistics*, 24, 209–39.

Spencer-Oatey, H. (2000) *Culturally Speaking: Managing Rapport through Talk across Cultures*, London: Continuum.

Stubbs, M. (2001) 'On inference theories and code theories: Corpus evidence for semantic schemas', *Text*, 21, 3, 437–65.

Stubbs, M. (2007) 'On texts, corpora and models of language', in Hoey, M., Mahlberg, M., Stubbs, M. and Teubert, W. (eds.) *Text, Discourse and Corpora*, London: Continuum, 163–90.

Vygotsky, L. (1978) *Mind in Society: The Development of Higher Psychological Processes*, Cambridge, MA: Harvard University Press.

Walsh, S. (2006) *Investigating Classroom Discourse*, London: Routledge.

Wenger, E. (1998) *Communities of Practice: Learning, Meaning and Identity*, Cambridge: Cambridge University Press.

Widdowson, H. (2000) 'On the limitations of linguistics applied', *Applied Linguistics*, **21**, 1, 3–25.

Williams, M. (1988) 'Language taught for meetings and language used in meetings: Is there anything in common?', *Applied Linguistics*, **9**, 1, 45–58.

Wray, A. (2002) *Formulaic Language and the Lexicon*, Cambridge: Cambridge University Press.

Appendix: Breakdown of the CANBEC sub-corpus

Company type (size*)	Words	Topic	Purpose	No. of speakers
Internal meetings (manager–subordinate)				
Foam manufacturer (3)	12,192	sales	reviewing	5
Consultants (4)	11,089	HRM	planning; reviewing; giving and receiving information/advice	2
Internal meetings (peer)				
Foam manufacturer (3)	5,772	strategy; production	planning	4
Bank (in Japan) (1)	11,276	technical; procedure	planning; task-/problem-oriented	6
Museum (4)	7,330	marketing; production	reviewing	4
External meetings (contractually bound)				
Pharmaceutical company (1); pharmaceutical company (1)	11,007	logistics; production	planning; reviewing	5
Pub chain (2); brewer (1)	3,250	procedure; logistics	task-/problem-oriented; giving and receiving information/advice	2
External meetings (non-contractually bound)				
Hydraulics manufacturer (3); magazine (2)	10,176	marketing; sales	negotiating	3
ISP provider (3); ISP reseller (4)	16,400	technical	task-/problem-oriented; giving and receiving information/advice	5

Total words: Internal meetings: 47,659, External meetings: 40,833; Combined: 88,492.

*Company size: 1: 10,000+ employees; 2: 1,001–9,999 employees; 3: 101–1,000 employees; 4: 11–100 employees

Index